The Art of Comics

New Directions in Aesthetics

Series editors: Dominic McIver Lopes, University of British Columbia, and Berys Gaut, University of St Andrews

Blackwell's New Directions in Aesthetics series highlights ambitious single- and multiple-author books that confront the most intriguing and pressing problems in aesthetics and the philosophy of art today. Each book is written in a way that advances understanding of the subject at hand and is accessible to upper-undergraduate and graduate students.

The Art of Comics

A Philosophical Approach

Edited by

AARON MESKIN AND ROY T. COOK

WILEY-BLACKWELL

A John Wiley & Sons, Ltd., Publication

This edition first published 2012
© 2012 Blackwell Publishing Ltd.

Blackwell Publishing was acquired by John Wiley & Sons in February 2007. Blackwell's publishing program has been merged with Wiley's global Scientific, Technical, and Medical business to form Wiley-Blackwell.

Registered Office
John Wiley & Sons Ltd, The Atrium, Southern Gate, Chichester, West Sussex, PO19 8SQ, UK

Editorial Offices
350 Main Street, Malden, MA 02148-5020, USA
9600 Garsington Road, Oxford, OX4 2DQ, UK
The Atrium, Southern Gate, Chichester, West Sussex, PO19 8SQ, UK

For details of our global editorial offices, for customer services, and for information about how to apply for permission to reuse the copyright material in this book please see our website at www.wiley.com/wiley-blackwell.

The right of Aaron Meskin and Roy T. Cook to be identified as the authors of the editorial material in this work has been asserted in accordance with the UK Copyright, Designs and Patents Act 1988.

Wiley also publishes its books in a variety of electronic formats. Some content that appears in print may not be available in electronic books.

Designations used by companies to distinguish their products are often claimed as trademarks. All brand names and product names used in this book are trade names, service marks, trademarks or registered trademarks of their respective owners. The publisher is not associated with any product or vendor mentioned in this book. This publication is designed to provide accurate and authoritative information in regard to the subject matter covered. It is sold on the understanding that the publisher is not engaged in rendering professional services. If professional advice or other expert assistance is required, the services of a competent professional should be sought.

Library of Congress Cataloging-in-Publication Data

The art of comics: a philosophical approach / edited by Aaron Meskin and Roy T. Cook. – 1
    p.   cm. –   (New directions in aesthetics; 12)
  Includes bibliographical references and index.
  ISBN 978-1-4443-3464-7 (hardback)
1. Comic books, strips, etc.–History and criticism.   2. Philosophy in literature.
I. Meskin, Aaron.   II. Cook, Roy T., 1972–
  PN6710.A86 2012
  741.5'9–dc23
                                              2011036428

A catalogue record for this book is available from the British Library.

This book is published in the following electronic formats: ePDFs 9781444354812; Wiley Online Library 9781444354843; ePub 9781444354829; Mobi 9781444354836

Set in 10/12.5pt ITC Galliard Std by SPi Publisher Services, Pondicherry, India

1   2012

Contents

Editors' Acknowledgments

Our primary debt of gratitude is to the authors of the papers in this volume. Not only did they contribute great philosophical work but, many of them provided useful feedback to other authors. John Holbo deserves special mention for going above and beyond in commenting on others' articles. We are grateful to Matthew Kieran and Kathleen Stock for useful feedback on our introduction. David Heatley provided us with a fabulous cover, and Warren Ellis wrote a fantastic preface; we owe thanks to both of them. Aaron also owes David thanks for reintroducing him to comics about a decade ago. Thanks also to MontiLee Stormer and Rob Callahan. We would also like to thank Jeff Dean (editor-aesthetician extraordinaire) and the rest of the staff at Wiley-Blackwell for all their support in getting this book out. Finally, we'd like to thank our families – Alice, Sheryl, and Ethan. Without their support and tolerance the book simply wouldn't have gotten done. Excelsior!

Aaron Meskin
Roy T. Cook

Figures

Contributors

Catharine Abell is a lecturer in philosophy at the University of Manchester. She has published articles on a variety of issues in aesthetics including the nature of depiction, the definition of art and cinematic representation, in journals including *Philosophical Review, Philosophy and Phenomenological Research, Australasian Journal of Philosophy, American Philosophical Quarterly*, and the *British Journal of Aesthetics*. Together with Katerina Bantinaki, she co-edited *Philosophical Perspectives on Depiction* (OUP, 2010). Her current research focuses on the philosophy of the representational arts and, in particular, on issues concerning fiction, such as the nature of the act of fiction making, the ontological status of fictional characters, and the scope and determinants of narrative content.

David Carrier is Champney Family Professor, Case Western Reserve University/Cleveland Institute of Art. His books include *Artwriting, Principles of Art History Writing, The Aesthetics of Comics, Writing About Visual Art, Museum Skepticism, A World Art History* and *Proust/Warhol*.

Roy T. Cook is associate professor of philosophy at the University of Minnesota – Twin Cities, a resident fellow at the Minnesota Center for Philosophy of Science, and an associate fellow of the Northern Institute of Philosophy at the University of Aberdeen. He has published numerous articles and book chapters on philosophical logic, mathematical logic, philosophy of mathematics, and more recently on the aesthetics of comics. He previously edited The *Arché Papers on the Mathematics of Abstraction* (Springer 2007), and is the author of *A Dictionary of Philosophical Logic* (Edinburgh University Press 2009).

Darren Hudson Hick (PhD, University of Maryland) is an Assistant Professor of Philosophy at Susquehanna University, where he specializes in issues in the ontology of art, philosophical problems in intellectual property, and their overlap. Occasionally, he writes philosophical papers about things like comics, zombies, and *Guitar Hero*. His work appears in a range of philosophy journals, law journals, and anthologies. He is the author of the forthcoming *Introducing Aesthetics and the Philosophy of Art* (Continuum), a former managing editor of *The Comics Journal*, and has received a great deal of press for an essay he wrote on what it would cost to become Batman.

John Holbo is associate professor of philosophy at the National University of Singapore. His most recent book is *Reason and Persuasion: Three Dialogues By Plato* (Pearson, 2009), an illustrated introduction. He is the co-editor of a forthcoming anthology, *Reading Graphs, Maps and Trees: Responses To Franco Moretti* (Parlor Press, 2011). His personal contribution to comics artistry (self-published) is *Squid and Owl* (Blurb, 2010). He is well-known as a blogger at www.crookedtimber.org.

Christy Mag Uidhir received his PhD in philosophy from Rutgers University in 2007. He is a former postdoctoral associate at the Cornell University Sage School of Philosophy and currently an assistant professor of philosophy at University of Houston. His main areas of research are artistic intentions and the ontology of art, with a special interest in printmaking and print-related areas such as comics and photography. He has published articles in journals such as *Philosophical Studies, Australasian Journal of Philosophy, American Philosophical Quarterly, The Journal of Aesthetics and Art Criticism*, and the *British Journal of Aesthetics*, and is currently editing the volume *Art and Abstract Objects* for Oxford University Press.

Patrick Maynard, emeritus full professor of Philosophy, University of Western Ontario, taught most subjects in Philosophy at all levels there, also as visiting professor at the universities of Michigan-Ann Arbor and California-Berkeley, and Simon Fraser University. He is author of *The Engine of Visualization: Thinking Through Photography* and *Drawing Distinctions: The Varieties of Graphic Expression* – both the only full philosophy treatises on their subjects – and co-editor of *Aesthetics (Oxford Readers)*. Works in progress include *Plato's Republic and Ours, Fly the Ocean in a Silver Plane, Many Aesthetics* (including an essay on paper-folding, based on translation of Unamuno) and a collection of papers, *Planes of Focus*. An active visual artist and photographer, he is particularly interested in visual (including information) design. He has written or edited many Wikipedia articles, and has drawn cartoons steadily since childhood.

Aaron Meskin is senior lecturer in philosophy at the University of Leeds. He is the author of numerous journal articles and book chapters on aesthetics and other philosophical subjects. His work on comics has been published in *The Journal of Aesthetics and Art Criticism*, the *British Journal of Aesthetics* and two previous anthologies. He was the first aesthetics editor for the online journal *Philosophy Compass*, and he co-edited *Aesthetics: A Comprehensive Anthology* (Wiley-Blackwell, 2007). He is a former Trustee of the American Society for Aesthetics and is Treasurer of the British Society of Aesthetics.

Henry John Pratt received his PhD in philosophy from the Ohio State University in 2005 and is currently assistant professor of Philosophy at Marist College. His primary research interests include artistic value, comparing art-works across genres, and narrative. His work on comics began with an article co-written with Greg Hayman, "What Are Comics?" (in *Aesthetics: A Reader in Philosophy of the Arts*, 2nd. ed.). Since then, he has presented on comics at numerous conferences and has had his articles published in *The Journal of Aesthetics and Art Criticism*, *Storyworlds*, and the third edition of *Aesthetics: A Reader in Philosophy of the Arts*.

Thomas E. Wartenberg is professor of philosophy at Mount Holyoke College where he also teaches in the film studies program. His current research focuses on issues in the philosophy of film and philosophy for children. He is the author of two books on film: *Unlikely Couples: Movie Romance as Social Criticism* (Westview) and *Thinking On Screen: Film as Philosophy* (Routledge). He has recently edited three books: *The Nature of Art* (Cengage 3rd edition), *The Philosophy of Film: Introductory Text and Readings* (Blackwell with Angela Curran), and *Thinking Through Cinema: Film as Philosophy* (Blackwell with Murray Smith). His most recent publications include *Existentialism: A Beginner's Guide* (Oneworld) and *Big Ideas for Little Kids: Teaching Philosophy Through Children's Literature* (Rowman and Littlefield Education). He has published widely on topics ranging from the history of philosophy and social theory to the philosophy of art. He maintains a popular website for teaching philosophy through children's literature: www.teachingchildrenphilosophy.org.

Foreword

Comics are a strange beast. It's a strange attractor of an artform, and almost everything that sticks to it is a source of continual argument, including the term "comics." From one perspective, comics take things from all other artforms and sew them together into a weird hybrid animal. Comics comprise illustration and prose and theatre and sloganeering and graphic design and any other damn thing you want to sling into the pot. From another, it's the first and simplest way we did visual narrative. Cave paintings are sequential art. So is the Bayeux Tapestry. Someone once argued that the Stations Of The Cross constitute a comic strip.

Comics have been around for so long that no-one can find a convincing start point for them anymore. In the West they're considered a niche art at best, but there's a comic packed into every airplane seat in the world that explains how to not die if the damn thing catches fire. Comics are often regarded as fringe-y and "alternative," and yet the US Army used them for operating manuals and the CIA dropped them on unfavoured countries to teach dissent to their populations. As pervasive as air and yet somehow as shameful as crack, comics win literary prizes and reshape the cultural landscape at the same time as we're told that comics are "just movies on paper," and therefore unworthy of special or separate consideration as an artform.

That last one ... that's been sticky, that epithet. Like all genuinely ignorant comments, it seems to have a half-life that outlasts more aware and less toxic observations. The shaky development of comics criticism and theory from inside the field has been too scattershot, too stop-start and often too fraught with industry politics to make any real headway against statements like that.

Which is just one reason why I'm so pleased to have this volume in my hands. In many ways, it feels like a fresh start for comics theory. Its strong and reasoned explanation of why comics are *not* paper movies alone make it a valuable contribution, and represents the sort of accessibly-presented clarity the field's been crying out for. Even when arguing that comics are the best material for film adaptation due to their similarities, there is a sharp understanding of what separates the two arts.

It's the book I would have wished for twenty years ago, when I was just entering the field, and the last in a depressing series of false starts for the medium as an intellectual art (or even as provider of half-smart entertainment) was burning away again. A rock-solid collection of thinking about what defines the medium and what it's capable of, and a fine foundation for building a new critical and theoretical language to explore comics' corridors. To have been able to place this book in front of people who didn't even understand why I'd want to involve myself in a thing like comics: that would have been delightful.

This book is a wonderful reader, and a superb set of argument-starters and positions that reveal intent and rigorous thinking about my medium. I hope you enjoy it as much as I did.

Warren Ellis
England
Hallowe'en 2010

The Art and Philosophy of Comics: An Introduction

Aaron Meskin and Roy T. Cook

1 Introduction to the Introduction

You hold in your hands (or view on a screen) the first-ever anthology of essays on the philosophy of comics written from the perspective of Anglo-American philosophy. An introduction to any such volume is intended to give the reader an overview of the subject and a feel for what is to be found in the remainder of the volume. Being the first anthology of this sort, however, places additional burdens on an adequate introduction. In addition to sketching what it is that we shall be doing in the remainder of the book, it will also be useful to indicate why the time has finally come for such a volume and how the essays contained in it connect to larger themes within research into both art in general and comics in particular.

With this in mind, this introduction will be structured as follows. First, we shall outline, in Section 2, what we take to be the subject matter of the philosophy of comics and of this volume, and why these issues and questions should be of interest to philosophers of art, philosophers more generally, and comics fans and scholars of all kinds. Once we have a better idea of what our target questions and controversies are, this introduction will take a somewhat historical turn. Although there has been little philosophical work until now on comics within the analytic Anglo-American tradition, both comics and comics scholarship have histories that inform the essays in this volume. Thus, we shall provide a short history of comics in Section 3, one that emphasizes aspects of that history that are relevant to the tasks at hand; and in Section 4 we shall provide a brief overview of recent comics scholarship with a particular

The Art of Comics: A Philosophical Approach, First Edition.
Edited by Aaron Meskin and Roy T. Cook.
© 2012 Blackwell Publishing Ltd. Published 2012 by Blackwell Publishing Ltd.

emphasis on the small amount of pre-existing philosophical work on comics within the Anglo-American philosophical tradition. The introduction will then conclude with an overview of the contents of the volume, summarizing each essay and forging links, when possible, between these essays and the larger picture sketched here.

2 What We Are Doing, and Why

The first and most important aspect of saying what it is that we are doing in this volume is to first say what we are not doing. Philosophical writing on comics can mean many things, but there are two particular types of scholarly work that have become most associated with the conjunction of philosophy and comics[1]:

> *Philosophy in or through comics:* The study of philosophical themes and ideas as they are represented and explored within particular comics.

> *Philosophy of comics:* The study – primarily aesthetic, but also perhaps semantic, metaphysical, or epistemological – of the nature and functioning of comics.

Studying the existential themes expressed by Alan Moore's characterization of Dr Manhattan in *Watchmen* (1995) is an instance of philosophy in comics, while examining the collaborative nature of authorship within that same comic would be an instance of philosophy of comics. This volume is primarily concerned with the second of these tasks: the authors of the essays herein pursue the philosophical study of comics as an art form, and the analysis of how this art form works, how it connects to other art forms, and how it poses novel questions and puzzles for the philosopher of art.

This is not meant to imply either that the study of philosophy in comics is somehow inferior to the study of the philosophy of comics, or that the two philosophical approaches to comics can be sharply and completely separated. With regard to the first issue, it is worth noting that the publisher of the present anthology also publishes the well-received *Philosophy and Pop Culture* series of volumes that includes a number of volumes squarely within the philosophy in comics vein (including volumes on *Batman, Green Lantern, Iron Man, X-Men,* and *Watchmen*), and that one of the editors of the present volume has written a paper for one of these volumes (Meskin 2009). That being said, it is probably safe to say that most of the extant work in the philosophy in comics vein does not attempt to break new philosophical ground; rather, the goal of the majority of this work is to popularize philosophy rather than further philosophical research. With regard to the second issue – a sharp contrast between philosophy in comics and philosophy of comics – it is likely that there are at least some cases where the philosophical themes explored within a comic will be relevant to examining, understanding and answering philosophical questions regarding that comic (or comics in general), and vice versa – *Watchmen* again comes to mind here, as do various experimental and avant-garde comics that explore arguably philosophical questions about the nature and limitations of the art form. (See Spiegelman (2008) and Molotiu (2009) for examples.) Nevertheless, the concerns of the essays collected in this volume fall for the most part squarely on the philosophy of comics side of the divide.

Note that we (and most of the authors included in this volume) simply assume that comics are an art form. This does not imply that that any of us think *all* comics are works of art, although some theorists might think so. Film is an art form, but not all films are art – the same goes for photography and painting. We think the same goes for comics – although many comics are art, at least some comics (e.g., various instructional comics, perhaps some crude pornographic comics) are not properly considered art. And, of course, even among the comics that are art there are many that are not very good.

Moreover, like film and photography, we believe that comics comprise a significant *category* of art – it is the sort of category that is invoked regularly in critical discourse. That is, critics and ordinary consumers appreciate, evaluate and interpret comics as *comics*. This supports the view that there really is an art form of comics, a view underwriting much of the work in this volume. In fact, we think this should be non-controversial – the existence of comics that meet the conditions for being art, and the further existence of a genuine, substantial category of art under which comics fall, is hard to deny (at least, by anyone who knows anything about comics and about art more generally). We are hard pressed to think of a reasonable theory of art that would necessarily exclude comics. But there has not been serious philosophical discussion of this issue, and we would not be surprised if there were skeptics about the art status of comics out there. (In fact we look forward to philosophical engagement with such skeptics!)

Thus, the topic of interest here is the philosophical – primarily aesthetic and metaphysical – study of comics as art. Unsurprisingly then, the essays largely fall into the sub-field of philosophy known as aesthetics (or the philosophy of art), especially where that domain of enquiry intersects with the sub-field of metaphysics. Hence many of the questions asked here will be of a familiar sort, similar to questions that philosophers have asked about other art forms, or concerning the connections that hold between comics and other art forms, such as:

What makes comics art?
How do comics relate to other art forms?

> How does collaborative creation affect the nature of comics?
> What can we learn about comics from the practice of adaptation?

Of course, given that comics are a distinct art form from those forms that have received extended and extensive attention from philosophers of art up to now, it should also be unsurprising that there are completely new questions that arise due to the unique characteristics of the comics medium itself, such as:

> What are comics?
> How do images and text interact to produce content in comics?
> What role does printing play in the metaphysics of comics?
> What different kinds of comics exist? How do these types differ?
> What is the significance of sequence and serialization in comics?

As is often the case in philosophy, the distinction here need not be a sharp one. In particular, answers to questions in one of these categories may well be intimately connected to answers to questions in the other. We shall return to a more detailed examination of these questions and concerns in Sections 4 and 5 below.

Now that we have a bit of a better idea of what it is we are, and are not, interested in here, it is worth examining *why* we should be interested in these issues. The first cluster of issues motivating the philosophical examination of comics as an art form has to do with the fruitful connections that can be drawn between work specifically on the aesthetics of comics and important more general themes in the philosophy of art. The following four examples are typical of such connections, but by no means constitute a comprehensive list.

First, there has been a notable increase of interest in the study of *philosophies of arts*, rather than simply the philosophy of art, in recent years (see Kivy (1993) and (1997) for arguments in favor of this turn). In other words, philosophers have increasingly paid attention to the specific problems raised by particular art forms rather than concentrating solely on a monolithic account of all art. Moreover, recent research on the philosophies of film, literature, music, theatre, computer art, and videogames – research focusing in part on problems and issues that are particular to each of these art forms – has been among the most fruitful research in philosophical aesthetics. Not only has such work unearthed intriguing and distinctive issues raised by those art forms, but it has gone some way to counteracting a natural tendency – evident in ordinary discourse and to some extent in philosophy – to over-generalize about the arts. A philosophical focus on comics, which asks not just general questions about comics as one of many art forms, but which also focuses on those aspects of comics that differentiate comics from other art forms, fits well with this developmental trend. In other words, a philosophy of comics that concentrates on the second kind of question alluded to above would constitute an additional important chapter in the increasingly central and increasingly important study of individual art forms.

Second, although traditional aesthetics tended to focus its attention on "high" or "fine" art, there has in recent years been an increasing amount of attention paid within academic philosophy of art to popular or mass art – see, for example, Noël Carroll's *A Philosophy of Mass Art* (1998) and Theodore Gracyk's *Rhythm and Noise: An Aesthetics of Rock* (1996). This work has shown that careful attention to the popular arts can be philosophically fruitful – both in bringing to light previously unnoticed questions of philosophical interest and in providing a more accurate picture of the nature of – and our engagement with – the arts more generally. A philosophical focus on comics would constitute a significant contribution to this area, if only because comics arguably pre-date many of the other typical examples of popular arts, including film and television. In addition, comics are subdivided into a number of distinct, robust regional variants and traditions with, for example, Franco-Belgian and Japanese comics differing from North American comics and from each other both in terms of their production and, most importantly for the study of popular arts, in terms of their reception. The fact that reading comics has, traditionally, been a more socially acceptable pastime for adults in some parts of Western Europe and in Japan than it has been for adults in North America may be an important datum for the philosopher wishing to understand the "popular" in popular arts.

Third, comics promise to be a particularly important example of the notion of a hybrid art form. Jerrold Levinson defines hybrid art forms as follows:

> Hybrid art forms are art forms arising from the actual combination or inter-penetration of earlier art forms. (1984: 6).[2]

Although some comics scholars have explicitly rejected the claim that comics are hybrids (e.g., McCloud (1993) and Sabin (1993)), the comics art form is clearly a hybrid art form in *this* sense, since it arose from a combination of technologies and techniques associated with drawing and caricature, prose storytelling, and printmaking. Hybrid art forms raise questions about standard approaches to art evaluation and ontology which often seem to implicitly assume that art forms are pure (i.e., that they are not hybrid). The study of comics and their hybridity promises to shed new light onto these debates and issues.

Finally, comics are a particularly interesting instance of hybridity, since the result of so combining these pre-existing art forms amounted, in the end, to something that is much more than merely the sum of its parts. In particular, as the comics art form evolved from its heterogeneous origins, a wealth of conventions evolved – conventions governing panel placement, panel borders (or frames), speech and thought balloons, narration boxes, sound effects, motion lines and other *emanata*, and a host of other characteristics. One underinvestigated, but particularly important, aspect of this phenomenon is the fact that these conventions vary considerably from culture to culture and from comics tradition to comics tradition (as anyone who reads both manga and western comics is aware). Arguably, comics are saturated with convention, and cultural variation of convention, to a degree unmatched by any other visual art form. As a result, philosophers interested in the role of conventions within art will not find a better test-lab than the comics.

Thus, there are a number of interconnected reasons why comics should be of central concern to philosophers of art, to art historians, to art and comics critics, and to anyone interested in the nature and development of contemporary art in general or comics in particular. This volume will not merely serve the specialist scholar. We predict that it will be of interest to a wide range of comics readers and creators. To a large extent this is because philosophical questions and concerns are not just of interest to philosophers. One does not, after all, have to be a professional academic to be interested in the definition of comics or the status of comics as an art.

More specifically, the theoretical investigation of comics found in this volume, may help the reader, or the creator, to (among other things):

(1) Better understand the significance and potential value of various avantgarde strategies for making comics.
(2) Better understand the choices and difficulties involved in adapting comics to other art forms, or vice versa.
(3) Better understand the connections between comics and other popular art forms, and the much-discussed connections between comics and Pop Art.
(4) Better understand the nature of contemporary comics in virtue of their historical connection both to earlier comic traditions and to distinct, prior artistic traditions out of which comics developed.

This is clearly only a partial list, but it nevertheless suggests that the theoretical work carried out in the chapters below will help the reader or creator to form a richer picture of how comics work, and how they might work, and as a result should be of interest to anyone who takes comics seriously.

Of course, philosophical work on comics is not the only type of work that can illuminate the sorts of issues outlined above. In particular, there is a continuously growing literature on comics in fields other than philosophy, including work by historians, literary theorists, communications scholars, and film theorists, that is relevant to many, if not all, of the topics discussed above. (For useful recent surveys of this literature see Chute (2008), Lent (2010), and Hatfield (2010)). We shall touch on such work in Section 4 below. Nevertheless, there has, until now, been a comparative lack of study of these issues from a *philosophical* perspective, resulting in a lop sided account. With this in mind, the present volume is not meant to answer these questions in full, nor is it meant to "fix" or replace pre-existing work on these topics by scholars from other disciplines. Instead, it is meant to provide insights, answers, and accounts relevant to these issues from the perspective of philosophers of art. We hope the comments above (and, more importantly, the chapters below) will convince the reader that this until-now under-represented perspective is worth the time and attention that we have devoted to it here.

3 A Short History of Comics

Our next task is to provide a brief, historically-oriented guide to the subject matter of this volume: comics. In general, we treat the term "comics" quite broadly, and understand this term to cover graphic novels, newspaper strips, single-panel gag cartoons, superhero comics, romance comics, western comics, underground comix, web-comics, manga, alternative comics, and a wealth of related phenomenon (this is not to say, of course, that every chapter below is intended by its author to address all of these sub-forms). Of course, treating the term "comics" as applying quite broadly is not the same as treating it as applying as broadly as is possible. Some art works, regardless of their superficial similarity to comics, are not, in fact, comics, and it will serve us well not to spread our net too widely.

Of course, it is difficult to draw a sharp line between those works that are comics and those that are not without a precise definition of "comic." The correct formulation of such a precise definition, however, is a matter of some contention, and is a subject addressed, either directly or indirectly, in a number of the chapters below. Here we shall take a different approach, and instead take a tour of the highlights in the history of comics-like art, looking at clear instances of comics but also at a few borderline cases, thus emphasizing the historical development of comics as they arose from pre-existing art forms (i.e., their hybridity) instead of attempting to demarcate their essential characteristics.

But where to begin? Scott McCloud (1993), emphasizing the sequential nature of comics, suggests that Egyptian tomb paintings from the thirteenth century BC are comics (1993: 12–15), and that the much more recent Bayeux Tapestry, which was created in the eleventh century AD, is also a comic (1993: 12–13). Inclusion of these examples on McCloud's part is as likely motivated by polemical goals – to justify the cultural and aesthetic importance of comics by identifying, as comics, artifacts whose cultural and aesthetic importance is secure – than it is by any genuine commitment to these examples as genuine instances of comics (see Meskin (2007) for relevant discussion). After all, regardless of any superficial similarity between these art works and comics, there seems to be no substantial historical connections between these and modern-day comics (nor does critical practice seem to treat those art works as comics), and, as a result, many will find it difficult to take seriously the idea that the creators of these works were working within the same art form as Charles Schulz.

At any rate, immediately after discussing these examples, McCloud moves on to another topic central to the nature of comics – printing (McCloud 15). And it is with the invention of printing that we get the first genuine proto-comics – artworks that are (1) similar to comics, and (2) out of which modern-day comics traditions evolved. Between the fifteenth-century development of the printing press and the nineteenth century, a number of artists experimented with telling stories through a combination of drawings and text. William Hogarth's eighteenth-century illustrated narrative print sequences (such as *A Harlot's Progress* and *Marriage A-La-Mode*) are perhaps the best known of these precursors of modern comics although many would resist characterizing them as actual comics. (But there are conflicting views, see below.)

Leaving aside Hogarth, the most notable of these proto-comics – and, according to many comics historians, the works that mark the first genuine comics in the modern sense of the term – are the picture stories created by Rodolphe Töpffer in the mid-nineteenth century (collected in Töpffer (2007). These stories introduced and standardized a number of innovations that would be crucial to comics as an art form, including panel borders and interdependent text and image – so much so that David Kunzle's critical study of Töpffer's life and work is titled *Father of the Comic Strip: Rodolphe Töpffer.* Similar early works were produced by Wilhelm Busch, Cham (Charles Henri Amédée de Noé), George Cruikshank, Léonce Petit, and Adolphe Willette (see Kunzle 1973: 1990) for details on the pre-Töpffer and early post-Töpffer comics tradition).

With the basic components of the comic in place, the art form developed in fits and starts until the late nineteenth century, where we can find a number of milestones leading up to the development of modern comics. The earliest of these was the development of the modern newspaper strip. R.F. Outcault's *Hogan's Alley,* featuring the Yellow Kid and first published in 1895, is traditionally credited with being the first modern newspaper strip, although other comics have also claimed this title. Outcault's strip is typically mobilized to defend the claim that the comic strip is an American invention (see Harvey 1999), although serialized strips with recurring characters, such as Charles H. Ross's *Ally Sloper*, had appeared in magazines in Britain as early as 1884. Thus, the strip form is not an American invention, although the *newspaper* strip might be. Nevertheless, the inclusion of regular strips in American newspapers, which exposed the comics form to a much wider audience than it had been able to access before, certainly marks a watershed in the development of this art form (for an analysis of *Hogan's Alley* and the subsequent American newspaper comics tradition, see Harvey 1999, for discussion of *Ally Sloper*, see Sabin 2003).

From these fairly humble beginnings, the strip form eventually developed into a serious art in the first few decades of the twentieth century. Winsor McCay's *Little Nemo in Slumberland* and *Dreams of the Rarebit Fiend*, Lionel Feininger's *Kin-der-Kids* and *Wee Willie Winkie's World*, and George Herriman's *Krazy Kat* are all still recognized masterpieces. In fact, outside of Art Spiegelman and his *Maus*, it would be hard to find a comics artist more respected than Herriman and a comic more lauded than *Krazy Kat* (see Seldes (1924) and Warshow (1946) for examples of laudatory statements about the work).

The next major development in the art form was the invention of the modern comic book – a standardized booklet format for distributing comics. The first comic book is traditionally considered to be *Famous Funnies: Carnival of Comics*, a volume reprinting newspaper strips and published in 1934 by Eastern Color (although, again, there are competing claims for this honor, some tracing as far back as the book-length *The Adventures of Obadiah Oldbuck* in 1842, an unauthorized booklet-sized American reprint of one of Töpffer's stories). Shortly afterwards in 1935 Major Malcolm Wheeler-Nicholson's company, National Allied Publications (now DC Comics), published *New Fun: The Big Comic Magazine* #1, the first comic book consisting entirely of original content instead of reprints of newspaper strips.

Roughly at the same time, a number of American artists – following the early twentieth-century example of Belgian Frans Masereel and others – began exploring the potential of wordless woodcut novels to tell serious (i.e., adult) stories. These works of pictorial narrative achieved a brief period of minor popularity in the 1930s, and although the genre has never been a central one, these artists did show the potential for comics to address "serious" social and political themes – something that was taken up by mainstream comics some decades later. Well- known authors of such works include Lynd Ward and Milt Gross.

At this point, all of the ingredients necessary for the development of modern mainstream comics were in place, except for their most famous subject matter – superheroes. Jerry Siegel and Joe Shuster introduced Superman to comic readers in *Action Comics* #1 in 1938. Batman, created by

Bob Kane and Bill Finger, followed shortly afterwards in *Detective Comics* #27, published in 1939. In actuality, there were other, proto-superheroes published earlier, and recently collected and discussed in Sadowski (2009). Nevertheless, regardless of which character one counts as the first genuine superhero, there is no doubt that the near-simultaneous introduction of Batman and Superman by what would become DC Comics is the first important milestone in what would become the super-hero dominated mainstream comic book industry.

The comic book industry passed through a number of distinct historical periods, or *ages*, over the next seven decades (The period dominated by newspaper comics strips, and comic books reprinting them – from roughly 1885–1938, is sometimes referred to as the *platinum age*) The *golden age*, roughly 1938 to 1945, was characterized primarily by the introduction of a pantheon of new superheroes and a solidification of the characteristics of the superhero genre, including secret identities, sidekicks, and superhero societies.

The post-war decade, called the *atomic age*, was characterized by a temporary shift away from superhero comics (although they never completely disappeared) and a proliferation of other genres, including romance, westerns, science fiction, and, notably, crime and horror comics. It is the horror and crime comics that proved to be the end of the atomic age, as the (alleged) excesses of sexual innuendo and violent content in these comics, along with the overblown rhetoric of anti-comics literature such as Fredric Wertham's *Seduction of the Innocent* (1954), led, after hearings of the Senate Subcommittee on Juvenile Delinquency, to the voluntary creation of the Comics Code Authority (CCA) in 1954. The CCA strictly censored the content of comics created by participating publishers, although a few publishers, including Dell, who published the clean-cut Disney line of comics, managed to continue to operate independently of the CCA.

Although some publishers left comics to concentrate on other ventures (such as EC Comics famous shift to Harvey Kurtzman's humor publication *Mad Magazine*), most of the publishers that survived the backlash of attacks by Wertham and others continued to publish comic books, albeit comics that now met the stringent restrictions of the CCA. Without the ability to tackle serious, controversial, or "adult" issues or storylines, the comics of the subsequent *silver age* (roughly 1956–1969) often resorted to silly plot devices, but the results of the CCA-imposed limitations were not all negative. This period saw an increase in the mean level of both artistic and storytelling skill in comics, and perhaps more importantly it saw the rise of Stan Lee's Marvel Comics. Lee's engaging stories, more often than not illustrated by Jack Kirby or Steve Ditko, spearheaded a new and important trend in mainstream superhero comics: a focus on the problems and issues faced by superheroes when in their everyday (i.e., "secret identity") personas.

Over the next couple of decades, there was a gradual weakening of the constraints enforced by the CCA and as a result, comic book publishers attempted to address more serious themes. This trend culminated in the publication, in 1986, of three notable comics which were to profoundly influence the development of the art form: Alan Moore and Dave Gibbon's *Watchmen*, Frank Miller's *Batman: The Dark Knight Returns*, and Art Spiegelman's *Maus: A Survivor's Tale Volume* I: *My Father Bleeds History*. (*Volume* II: *And Here My Troubles Began* would not be published until 1991). The first two of these ushered in the *modern age* of mainstream comics, which continues into the present and is characterized by darker, more psychologically driven stories and by anti-hero protagonists that blur the line between hero and villain.

Spiegelman's *Maus*, on the other hand, which did not concern spandex-clad superheroes, eventually went on to win a Pulitzer Prize in 1992, and it would be hard to exaggerate its significance to the art form. There is literally a cottage industry of academic research on *Maus* (see Chute 2008), it appears on a variety of popular best book lists, and it is plausible that it has done more than any other work to establish comics as an art form worthy of serious study. In addition, the non-fiction nature and autobiographical elements of Spiegelman's comic have been tremendously influential – a remarkable number of the most lauded comics produced in the last two decades have followed Spiegelman in exploring both the documentary capacities of comics and the memoir form. It is widely claimed that the success of the three works that ushered in the modern age is responsible both for the widening popularity of comic books and their eventual inclusion in libraries and mainstream bookstores.

This brief history covers the development of mainstream comics – particularly superhero comics – but leaves out a number of equally important parallel developments. In particular, there are five additional traditions that are worth noting here: Underground comics, alternative comics, single-panel gag cartoons, webcomics, and manga.

First, there are the underground comics (or comix, or commix) that grew out of the counterculture scene centered in the San Francisco area during the late 1960s and early-to-mid 1970s, although not all of the comics produced as parts of this alternative movement were necessarily produced or distributed in San Francisco. A number of artists who were interested in the comics form but disillusioned by mainstream comics and, in particular, the tame comics being produced under the CCA seal, began to produce and distribute their own comics, often in the form of anthology series such as Robert Crumb's *Jiz*, *Snatch*, and *Zap Comix*, Jay Lynch's *Bijou Funnies*, and Trina Robbins' *Wimmen's Comix*. For the most part, the stories revolved around and glorified the concerns of the counterculture movement including sex, drugs, and violence. *Mad Magazine*, with its subversive subtext and comics-code free content, was a particularly strong influence on the underground scene, although the edgy content of *Mad* pales in comparison to the intended-to-offend comics eventually created by Crumb, Denis Kitchen, Gilbert Shelton, Frank Stack, S. Clay Wilson, and others.

Second, there are contemporary alternative comics (or literary comics), although it is difficult to formulate a precise division between alternative comics and their San Francisco predecessors. The underground comix scene did not end so much as it metamorphasized, in concert with the interests of non-mainstream creators and the fading of the counterculture scene, into the contemporary alternative comics scene. These comics, like the undergrounds, can be characterized at least in part as a reaction against the mainstream comics industry and its emphasis on mythic, superheroic stories and mesomorphic anatomy, but the alternative comics scene is characterized by an emphasis on less reactionary, more mature themes. This evolution is not so much a rejection of the concerns of the underground so much as an evolution and maturation of the creators involved, and a number of artists associated with underground comix now produce less sex-and-drug fuelled comics squarely within the alternative tradition, including Lynda Barry (*What It Is*), Robert Crumb (*The Book of Genesis Illustrated by R. Crumb*), Bill Griffith (*Zippy: Ding Dong Daddy*), Art Spiegelman (*In the Shadow of No Towers*), and Trina Robbins (*Go Girl! Vol.* I–II, with Anne Timmons).

A discussion of alternative comics brings us to the second important year in contemporary comics history. As Ben Schwartz points out in his introduction to the critical anthology *Best American Comics Criticism* (2010), 2000 marked a watershed year for alternative comics, as it saw the publication of two of the most important, and admired, comics within this tradition by what were are the time a pair of such young up-and-comers: Chris Ware's *Jimmy Corrigan: The Smartest Kid on Earth*, and Daniel Clowes' *David Boring*. According to Schwartz, it was only with the publication of these works that comics were transformed from a niche market into a self-subsistent form of literature or art that could exist, not as a part or outgrowth of so-called mainstream comics, but instead as an independent tradition, sold in bookstores and widely read and studied.

Regardless of whether Schwartz is right regarding the comparative cultural impact of year-1986 comics versus year-2000 comics, there is no doubt that an explosion of quality alternative comics appeared during the decade after *Jimmy Corrigan* and *David Boring*. Notable creators include Alison Bechdel (*Fun Home: A Family Tragicomic*), Charles Burns (*Black Hole*), David Heatley (*My Brain is Hanging Upside Down*),[3] David Mazzucchelli (*Asterios Polyp*), Jeff Smith (*Bone*), Seth (*It's a Good Life if You Don't Weaken*), and Craig Thompson (*Blankets*). As mentioned earlier, comics with autobiographical elements have made up a particularly significant genre (arguably the most important genre) among recent alternative comics. In addition to comics memoirs by Bechdel, Heatley, and Thompson, creators such as David B, Marjane Satrapi, Jeffrey Brown, Guy Delisle, and Aline Kominsky-Crumb have explored this form. And Harvey Pekar produced important and influential autobiographical comics in his *American Splendor* series for more than thirty years between 1976 and 2008.

A third tradition within comics that deserves attention here are single-panel gag cartoons. Although the deceivingly simple structure of single-panels cartoons have tempted some to treat them as a distinct art form (see, e.g., McCloud 1993), the overlap of techniques combined with the fact than many creators work in both the single-panel format and in sequential comics seems to justify treating these as one of many formats within comics rather than as a distinct art form. Single-panel gag cartoons can be traced back to humorous illustrations found in nineteenth-century magazines such as *Punch*, and the modern editorial cartoon is a direct outgrowth of this tradition. Although once common in magazines and on the daily and Sunday newspaper pages (e.g., Hank Ketcham's *Dennis the Menace* and Gary Larson's *The Far Side*), single-panel cartoons are quickly disappearing, with the exception of single-panel editorial cartoons (and a small number of alternative cartoonists who work in the format, such as Ivan Brunetti). At present, very few American magazines regularly publish single-panel gag cartoons, with *Playboy* and the *New Yorker* being perhaps the most influential. Notable artists within this tradition include Charles Addams, Peter Arno, Charles Barsotti, Roz Chast, Leo Cullum, Will Elder, Rube Goldberg, Virgil Partch, William Steig, Saul Steinberg, James Thurber, and Gahan Wilson (see Topliss (2005) for detailed examinations of the work of Addams, Arno, Steig, and Steinberg).

Fourth, we should say something about webcomics. Although webcomics began merely as a means for comics artists to distribute their comic as widely and as cheaply as possible, this sub-category of comics has quickly outgrown its origins. In particular, webcomics provide creators with a new set of tools with which to create and share their comics, and this mode of production and distribution also lifts some of restrictions inherent in more traditional methods. Scott McCloud, in *Reinventing Comics* (2000), explores how the digital canvas can change the nature of comics by allowing us to link up panels in new, non-two-dimensional patterns (2000: 223). In addition, McCloud argues that by eliminating the need for physically printing comics, we thereby eliminate many of the restrictions imposed by printing, such as limits on the length of tiers of panels (i.e., how many panels can be strung together in a row), limits on the size and arrangement of pages, and fixed size ratios between panels (2000: 223–224).

Fifth, and finally, we should say a bit about other comics traditions. Comics have a varied history, with most contemporary cultures supporting some form of comics. One particularly interesting form not frequently found in the Anglo-American comics tradition is the photographic comic – these are called *fotoromanzi* in Italy and *fotonovelas* in Latin America where they are extremely popular. As alluded to above, the *bande dessinée* tradition found in France and Belgium has a distinctively higher cultural status than does the comics tradition in Britain and the United States (see Beaty 2007, McKinney 2008, and Vessels (2010)), and there is a closely connected, adult-oriented and artistically robust, comics tradition in Canada (see Bell 2006). Other comics traditions that have received substantial academic attention include Italy (Castaldi 2010), Mexico (Rubenstein 1998 and Campbell 2009), and Russia (Alaniz 2010 and McKenna 2001).

The tradition that has had the most impact both on Anglo-American comics and Anglo-American culture more generally, however, is Japanese manga. Manga has a rich history, tracing its origin to two competing influences. The first of these is the tradition of Japanese woodblock prints known as ukiyo-e, and kibyôshi – woodblock-illustrated books such as that explicitly aimed for harmonious balance between image and text. The other is the Western influence – in this case, primarily American comic books – that shaped Japanese culture in the post-World War II occupation of Japan. The combination of traditional Japanese art forms and Western comics resulted in a comics tradition that combined aspects of each, and which developed its own artistic and narrative styles as well as its own set of formal conventions (see Gravett 2004 for a useful overview of manga, and Power 2009 for a study of Osamu Tezuka, the most important figure in post-World War II Japanese comics).

Of course, understanding manga both as an art form and as a culture requires more than the embarrassingly brief sketch just provided. Unfortunately, space concerns preclude us from a proper treatment of this tradition. We will, however, emphasize that anyone interested in comics and the study of comics, no matter what one's narrower concerns are, would do well to study manga, and the traditions that have sprung from it (including Chinese manhua and Korean manhwa, as well as the growing original English language (OEL) manga literature) as closely as possible. The reason is simple: Younger readers, no matter what their backgrounds, are becoming attracted to manga in increasing numbers, so much so that complaints one heard ten or twenty years ago, regarding the lack of a serious comics section at major bookstores, have now been replaced by worries regarding the large fraction of that section now given over to manga. While we think that there is no real danger that mainstream superhero comics or alternative comics will disappear anytime in the near future, it is clear that manga will continue to grow in popularity, and as a result, comics scholars should devote equally substantial efforts towards its study.

4 Comics Scholarship and the Philosophy of Comics: A Brief History

Relative to the development of the comics art form itself, comics scholarship has been slow to develop, and the serious study of comics within Anglo-American Philosophy has been slower still when compared to the exciting work done in other disciplines such as Literature Studies, Film Studies, Communications, and History. Surely the low cultural status of comics has something to do with their general neglect by the Academy as does their ephemerality. (It can be difficult to study things that are often thrown away so quickly.) Relatedly, the lack of an established corpus of masterpieces prior to the publication of *Maus* certainly had a retarding affect. In the case of philosophical aesthetics, as suggested above, the tendency to focus on general questions about art (especially of the "fine" or "high" varieties) rather than on questions about individual arts was also a significant contributing factor in its neglect of comics. But we suspect this is not the whole story. The recent shift in aesthetics from the philosophy of art to the philosophies of arts is bound up with the idea that philosophers ought to purse the *distinctive* issues raised by the individual arts. We are not completely persuaded by the idea (since philosophy of literature seems to proceed quite nicely even when it does not focus on distinctive issues raised by literature), but we suspect that much of the neglect of comics stems from something like it. And so on our account it is a failure to recognize the sorts of genuine and distinctive philosophical problems raised by comics that explains why philosophers have been so slow to engage with the art form. If this is right, then a compelling defense of the philosophy of comics looks like it must provide an account of some genuine philosophical problems that are raised by the art form; problems that are not so generic that they are not properly dealt with simply by the general philosophy of art nor so familiar that they are not already dealt with by other subfields within philosophical aesthetics. We think the work described in this section and the one following provide the basis for such a defense. In the remainder of this section, then, we shall sketch, in rough outline, the philosophical work on comics that has been carried out so far. In the final section we turn to the work contained in this very volume.

Perhaps the single most influential work in the burgeoning field of the philosophy of comics is a comic book. Scott McCloud's previously mentioned brilliant investigation of the comics medium by means of the comics medium – his 1993 *Understanding Comics: The Invisible Art* – addresses a wide range of important issues raised by comics, but the book is arguably best known for articulating a sophisticated and much-discussed definition of comics. McCloud argues that comics are "juxtaposed pictorial and other images in deliberate sequence, intended to convey information and/or to produce an aesthetic response in the viewer" (p. 9). It is notable that this definition is neutral with respect to both content and technological medium (as opposed, for example, to art historian David Kunzle's definition which appeals to both a "mass medium" and the putatively "moral and topical" nature of comics (Kunzle 1973), and it is arguably this formalism that has led to its enduring appeal. Other key elements of McCloud's seminal work include his argument for the artistic significance of "closure" in comics, his popular but controversial claim that cartooning enhances viewer-identification, his exploration of the various means by which comics may represent motion and time, and his brilliant cataloguing of both the kinds of panel transitions that can be found in comics and the sorts of word/picture combinations that one can find in them. This is just a taste of the riches to be found in McCloud's work – the book is required reading for anyone seriously interested in the art form. Later work by McCloud, such as the previously discussed *Reinventing Comics* (2000) and his more recent how-to book *Making Comics* (2006) are full of additional interesting ideas although neither has yet had the kind of influence on philosophers that his first book did.

McCloud is not the only comics artist who has produced theoretical works of interest to philosophers. Will Eisner, author of the classic comic strip *The Spirit* as well as one of the first self-identified graphic novels, *A Contract with God*, wrote two important works devoted to the subject. His *Comics and Sequential Art* (1985/1990) famously argued that comics are a "form of reading" but also emphasized the visual aspects of their textual elements. Also of special interest in this book are Eisner's careful examination of the various expressive, representational and aesthetic functions of panel and frame design, his investigation of "expressive anatomy" (i.e., the way in which the representation of the human form and human action function expressively), and his attempt to catalogue some of the broadest genres of comics. His follow-up, *Graphic Storytelling* (1996/2008), although more of a how-to book focusing on the construction of narrative in the comics medium (as well as in other visual media), also contains important insights into the comics art form.

In *The Aesthetics of Comics* (2000), David Carrier produced the first full-length philosophical treatment of the art of comics. Carrier is an analytic philosopher, art historian and well-known art critic, and his work can be usefully seen as focusing on the relationship between comics and the more traditional visual art of painting. The first part of the work involves an extended argument for Carrier's intriguing and much-criticized account of comics in terms of three putatively essential features – speech balloons, closely-linked narrative and book-size scale – as well as the development of the intriguing suggestion that comics are properly seen as an artistic solution to a problem raised by traditional narrative painting (i.e., how to tell a story by means of pictures "without reference to some prior text" (2000: 74)). In the second section of the book, Carrier goes on to argue for a number of other controversial theses including the suggestion that the interpretation of comics (as a mass-culture art) differs radically from the interpretation of "high" art and that comics are essentially "self-interpreting pictures." Finally, Carrier argues that comics are a post-historical art "not needing or being able to progress" (2000: 121). Unsurprisingly Carrier's claims have been controversial, but it has to be said that contemporary philosophical work on comics owes much to the example of serious investigation into the art form that he provided.

The definitions proposed by McCloud and Carrier are criticized in Greg Hayman and Henry John Pratt's "What Are Comics?" (2005) although they ultimately propose a formalist definition that is fairly close to McCloud's, differing primarily in the emphasis they place on narrative. Hayman and Pratt argue that comics are essentially sequential pictorial narratives, and it is this approach that Meskin takes as his primary target in his "Defining Comics?" (2007). In that chapter, Meskin argues that a range of proposed definitions of comics (including those offered by Kunzle, McCloud and Carrier) suffer from straightforward counterexamples, and he suggests that theorists might do better to eschew the definitional project altogether since there is little reason to think that there exist any serious theoretical undertakings that require having such a definition to hand. Picking up on Meskin's skepticism about extant definitions of comics, Roy T. Cook's "Do Comics Require Pictures? Or, Why *Batman* #663 is a Comic" (2011) focuses on the pictorial thesis (i.e., the view that comics are or contain a sequence of pictures) – a view that is accepted by pretty much everyone who has offered a definition of comics. Cook criticizes standard forms of the pictorial thesis and goes on to argue that a very weak version of the thesis is true (roughly that something is a comic only if it is part of some (possibly larger) comic that has a sequence of pictures in it).

In other work, Meskin and Pratt have explored the relationship between comics and other art forms. In his "Comics as Literature?" (2009), Meskin explores the widespread assumption that comics are a form of literature and investigates the connections between comics and literature. After exploring arguments both for and against the "comics as literature" thesis, Meskin concludes that the answer to these questions may be indeterminate. In a more positive vein, Meskin ultimately argues that the art of comics is (contra McCloud and Sabin, see above) a hybrid art form descended from the arts of literature and printmaking. Furthermore, he suggests that this has implications for how comics are properly understood and appreciated. (A simplified, "popular" version of Meskin's argument is presented in his "'Why Don't You Go Read a Book Or Something' *Watchmen* as Literature" 2009.) In his

"Relating Comics, Cartoons, and Animation" (2011), Pratt recants his earlier definition of comics in the course of exploring the relationship between the arts of comics and animation and the artistic style of the cartoon.

Although there are good reasons to think that comics need not be narrative, it is certainly the case that narrativity is a feature of the vast majority of comics. In his "Narrative in Comics" (2009a), Pratt investigates the nature of narrative in comics and, after pointing out the significant similarities between comics and film narration, he ultimately argues that there is a distinctive form of narration associated with comics. In "Medium Specificity and the Ethics of Narrative in Comics" (2009b), Pratt explores the question of whether there is something essentially morally problematic about the medium of comics. Perhaps unsurprisingly, his answer is that there is not.

Brian Boyd, a professor of literature and an evolutionary aesthetician, has published work on comics in a philosophy journal as well as a new journal devoted to evolution, art, and culture. "Art and Evolution: Spiegelman's *The Narrative Corpse*" (2008) and his more recent "On the Origins of Comics: New York Double-Take" (2010) both investigate comics from the perspective of evolutionary theories (both biological and cultural).

In addition to philosophers who have focused their attention specifically on comics, a number of philosophers have addressed comics in the course of their discussion of other issues in the philosophy of art. Here are two notable examples: Dominic McIver Lopes recently offered a argument to the effect that at least some of Hogarth's narrative works (e.g., *Rake's Progress*) are, in fact, comics (2010: 17). And in the course of his influential discussion of cinematic narration and cinematic narrators, George Wilson argues that, although ordinary comics (unlike ordinary films) do not involve "fictional showings," it "is easy to think of possible comic strips in which a fictional showing would be implicated" (Wilson 1997).

Outside of Anglo-American philosophy, the recent growth in scholarship on comics is extraordinary. We have already mentioned a few recent overviews of this literature, and it would be impossible to summarize this work in the space we have available to us here, but it might be useful to conclude this section by indicating some of the most significant contemporary outlets for comics scholarship. The University Press of Mississippi has been a notable publisher of academic work in the field. Not only has the press published numerous important anthologies such as Varnum and Gibbons (2001) which addresses the relationship between words and images in comics and the Heer and Worcester (2004) volume collecting early twentieth-century writing on comics, but it has also published monographs on such topics as alternative comics (Hatfield 2005) and Rudolf Töppfer (Kunzle 2007), as well as occasional translations of important works into English (such as Thierry Groensteen's *The System of Comics* 1999). The last few years have also seen the birth of at least three new English language print journals solely devoted to scholarly research on comics: the *Journal of Graphic Novels and Comics*, *European Comic Art*, and *Studies in Comics*. This is in addition to various peer-reviewed online journals such as *ImageText* and *Image and Narrative*, and two important and longer-running print journals, the *International Journal of Comic Art* and the more popular (and less academic) *Comics Journal*. Furthermore, articles on comics appear regularly in journals that do not specialize in comics, such as *Word and Image* and the *Journal of Popular Culture*. Comics have also been the focus of recent special issues of *English Language Notes*, *Modern Fiction Studies* and the online journal *Scan*.

5 The Contributions

The volume is divided into three sections: Part One: The Nature and Kinds of Comics; Part Two: Comics and Representation, and Part Three: Comics and the Other Arts.

The first part of the volume focuses on issues surrounding the nature and kinds of comics: What is the definition of comics? What sort of thing (in the broadest sense) is a comic? How should we think about authorship in the case of comics? What are comics genres?

As discussed above, the definition of comics has been a central concern (arguably *the* central concern) of philosophers who have paid attention to the art form. In his essay, John Holbo (Chapter 1) returns to this issue and offers a sustained meditation on the implications of Scott McCloud's famous formalist definition of the medium. That is, rather than once again dismissing McCloud's definition for its apparent flaws (most notably that it looks to be straightforwardly falsified by a range of counterexamples), Holbo seeks to show that the account provides important insights into a wide range of art works. Holbo starts by arguing that despite McCloud's best intentions, his definition leads to the radically revisionist conclusion that all (or almost all) pictures are comics since all (or almost all) pictures include spatially juxtaposed images and sequences can consist of just one element. Rather than treating this as a *reductio ad absurdum* of McCloud's approach, Holbo treats it as telling us something important about the nature of pictures. Perhaps even more radically, Holbo flirts with the idea that novels may be understood to be a kind of comic (or at least on a continuum with comics) since they are graphic products in virtue of the fact that letters and printed words are images. Ultimately, Holbo suggests that we might best think of McCloud's definition as picking out the very significant category of the "graphical work" which is designed for visual reading and consists of a mixture of image types.

In Chapter 2, Aaron Meskin addresses a variety of ontological issues raised by comics. While expressing agnosticism about the fundamental metaphysical category to which comics belong, Meskin argues that comics are not essentially multiples which admit of instances. Rather, he argues that it is plausible that comics must be either multiples or self-conscious anti-multiples (i.e., works which are intended to subvert the expectation that comics are multiples). He goes on to argue that the art of comics is normally a two-stage art (the comic artist is finished when she has produced the original art even though that does not count as the artistic end-product) and that it is typically produced and disseminated by means of what Stephen Davies (2005) has referred to as "encoding" and "decoding." But Meskin goes on to point out that there are complications with these general claims. Some comics are made in a one-stage process, and (contra Davies) in some cases the encodings from which instances of comics are produced count as instances of those comics themselves. In the final section of his chapter, Meskin explores the conditions under which something counts as an authentic instance of a comic. Meskin argues that comics are what Nelson Goodman has called an "autographic" art – exact duplicates of authentic instances do not count as authentic instances unless they are produced in the right way and, hence, certain forms of forgery are possible in comics which are not typically possible in "allographic" forms such as literature and music.

Christy Mag Uidhir (Chapter 3) addresses another key issue about which no previous philosophical work has been done – the nature of comics authorship. Despite (in)famous claims as to the death of the author, contemporary philosophers of art are generally agreed that the notion of authorship is crucial to the appreciation, evaluation, and interpretation of works of art. Moreover, as Mag Uidhir points out, authors have become crucially important to the marketing and consumption of contemporary comics. But while most popular comics are collectively produced, standard theoretical approaches to authorship focus on individually produced works of art and, hence, are ill-equipped to make sense of comics authorship. Mag Uidhir attempts to rectify this situation by offering an account of comics authorship which meets some independently plausible criteria (e.g., it makes sense of the fact that comics can, but need not, have authors) and is rooted in a powerful general theory of authorship. Central to Mag Uidhir's approach is the view that authorship is work-description relative – that is, authorship is a matter of responsibility for making a work that falls under a medium description (e.g., poem, novel, comic). One is not, then, merely an author of a comic – one is author of a work *as a comic*. And, Mag Uidhir argues, in order to be an author of a work as a comic one must be partly responsible for its possessing some of the features that are non-trivially essential for being a comic. This account provides a basis for recognizing both individually and collectively authored comics, as well as comics that lack authors altogether.

Genres are central to the comics art form, but heretofore there has been no serious philosophical attention paid to comics genres. In particular, is has become quite common for defenders of the art form to blame the bad reputation of comics on a confusion between the art form itself and a particular genre – superheroes (e.g., McCloud 1993). It is worth noting that this argument has had the unfortunate, and possibly unintended, effect of making superhero comics of little interest even to those who defend comics in general. In her essay, Catharine Abell (Chapter 4) criticizes two important recent philosophical theories of genre (by Gregory Currie 2004 and by Brian Laetz and Dominic Lopes 2008) and offers her own alternative account. For Abell, genres are historically established sets of conventions which generate evaluative and interpretive expectations among audience members. Membership in a genre requires production in a community where those conventions are established as well as production in accordance to those conventions. So, for example, superhero comics are a genre in part because they involve conventions which generate expectations in audience members (e.g., that the costumed characters in them will have special powers or abilities). Grant Morrison's *Seven Soldiers of Victory* belongs to the superhero genre because it is made in a community in which those conventions are established and because it was produced in accordance with those conventions (i.e., it was intended to have features that underwrite the applicability of those conventions). Abell goes on to use her account both to explain how genre membership affects content and to distinguish genres from both styles and media. The last distinction is used by her to make the case that both graphic novels and fumetti (i.e., photo-comics) count as media rather than genres.

How do comics represent? The essays in the second part of the volume address questions having to do with the nature of representation in the medium. How do words and image relate in comics? How do comics express mental content? Is there a language of comics?

In his contribution to the volume (Chapter 5), Thomas E. Wartenberg addresses the complex relationship between words and images in comics. Wartenberg begins by distinguishing two ways that words and images relate in other art forms. In illustrated books, images – that is, illustrations – typically function, well, as mere illustrations. Wartenberg argues that mere illustrations are ontologically dependent on (and subordinate to) the text which they illustrate. By this, he means that the text alone fixes the associated story-world, and that the illustrations must be faithful to that text and what that text tells us about the story-world with which it is associated. In many children's picture books, on the other hand, the images (although still illustrations and still subject to the constraint of faithfulness) are canonical in that they codetermine the story-world along with the text. But how then do words and images relate in comics? Wartenberg argues that it is distinctive of the images in comics that they "are not illustrations of a story-world determined by the text with which they appear" (Wartenberg: this volume). In other words, in comics the images and words work together to generate content – neither is more fundamental than the other, neither is dependent on nor subordinate to the other.

Patrick Maynard's essay (Chapter 6) explores the means by which comics express mental content. He focuses on funny or light comics and asks how it is possible for comics to be appropriately described as such. An obvious answer is that comics are funny or light in virtue of their subject matter, and this is surely part of the answer to that question. But Maynard is interested in something deeper and more interesting – the way in which some comics *present* their subject matter in a funny or light manner; that is, how they may be seen as manifesting mental attitudes towards situations or subject-matter. (Maynard talks picturesquely of "the shape of a mental "bubble" enclosing the entire cartoon, which expresses the depiction's conception and attitude regarding its contents" (Maynard: this volume.)) Maynard argues that various theories of depiction have difficulty making sense of this sort of phenomenon since they have an inappropriate tendency to treat the experience of depiction as analogous to ordinary looking and seeing. This is, Maynard argues, true even of most contemporary scientific (and scientifically-informed) approaches to depiction which also fail to make sense of the way depictions "express visual conceptions of things" (Maynard: this volume). The cure, he claims, is to take the artifactuality of pictures and, hence, comics seriously. By focusing on the ways in which comics as artifacts are designed to present us with affordances (i.e., functional or useful aspects) we will be better able to make sense of the various techniques by which a comic may depict a scene in a light or irreverent manner and, hence, may express various ways of taking things.

It is not uncommon for theorists to talk about there being a "language of comics" distinct from the language of the text of the comics (see, e.g., McCloud 1993, 2000, 2006; Saraceni 2003; and the essays collected in Varnum and Gibbons 2001), but contemporary analytic philosophers have often been skeptical of the extension of the term "language" (used most clearly to describe natural languages such as English and Swahili) to characterize representation in various art forms. In his essay (Chapter 7), Darren Hudson Hick addresses this issue by first exploring and criticizing Gregory Currie's attack on the popular film-as-language hypothesis. Hick argues that Currie is wrong to think that natural language representation is entirely arbitrary and also mistaken in thinking that image meaning is not at all conventional. These points, as well as the fact that comics use a great deal of conventional representation, suggest that one line of Currie's argument (rooted in the distinction between symbols and icons) will not by itself establish the rejection of the comics-as-language hypothesis. Hick goes on to argue that the supposed independence from context of linguistic meaning cannot be harnessed to draw a sharp distinction between semantic representation and the representation one finds in comics since, like linguistic utterances, comics express propositions in virtue of the arrangement of basic units (words in the case of utterances, panels in the case of comics). Ultimately, however, Hick argues that comics are not properly understood as linguistic since the idea of a comics syntax "is a difficult concept to even wrap one's head around" (Hick: this volume). Nevertheless, Hick concludes by suggesting that comics are reasonably characterized as "language-like – as constituting a pseudo-language" (Hick: this volume) and as functioning like natural languages in many ways.

In the third and final part of the book, the contributors turn their attention to the relationship between comics and two art forms with which they are often compared, film and literature.

One cannot help but notice the number of recent movies that are based on comics – in addition to the plethora of superhero comics that have been recently adapted into film, there are a multitude of comics from outside that genre that have also been adapted (e.g., *Ghost World, American Splendor, Persepolis, A History of Violence, 300, Tamara Drewe, From Hell, Gainsbourg*). Henry John Pratt (Chapter 8) explores the question of why comics have recently become so popular as a source of material for film adaptation. Although he points to a range of factors, Pratt's central contention is that, in virtue of a range of similarities between the comics and cinematic media, comics are more suited than any other medium for cinematic adaptation. Pratt contends that medium-specific qualities of both comics and films exert a bias towards narrative. In fact, since both art forms utilize visual media, they both tend to narrative of a particular sort – mimetic narrative in which stories are told by showing rather than by telling. Additionally, comics and film are typically "gappy" in that relations between viewers and the represented space and time regularly shifts. And it is central to both art forms that these gaps are manipulated for artistic effect. Finally, comics and film have very similar means of directing audience attention and share a high capacity for exerting visual control in virtue of those means.

Addressing a related topic, Roy T. Cook (Chapter 9) argues that, regardless of the many similarities between comics and film, it is a mistake to think that the theories, techniques, and tools developed to make sense of film are all that are needed to make sense of comics. In other words, we need a separate and distinct theory of comics to make sense of works in that art form. Cook makes his case by criticizing what he calls the "filmstrip argument." The filmstrip argument holds (roughly) that (1) since we can imagine turning any comic into a film by means of projection and (2) since such a film would be aesthetically identical to the original comic and (3) completely understandable in terms of film theory, we do not need to develop a distinctive theory of comics to understand them. Cook points out a number of flaws with this argument but his primary focus is on the challenge posed to it by metafictional comics (i.e., comics that are about comics). Metafictional comics are all the rage these days (see, for example, the Grant Morrison oeuvre for many examples, and Inge (1995) for a discussion of metafiction in comic strips), and Cook argues that a particular species of metacomic – formal metacomics in which there is "formal manipulation of the conventions of the comic medium" (Cook: this volume) – pose a devastating objection to the filmstrip argument. In brief, the effects produced by metafictional elements of these comics (for example, thought balloons that characters can see) simply cannot be replicated by film because of the different conventions found in the two forms. If Cook is right, comics call for the development of distinctive theoretical tools.

Comics do not just provide material for adaptation into other media; they often are the products of adaptation *from* other media. In his contribution to the volume, David Carrier (Chapter 10) sheds light on the nature of the comics form by investigating the relationship between Marcel Proust's *In Search of Lost Time* and the recent comic-book adaptation of that work by Stéphane Heuet (2001), (2007), and (2008). By means of careful analysis and comparison of the two works, Carrier shows us both how successful Heuet is in achieving the difficult task of translating Proust into the comics form as well as how comics differ from novels when it comes to both artistic resources and to their effects. Although Carrier holds that any story that can be told by means of literature can be told in comics, the capacity of comics – a "bastard art form" in his words (see the discussion of hybrid art forms above) – to *show* rather than merely tell means they possess aesthetic resources and face aesthetic constraints that novels (ordinary novels at least) lack.

Notes

1 There are also a number of comics *about* philosophy; notable recent examples include *Logicomix*, the *Action Philosophers!* series, or the often hilarious and disarmingly sophisticated *Dinosaur Comics* webcomic. But it cannot be said that these are scholarly works.

2 Levinson also holds that we typically treat an art form as hybrid only if it is descended from its ancestors in the recent past (1984: 8).

3 Heatley also provided the fabulous cover art for this volume!

References

Alaniz, J. *Komiks: Comic Art and Russia*, Jackson, MS: University Press of Mississippi, 2010.

Beaty, B. *Unpopular Culture: Transforming the European Comic Book in the 1990s*, Toronto: University of Toronto Press, 2007.

Bell, J. *Invaders From the North: How Canada Conquered the Comic Book Universe*, Toronto: Dundurn Press, 2006.

Boyd, B. "Art and Evolution: Spiegelman's The Narrative Corpse." *Philosophy and Literature* 32, 2008: 31–57.

Boyd, B. "On the Origin of Comics: New York Double-take." *The Evolutionary Review* 1, 2010.

Campbell, B. *¡Viva la Historieta! Mexican Comics, NAFTA, and the Politics of Globalization*, Jackson, MS: University Press of Mississippi, 2009.

Carrier, D. *The Aesthetics of Comics*, Pittsburgh, PA: Penn State University Press, 2000.

Castaldi, S. *Drawn and Dangerous: Italian Comics of the 1970s and 1980s*, Jackson, MS: University Press of Mississippi, 2010.

Carroll, N. *A Philosophy of Mass Art*, Oxford: Oxford University Press, 1998.

Chute, H. "Comics as Literature? Reading Graphic Narrative." *PMLA* 123.2, 2008: 452–465.

Cook, R.T. "Do Comics Requre Pictures, or, Why Batman #663 is a Comic," *The Journal of Aesthetics and Art Criticism* 69.3, 2011: 285–296.

Currie, G. "*Genre*." In *Arts and Minds*, Oxford: Oxford University Press, 2004.

Davies, S. "Ontology of Art" in Jerrold Levinson (ed.) *The Oxford Handbook of Aesthetics*, Oxford: Oxford University Press, 2005.

Eisner, W. *Comics and Sequential Art*, Tamarac, FL: Poorhouse Press, 1985.

Eisner, W.. *Graphic Storytelling*, Tamarac, FL: Poorhouse Press, 1996. Reprinted as *Graphic Storytelling and Visual Narrative: Principles and Practices from the Legendary Cartoonist Will Eisner*, New York: W.W. Norton and Company, 2008.

Gracyk, T. *Rhythm and Noise: An Aesthetics of Rock*, Durham, NC: Duke University Press, 1996.

Gravett, P. *Manga: Sixty Years of Japanese Comics*, London: Laurence King Publishing, 2004.

Goodman, N. *Languages of Art.* Indianapolis, IN: Hackett Publishing Company, Inc., 1976.

Groensteen, T. *The System of Comics*, trans. B. Beaty and N. Nguyen, Jackson, MS: University Press of Mississippi, 1999.

Harvey, R.C. *Children of the Yellow Kid: The Evolution of the American Comic Strip*, Seattle, WA: University of Washington Press, 1999.

Hatfield, C. *Alternative Comics: An Emerging Literature*, Jackson, MS: University of Mississippi Press, 2005.

Hatfield, C. "Indiscipline, or, The Condition of Comics Studies.," *Transatlantica*, 1 2010, Accessed 1 March 2011.Available online at http://transatlantica.revues. org/4933 (accessed March 1, 2011).

Hayman, G. and H.J. Pratt. "What Are Comics?," in D. Goldblatt and L.B. Brown (eds), *Aesthetics: A Reader in Philosophy*, 2nd ed., Upper Saddle River, NJ: Pearson Prentice Hall, 2005: 419–424.

Heer, J. and K. Worcester (eds), *Arguing Comics: Literary Masters on a Popular Medium*, Jackson, MS: University of Mississippi Press, 2004.

Heuet, S. *Remembrance of Things Past: Combray, trans.* Joe Johnson, New York: ComicsLit, 2001.

Heuet, S. *Remembrance of Things Past: Swann in Love*, New York: ComicsLit, 2007.

Heuet. S. *Remembrance of Things Past: Within a Budding Grove*, New York: ComicsLit, 2008.

Inge, M.T. *Anything Can Happen in a Comic Strip: Centennial Reflections on an American Art Form*, Jackson: University Press of Mississippi, 1995.

Irwin, W. and M.D. White (eds), *Watchmen and Philosophy: A Rorschach Test*, Oxford: Wiley-Blackwell, 2008.

Kivy, P. "Differences" *Journal of Aesthetics and Art Criticism* 51(2), 1993: 123–132.

Kivy, P. *Philosophies of Arts: An Essay in Differences*, Cambridge: Cambridge University Press, 1997.

Kunzle, D. *The Early Comic Strip: Narrative Strips and Picture Stories in the European Broadsheet from c. 1450 to 1825: The History of the Comic Strip Vol.* I, Berkeley, CA: University of California Press, 1973.

Kunzle, D. *The Nineteenth Century: The History of the Comic Strip Vol.* II. Berkeley, CA: University of California Press, 1990.

Kunzle, D. *Father of the Comic Strip: Rodolphe Töpffer*, Jackson, MS: University Press of Mississippi, 2007.

Laetz, B. and D. McIver Lopes. "Genre" in Paisley Livingston and Carl Plantinga (eds), *The Routledge Companion to Philosophy and Film*. Routledge, 2008.

Lent, J.A. "The Winding, Pot-holed Road of Comic Art Scholarship," *Studies in Comics* 1 (1) 2010: 17–33.

Levinson, J. "Hybrid Art Forms," *Journal of Aesthetic Education* 18 (4), 1984: 5–13.

Lopes, D. McIver. *A Philosophy of Computer Art*, London: Routledge, 2009.

McCloud, Scott. *Understanding Comics: The Invisible Art*, New York: Harper Collins, 1993.

McCloud, S. *Reinventing Comics: How Imagination and Technology are Revolutionizing an Art Form*, New York: Harper Collins, 2000.

McCloud, S. *Making Comics: Storytelling Secrets of Comics, Manga, and Graphic Novels*, New York: Harper Collins, 2006.

McKenna, K.J. *All the Views Fit to Print: Changing Images of the US in Pravda Political Cartoons* 1917–1991, New York: Peter Lang Publishing, 2001.

McKinney, M. (ed.), *History and Politics in French-Language Comics and Graphic Novels*, Jackson, MS: University Press of Mississippi, 2008.

Meskin, A.. "Review of The Aesthetics of Comics." *British Journal of Aesthetics* 41 (4), 2001: 446–449.

Meskin, A. "Defining Comics?" *Journal of Aesthetics and Art Criticism* 65, 2007: 369–379.

Meskin, A. "Comics as Literature?" *British Journal of Aesthetics* 49 (3), 2009a: 219–239.

Meskin, A. "'Why Don't You Go Read a Book Or Something' Watchmen as Literature," in M.D. White (ed.) *Watchmen and Philosophy: A Rorshach Test.* Hoboken, NJ: John Wiley and Sons, Inc., 2009b: 157–171.

Molotiu, A. (ed.), *Abstract Comics: The Anthology*, Seattle, WA: Fantagraphics Books, 2009.

Moore, A. and D. Gibbons, *Watchmen*, New York: DC Comics, 1995.

Morris, T. and M. Morris (eds), *Superheroes and Philosophy: Truth, Justice and the American Way.* Chicago and LaSalle, IL: Open Court, 2005.

Power, N.O. *God of Comics: Osamu Tezuka and the Creation of Post-World War II Manga.* Jackson, MS: University Press of Mississippi, 2009.

Pratt, H.J. "Narrative in Comics." *Journal of Aesthetics and Art Criticism* 67, 2009a: 107–117.

Pratt, H.J. "Medium Specificity and the Ethics of Narrative in Comics" *StoryWorlds: A Journal of Narrative Studies* 1. 2009b: 97–113.

Pratt, H.J. "Relating Comics, Cartoons, and Animation," in D. Goldblatt and L.B. Brown (eds), *Aesthetics: A Reader in Philosophy of the Arts*, 3rd ed. Upper Saddle River, NJ: Pearson-Prentice Hall, 2011.

Rubenstein, A. *Bad Language, Naked Ladies, and Other Threats to the Nation: A Political History of Comic Books in Mexico*, Durham, NC: Duke University Press, 1998.

Sabin, R. *Adult Comics*, London and New York: Routledge, 1993.

Sabin, R. "Ally Sloper: The First Comics Superstar," *Image & Narrative* 7: online at: Available online at http://www.imageandnarrative.be/inarchive/graphicnovel/rogersabin.htm (accessed August 25, 2011), 2003.

Sadowski, G. (ed.), *Supermen! The First Wave of Comic Book Heroes 1936–1941*, Fantagraphics, 2009.

Saraceni, M. *The Language of Comics*, London: Routledge, 2003.

Schwartz, B. (ed.), *The Best American Comics Criticism*, Seattle: Fantagraphics Books, 2010.

Seldes, G. "The Krazy Kat That Walks by Himself," in *The Seven Lively Arts.* New York: Harpers, 1974. Reprinted in Heer and Worcester (eds), *Arguing Comics.*

Spiegelman, A. *Maus: A Survivor's Tale: Vol I: My Father Bleeds History*, New York, Pantheon, 1986.

Spiegelman, A. *Maus: A Survivor's Tale: Vol II: And Here My Troubles Began*, New York, Pantheon, 1991.

Spiegelman A. *Breakdowns: Portrait of the Artist as a Young %@*! New York: Pantheon, 2008.

Töpffer, R. *Rodolphe Töpffer: The Complete Comic Strips*, David. Kunzle (ed.), Jackson, MS: University Press of Mississippi, 2007.

Topliss, I. *The Comic Worlds of Peter Arno, William Steig, Charles Addams, and Saul Steinberg.* Baltimore, MD: Johns Hopkins University Press, 2005.

Varnum, R. and C.T. Gibbons (eds.) *The Language of Comics: Word and Image*, Jackson, MS: University Press of Mississippi, 2001.

Vessels, J.E. *Drawing France: French Comics and the Republic*, Jackson, MS: University Press of Mississippi, 2010.

Warshow, R. "Woofed with Dreams," *Partisan Review* 13, 1946. Reprinted in Heer and Worcester (eds.) *Arguing Comics.*

Wertham, F. *Seduction of the Innocent: The Influence of Comic Books on Today's Youth,* New York: Reinhart and Company, 1954.

Wilson, G. "Le Grand Imagier Steps Out: The Primitive Basis of Film Narration," *Philosophical Topics* 25, 1997: 295–318.

Wolk, D. *Reading Comics: How Graphic Novels Work and What They Mean,* Cambridge, MA: Da Capo Press, 2007.

Part One

The Nature and Kinds of Comics

Redefining Comics

John Holbo

When we read a book for the first time the very process of laboriously moving our eyes from left to right, line after line, page after page, this complicated physical work upon the book, the very process of learning in terms of space and time what the book is about, this stands between us and artistic appreciation. When we look at a painting we do not have to move our eyes in a special way even if, as in a book, the picture contains elements of depth and development. The element of time does not really enter in a first contact with a painting. In reading a book, we must have time to acquaint ourselves with it. We have no physical organ (as we have the eye in regard to a painting) that takes in the whole picture and then can enjoy its details. But at a second, or third, or fourth reading we do, in a sense, behave towards a book as we do towards a painting.

Vladimir Nabokov[1]

Oh, that's not drawing – that's typography.

Chris Ware[2]

McCloud's Definition

We all know McCloud's definition: "juxtaposed pictorial and other images in deliberate sequence, intended to convey information and/or to produce an aesthetic response in the viewer."[3] But do we *like* it?

The Art of Comics: A Philosophical Approach, First Edition.
Edited by Aaron Meskin and Roy T. Cook.
© 2012 Blackwell Publishing Ltd. Published 2012 by Blackwell Publishing Ltd.

A good definition, McCloud says, should include the sorts of things we consider comics, while excluding things that are "clearly not" (1994: 4). His, however, lets in not just the likes of early twentieth-century woodcut novels by Masereel and Ward, whose authors had no notion they were "making comics," but also the Bayeux Tapestry and the Codex Nuttall.

A little revisionism is always welcome, but this looks to be *a lot*. What is worse, it looks *ad hoc*. McCloud doesn't want all illustrated books – most children's books – to turn out to be comics; but they satisfy the letter of his definition. On the other hand, McCloud holds the line at *The Family Circus* (one panel, hence not "juxtaposed"). Can it be easier for the Bayeux Tapestry to pass through the eye of the needle of comics-hood than a one-panel gag strip?

What's the alternative? If not formalism, historicism. Aaron Meskin provides the paradigm:

> The art of comics, which began in the middle of the nineteenth century and developed largely out of eighteenth- and nineteenth-century British humor magazines such as *Punch*, can and should be understood in its own terms and by reference to its own history.[4]

Adding another twist: even if this line is sound, does it follow that it's a good idea to *define* "comics" at all? Meskin himself is skeptical. The most he would commit to would be that *if* there is to be a definition, it should be historicist, on pain of being open to obvious counter-examples.

Let's start by ignoring this "if." Suppose we have done our diligent, historicist best to articulate a necessary (not sufficient) genealogical condition on comics-hood (as post-*Punch*-hood, say). That should keep out the Bayeux Tapestry. Will it exclude anything it should let in? Apparently, yes: *manga*.[5] But the *manga* point points both ways. If, following Meskin, we use "comics" in a manner analogous to "*manga*" – that is, to name a genealogically/ historically/institutionally/geographically-defined tradition – where's the nonsense in that? "Manga" is a fine and functional word.

What *is* the point of defining "comics"? McCloud suggests we need a proper definition to "give the lie to the stereotypes," to "show that the potential of comics is limitless and exciting" (1994: 3). McCloud wants "but shouldn't it have Batman in it?" (1994: 9) exposed for the sorry fallacy it is. But is a *definition* the tool for the job? Meskin is skeptical about definitions not just because he thinks none is forthcoming, but because he sees them as unlikely to provide what McCloud apparently thinks they are most apt to provide: real insight. Who's right?

Let me see if I can split the difference in two ways. First, let "comics" be ambiguous between *genus* (McCloud's medium) and *species* (Meskin's history). There is even a grammatical marker if we follow McCloud in letting "comics," in his sense, take a singular verb. (Comics *is* the medium.) History is important, so you have to have words to write it. But something like McCloud's historically revisionistic, formalistic definition seems to me necessary as well.

How so, and why? Because any historicist definition will be *ironic*. A definition should not afflict us with a sense that, even if it *was* so, it could have been different. One of the most distinctive features of this subject – comics – is: narrowness by birth, breadth by nature. The problem with understanding the tradition in "its own terms" is that those terms have a tradition of being, not to put too fine a point on it, *wrong*: too narrow. To a first approximation, comics are footnotes to *Punch*; yet most visual and much literary art is just footnotes to comics – in McCloud's sense. So I will argue.

Putting the point another way: while terms like "*manga*" – hence "comics," on Meskin's usage – are usable, they are *odd*.[6] "*Manga*" means – has meant – (1) works of a particular sort; (2) published in Japan. It's (2) that nags, though (1) would be hard enough to nail down. "Comics" has similar problems. You *can* create a social register of any comic that can trace its pedigree to *Punch*. But, supposing this keeps out *manga*, isn't it perverse to define apart two things that have, in the event, hybridized to the point where they are often hard to distinguish? And that have done so because, at a basic level, they *work the same*? Don't we need a term for *that*?

But here is a strong reply: yes, any good historicist account must allow for this sort of thing, but *going forward*. Admitting the city of post-*Punch* comics can form a megalopolis by sprawling to Japan does not commit one to insisting that, therefore, this has necessarily always already happened, by definition.

And here is an even stronger reply: the alternative is to take McCloud's definition seriously, not allowing *ad hoc* stops, and then we just slide and slide. Realizing a few things that weren't classed as "comics" *work like* comics is eye opening. Finding out nearly *everything* works like comics – hence *is* comics, by definition – means we made a stupid mistake somewhere and should go back to the drawing board. But not necessarily.

Which brings me to my second way of splitting the difference. What is a definition of "comics" *for*? You would need one for certain sorts of quantitative research. If you are counting comics, you must say what you count. But McCloud is not primarily concerned with quantitative research. Does that mean McCloud's definition isn't performing any proper function *for him*?

That goes too far: a definition makes a circle, in/out, center/perimeter. Our responses to works are informed by knowing where this circle – comics – is. Yes, but *do* we? Or do we just act as if we know, thereby pushing preferences and biases under cover of what appears to be a neutrally descriptive formula?

A fair concern, but at worst a definition like McCloud's is an economical way of encoding *a lot* of attitude.

But why is *that* good? Robert Venturi makes a shrewd observation about how this goes: "Louis Kahn has referred to "what a thing wants to be," but implicit in this statement is its opposite: what the architect wants the thing to be. In the tension and balance between these two lie many of the architect's decisions."[7] Mistaking what *you* want for what *it* wants may seem a silly error – even a lie – but it can bring out that tension and balance. So the point of this essay will be to articulate how a definition of "comics" that seems doomed to die the death of a thousand flyspecks – counter-examples, that is – can be a source of essential insight.

Pictures and Comics

I am looking at panels, separated by gutters, populated by active, attractive, albeit implausibly well-muscled, precariously clad persons of human and superhuman nature. The eye is invited to take in the whole page while the panels, in sequence, are read as narrating an origin story. I am gazing at the ceiling of the Sistine Chapel.

Oh, gerrymander around Michelangelo, if you must. Insist on paper; rule out religious material.[8] At the end of the day, the ceiling of the Sistine Chapel and a page from a superhero comic have a lot in common. This isn't to say they must be worth the same, but at a basic level they *work* the same.

Attempts to say what comics *is* by formal-functional analysis are going to have a natural tendency to expansive revisionism. Let me illustrate further. McCloud wants to keep out the bulk of children's picture books and illustrated books, nominally on the grounds that we don't call that sort of thing "comics." But we don't call the Bayeux Tapestry "comics" either. But McCloud does. So into the McCloudian comics longbox – with the Bayeux Tapestry and Codex Nuttall – go children's books, illustrated books, and (why not?) the ceiling of the Sistine Chapel.

Next case: *The Family Circus.* Can we keep it out? It is almost sufficient to note the absurdity of supposing the funnies page, with its traditional mix of single and multi-panel strips, is working in two distinct *media*. McCloud tries various angles: you *can't* have single-panel sequential art because there's no such thing as a sequence of *one*. But no. Mathematically, you can have a sequence of *none*, the so-called "null sequence." Resting an account of the nature of comics on the semantics of "sequence" simply doesn't satisfy.

It also won't do to suggest the single-panel items are cartoons – a style term for McCloud. Using one panel isn't a drawing style, it's a *narrative* style. Unpacking this point: a panel typically depicts only a single moment, but this need not be so. Or rather: it need be so only in a narrow sense we shouldn't get exclusively attached to. McCloud himself provides a quite brilliant illustration of how a single panel can have, as it were, an implied timeline, hence implied internal gutters (1994: 95).

Let me make McCloud's timeline point less elaborately, because it is important to see how truly simple a case can illustrate it. Here are two gentlemen from my own book, *Squid and Owl*. I have long felt they should have something to say for themselves. Now they do.

Figure 1.1 "Mommy, why ain't I juxtaposed?"
Copyright John Holbo, *Squid and Owl* (Blurb 2009).

In a left-right reading culture this might as well be:

Figure 1.2 "Mommy, why ain't I juxtaposed?" part II.
Copyright John Holbo, *Squid and Owl* (Blurb 2009).

Why not admit, as well, that a single panel can have implied gutters, side to side?

But don't we have to *see* things in implied panels for there to be implied gutters? That is, isn't it a leap from implied gutters, dividing a picture you can see into more pictures you can see, to *pictures you can't see*?

A fair point. But even if a panel depicts only an instant, it invites "seeing-in" of more than that instant. A panel is a work of narrative art if its function is to tell/imply a story (represent an event, or events). Bence Nanay puts forward a plausible framework for talking about how this goes.[9] But McCloud's own vocabulary of "closure" already commits him to conceding the point. He writes about "blood in the gutters." One panel of an axe murderer, closing in on his victim; in the next, we hear a scream. (Well, we don't *hear*. We *see*. As Shakespeare says, "to hear with eyes belongs to love's fine wit.") We "fill in" the gutters with what we know must be there.

Figure 1.3 Scott McCloud, *Understanding Comics: The Invisible Art* (1994) a. From McCloud, S., *Understanding Comics: The Invisible Art*, New York: Harper Paperbacks.

Compare McCloud's two-panel axe-murder to a one-panel *New Yorker* cartoon. Businessman at desk, axe-wielding executioner at door, ushered in by secretary: "Your four-o'-clock is here." Do the two cases work in completely different ways, due to the one-panel/two-panel difference? No. The function of depicting a single time-slice – in the *New Yorker*, even time-stamped – is to imply a sequential order of events. The not invariable but highly typical mechanism of the gag strip is to imply at least one unseen action or event: what happens next, or before.[10]

Here is a more mild-mannered illustration of the same point, again McCloud's own. What do you see?

Figure 1.4 Scott McCloud, *Understanding Comics: The Invisible Art* (1994) b. From McCloud, S., *Understanding Comics: The Invisible Art*, New York: Harper Paperbacks.

Suppose it were only one panel (take your pick). *Still* a man tipping his hat, isn't it? Place both in a line-up with the Bayeux Tapestry. The Bayeux Tapestry and the two panel hat-tip are like each other and unlike the single panel hat-tip? Hardly. So we have to let the *Family Circus* into the family of comics, if we are going to let even the Bayeux Tapestry in.

But once we do *that*, there is so much more we cannot keep out. Consider a less comic family circle:

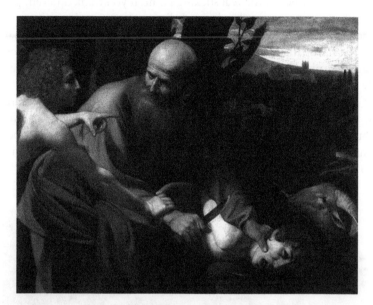

Figure 1.5 Caravaggio, *The Sacrifice of Isaac* (1603).
Image courtesy of Wikicommons/ibiblio, licensed under CC Attribution-ShareAlike 3.0

If a single panel can be comics, can we deny *this* is? Is a caption under a single panel in the *New Yorker* so formally or functionally different than "The Sacrifice of Isaac" on a plaque under a museum frame? ("But shouldn't it have a joke in it?" We cannot secure a fundamental difference by insisting on anything so incidental.[11])

Caravaggio's work does not work differently, blood in the gutters-wise, than a gag strip, or McCloud's axe murderer panels. But now, since we aren't going to enforce French Academy-grade snobbery about acceptable subjects, *any* image in which it can be seen what is happening is narrative art, ergo … comics?

Panels, Panels Everywhere

Let's step back and try to resist the slide in a different way. McCloud toys with the possibility that *The Family Circus* can be admitted on the grounds that, even with only one panel, there *is* image juxtaposition – of picture and caption. (Words – letterforms – are non-pictorial images.) This is just a *different way* to let in too many things, however. So many museum pieces have titles, even the ones just titled "Untitled." We *could* take down all the little plaques. But here's the real sticking point: if you think different *parts* of an overall composition can be deemed distinct images (picture/text), ergo the composition counts as comics, how can you avoid conceding that *any* image that has spatially well-delineated elements is, in effect, a juxtaposition of images? A picture of two people, side by side, is, in effect, two pictures. Nearly *everything* is coming up comics.

But without word balloons to imply a timeline and reading order, are two people standing side by side a *sequence*? A picture of two people is not *read*, left to right (right to left, if the style looks Japanese). But consider: is there perhaps a prominent, central figure or object seen *first*, whence the eye is drawn away, along a line?[12] Consider a Poussin painting, *Landscape with Saint John on Patmos*.

Figure 1.6   Nicolas Poussin, 1594–1665, Landscape with Saint John on Patmos, 1640, Oil on canvas, 100.3 × 136.4 cm (39½ × 53⅝ in.), A. A. Munger Collection, 1930.500, The Art Institute of Chicago. Photography © The Art Institute of Chicago.

Do you think the eye is supposed to start with the saint, then zig-zag up and back, eventually around? It seems to me so. In many landscapes, a river running through it functions as a gutter, not just in the sense that rivers, like gutters, are for carrying away excess fluid; rather, in the sense that they direct the eye's passage through the field. If we say things that *work this way* are comics, Poussin is comics. More weakly: if you want to insist it isn't, you can't just say it *obviously* isn't, because it's Poussin. You have to argue that the eye in fact *isn't* supposed to trace a path through the canvas.

Seeing-in and Closure

To sum up our slide so far: a one-panel gag strip is a multi-panel comic, merely minus the multi. And the museums are full of one-panel gag strips, merely minus the gag.[13]

My point is, despite appearances, serious: McCloud defines "comics" formally, but his account is functional. He wants to show how "juxtaposed pictorial and other images in deliberate sequence, intended to convey information and/or to produce an aesthetic response in the viewer" *work*. And the answer is: like pictures.

To drive this point home, let's turn back to that Poussin canvas, concerning which, it so happens, Richard Wollheim has posed a series of yes-or-no questions, and provided what he takes to be reasonable answers:

> Can you see those columns as having been thrown down hundreds of years ago? Yes. Can you see those columns as having been thrown down hundreds of years ago by barbarians? (with some difficulty) Yes. Can you see those columns as having been thrown down hundreds of years ago by barbarians wearing wild asses' skins? (with little difficulty) No.[14]

On the other hand, you *could* make this painting a comics panel. If an earlier page featured a glorious splash of barbarians in skins of wild asses, throwing down those columns, you might see that *in* the later panel, at least to the same extent that you can "see" these other things Wollheim claims to.

Wollheim's quiz is meant is to highlight a dilemma. If we get too fastidious about "seeing," we are driven to a view on which we never "see" anything but paint when we look at paintings (never anything but our own sense-data, if this retreat turns into a route). On the other hand, if we loosen up, we start "seeing" barbarians where they are not.

Wollheim's solution is to throw himself – but lightly – on both horns. "Seeing-in" is the Wollheimian duck-rabbit seen as duck *and* rabbit: paint *and* saint (no sense-data, no barbarians). Intuitively, it's plausible that when you appreciate a painting, appreciation *is* a function of simultaneous awareness of properties of the canvas *and* of what it is *of* (if anything). Whether you think you can "see" the ruins fell, or were pushed, you *do* see *ruins*. In general, if you are seeing-in *at all*, with regard to this picture, you are seeing-in space *and* time.[15] This is "closure." So if "in a very real sense" "comics *is* closure" (2003: 67), this picture *is* comics. Probably *all* pictures are.

Pictureless Comics?

That's not the worst of it, however. If you can have comics without words, why not comics without pictures?

McCloud's definition would seem to rule this out: "juxtaposed pictorial *and* other images in deliberate sequence." But he makes clear his "and" is more an *or* at heart. Wordless comics are OK. Why *not* pictureless ones?

Because then you have a novel. Precisely! Novels (and other pure word products) are one *kind* of comics.[16] Just as Frans Masereel's *Passionate Journey* is a wordless comic, so – oh, for example, Nabokov's *King, Queen, Knave* is a pictureless comic. These works should be seen as standing at opposite ends of the McCloudian sequentially juxtaposed image spectrum. They are the formal limit cases in which the quantity of one or the other of the two standard ingredients (pictorial and non-pictorial images) is reduced to zero. We should let McCloudian "comics" slide past all *ad hoc* stops until the term is basically synonymous with "graphic design." And isn't this the soul of reasonableness?

No, because – fishing but one counter-example from the vast sea – writing a novel, of the traditional sort, is not traditionally conceived of as an exercise in graphic design. But this just pushes the point back. Why not? Well, why *should* it be? Consider the so-called "emblem poem," combining one picture (traditionally a woodcut) and a short verse. Here is one such, from Robert Louis Stevenson's *Moral Emblems and other Poems*:

> Unlike the common run of men,
> I wield a double power to please,
> And use the GRAVER and the PEN
> With equal aptitude and ease.[17]

Why *don't* more novelists cultivate this power, coming to move with those Stevenson acclaims as "that illustrious crew/ The ambidextrous Kings of Art." Everyone says novelists should *show* not *say*. Anyway, as another Stevenson poem makes clear, it's not as though you can *cut* the cut, thereby casting off the burden of producing a handsome graphical product:

> They burned the nightly taper;
> But now the work is ripe –
> Observe the costly paper,
> Remark the perfect type!

Typography *is* graphic design. Novels, being typed, are *graphic* novels. If you think you can get around this by adopting, as authors and publishers do, a restrained and more or less self-effacing graphic design formula, you are making a mistake like that made by certain ladies. (Was it Wilde who mocked them?) In order to be perfectly spiritual, they try to become thin. (Descartes fell into a similar error with regard to the pineal gland.) We don't want to repeat the mistake with comics. It's not as though the perfect novel is *unpublished*, that is, is *not* a graphic product. (Anyway, a hand-written ms. is still a *calli-graphic novel.*)

Letterforms *are* images. They just aren't *pictures.*

Wordless Prints, Unprinted Words

Let's start again at the opposite end of the comics spectrum – with wordless, as opposed to pictureless graphic novels. Milt Gross' "cartoon novel," *He Done Her Wrong* (1930) aims to puncture the self-seriousness of wordless works of the early twentieth century, such as Lynd Ward's woodcut novels. Gross' subtitle: *The Great American Novel and Not a Word in It – No music, Too.* David Beronä suggests this is a reference to musical theater, which it may be.[18] It also seems like a send-up of the modernist dictum that purism to one's medium is presumptive virtue. Where's the sense in bragging about the perfectly nice things you could be doing, but aren't?

But the reference to music may bring us to our senses – one more, at least. A sound case can be made that the printed word should be regarded, not as a natively graphical product, but as a prosthetic extension of, or strayed expression of, *speech.*[19] Even if all juxtaposed imagery is, essentially, comics, the *written* word isn't, essentially, image. The only thing it is, essentially, is *word*; heir to an ancient, ear-oriented line.

This suggestion invites the further thought that words are more *properly* heard, not seen; which drags in its train suspicion that there is something wrong with writing, bad child. Plato has thoughts on the subject, you may recall. But let me quote James Hogg's mother, complaining to Sir Walter Scott that he ruined everything.

> There ware never ane o' my sangs prentit til ye prentit them yoursel', an' ye hae spoilt them awthegither. They were made for singin' an no for readin'; but ye hae broken the charm noo, an' they'll never sung mair. An' the worst thing of a', they're nouther richt spell'd nor rich't setten down.[20]

This complaint (minus that last line) is quoted in E.A. Levenston, *The Stuff of Literature*; an instructive book which, its author says, would have been subtitled (had it been a PhD thesis), "a study of the contribution made to the meaning and value of a work of literature at the level of graphic form, with particular reference to spelling, punctuation, typography, and layout." As this non-actual subtitle shows, the book has the wrong title. It should be: *The Stuff of Comics.* Then Levenston might have been moved to redress the odd omission of pictures from his list of likely graphical contributors. To be fair, he *does* discuss pictures, and argues – correctly – that Hoggs' mother is not right; but it takes a bit of showing.

"Literature" signals essential membership in two media with divergent essences, inducing us to apply schizophrenic value scales, possibly. "Oral literature" is an oxymoron – one that we nevertheless need, for more or less the same reason we employ the redundant "acoustic guitar." In both cases an original case has declined into a special case. Our choice of labels shows we are unsure what to regard as central, hence peripheral.

It is certainly possible to valorize sound/voice, especially if we value poetry. Even in this day and age, some still deem poetry the highest form of literature, although these new-fangled *graphic novels* – from up-and-comers like Richardson, Defoe, Swift, Spiegelman and Ware – have their partisans. And yet: despite the high status of poetry, there is a tendency to regard audiobooks (another of those funny words) as marginal denizens – resident aliens, not true citizens – of the republic of letters. No *letters.* Levenston remarks that "a secondary mode of existence for a novel would be a complete oral performance available on tape for the blind" (1992: 10). Why *even* secondary? Most consumers of audiobooks aren't blind.

Someone could resist my argument that all novels are, in effect, graphic novels, by asserting there is in fact *nothing* secondary about audiobooks. A novel or short story may be stripped of all graphic design elements and remain what it *is.* Not so for comics. *That's* the difference. But this is a mistake. Any attempt to draw a line between, say, novels and comics, on the grounds that the latter is an affair of the eye, the former of the ear, will fall foul of the consideration that there *is* a fairly bright line to be drawn, but novels and comics are on the same side of it.

Spaces Between Words

Let me tell you who *really* invented *comics,* by pioneering standard use of what McCloud identifies as "comics' most important icon" – which, he adds, is also its most overlooked: the panel. No, not Rodolphe Töpffer. Irish monks. As Thierry Groensteen writes, in *The System of Comics,* laying out what he takes to be the distinctive characteristics that make comics "well and truly a language":

What is put on view is always a space that has been divided up, compartmentalized, a collection of juxtaposed frames, where, to cite the fine formula of Henry Van Lier, a "multi-framed aircraft" sails in suspension, "in the white nothingness of the printed page." A page of comics is offered at first to a synthetic global vision, but that cannot be satisfactory. It demands to be traversed, crossed, glanced at, and analytically deciphered. This moment-to-moment reading does not take a lesser account of the totality of the panoptic field that constitutes the page (or the double-page), since the focal vision never ceases to be enriched by peripheral vision. (2008: 19)

Irish monks were first (at least in Europe) to add spaces between words, thereby launching the great, multi-framed flying fortress of comics. When you put space between words, the page becomes, for the first time, essentially an affair of panels.

It is almost incomprehensible to us today, looking back, that it took so long. Putting spaces between words is a small step, for a graphic designer, a huge leap for mankind. It is objectively harder – much harder – to read *scriptura continua* (unseparated text). Yet it was employed for centuries, despite awareness of the alternative and its advantages, in terms of visual affordances. As Paul Saenger writes in his landmark study: "stated summarily, the ancient world did not possess the desire, characteristic of the modern age, to make reading easier and swifter because the advantages that modern readers perceive as accruing from ease of reading were seldom viewed as advantages by the ancients."[21] You aren't *supposed* to be able to engage in skidding ocular saccades, peripherally and over page spreads. The thing is supposed to be *read*, not "looked at" (or whatever you call it, after you've changed proper reading material into a graphic design project).[22]

There was a time when *all* books were, in effect, *audiobooks* – composed orally; recorded (by a scribe: state of the art recording equipment; not as expensive as you think, providing reasonable fidelity); to be audibly replayed later; unreplayable without a speaker. Hence Augustine's oft-wondered-at wonderment at the spectacle of Ambrose, reading silently. As Saenger notes: it is virtually impossible that Ambrose really was reading in the swift and silent modern, visual mode. He would have been reading *scriptura continua*, an audiobook format. What impressed Augustine was Ambrose's invention of headphones.[23]

As Ellen Lupton writes in *Thinking With Type*: "Although many books define the purpose of typography as enhancing the readability of the written word, one of design's must humane functions is, in actuality, to help readers *avoid* reading."[24] By "design" she means, of course, *graphic* design. And so, once the Irish invented comics to do what comics have always been so justly charged with doing – teaching young people how *not* to read – it was possible, for the first time, to enjoy what has come to be known as "the reading experience." And pictures were added, as naturally they would be. Any work that exists to suit the eye will attract such things as suit eyes. Saenger writes:

> A miniature [illustration] containing a banderole, an unfurled banner that bears text, exemplifies an important new development brought about by the spread of word separation. This is the mixture of script and image.

The ancients did not illustrate texts that were, after all, aimed at the ear,

> the spread of separated writing broke down the perceptual barriers that had isolated the two activities. The first banderoles appeared in the ninth and tenth centuries, in the illuminations for codices, and beginning in northern France during the eleventh century, banderoles bearing text narrating the scenes depicted in miniature manuscripts illustrations, mural paintings, stained glass windows, sculpture, and tapestry became the hallmark of medieval art. (2000: 187)

The Air of Non-Pictures

I could have made the point ahistorically, citing not Saenger but, for example, Dominic Lopes' *Sight and Sensibility*. He has a chapter, "The Air of Pictures," concerned with "expression." Lopes distinguishes *figure* from *scene* expression (happy figure/sad figure; happy scene/sad scene); both are distinguished from *design* expression: "an expression [not necessarily emotional, but some "air"] that is wholly attributable to a picture's design or surface, and not to any figure or scene it depicts."[25] It is immediately noteworthy that design expression will not be a feature of *pictures* but of graphic design generally. (Lopes' epigraph is from Neil Young: "there's more to the picture than meets the eye." Also: there's more to what meets the eye than pictures).

I could have made the point a third way by quoting from writings just on typography. Robert Bringhurst's classic *Elements of Typographic Style* is eloquent on the subject of design expression:

> In a badly designed book the letters mill and stand like starved horses in a field. In a book designed by rote, they sit like stale bread and mutton on the page. In a well-made book … the letters are alive. They dance in their seats. Sometimes they rise and dance in the margins and aisles.[26]

Bringhurst says good typography is like "transparent statuary," affording a special "seeing-in" – *of* a beautiful surface and *through* that surface to what it is *of*. This is a recurrent paradox in writings on the subject of beautiful writing. It must be seen, to be beautiful, but can only be beautiful if seen *through*.

In short, typography works the way Wollheim says *paintings* work. And paintings, as we now know, are just comics.

Let me quote Edward Burne-Jones on how satisfactory he found it to have his illustrations ensconced in William Morris' "pocket cathedral" –the Kelmscott Chaucer. Burne-Jones sounds like Bringhurst, only the images with whose sequential juxtaposition he is concerned happen to be pictures; but without, he insists, ceasing to be typography:

> I love to be snugly cased in the borders and buttressed up by the vast initials – and once or twice when I have no letter under me I feel tottery and weak; if you drag me out of my encasings it will be like tearing a statue out of its niche and putting it in a museum.[27]

As William Morris himself writes, in the oft-quoted final paragraph of his essay on "The Ideal Book":

> The picture-book is not, perhaps, absolutely necessary to man's life, but it gives us such endless pleasure, and is so intimately connected with the other absolutely necessary art of imaginative literature that it must remain one of the very worthiest things toward the production of which reasonable men should strive.[28]

A Continuum of Cases

I have proceeded on two fronts. On the picture front I see no prospects for stopping a slippery slide. McCloud's account accounts for sequences of *n* juxtaposed images; 1 is a valid value for *n*. Pictures *are* comics. (As are print ads, magazines, newspapers, movie posters and album covers). But on the word front, my claim that the "and" in McCloud's definition – "juxtaposed pictorial *and* other images" – is an *or* at heart can be resisted. McCloud thinks you can have wordless comics. That needs an "or." But you *can* set this Boolean hinge to swing only one way. Pictures necessary. Words not. So if we think it's silly to have traditional novels turn out comics, we needn't let them.

But do we think this is silly for any reason to do with *comics* and *novels* – as opposed to "comics" and "novels"? Is there a problem with what I am thinking, which is pretty much that we confront a continuum, with novels at one end of the comics spectrum? Or is it just odd to say it this way? What is clouding my McCloudian message may be his medium. What *is* an artistic medium? Something like the Platonic Form of the material basis. (An ideal tendency to the Good – higher function of the force vectors of what it and I want it to be?) Put it that way, its existence is less than self-evident. But let's *suppose*. If there *is* such a thing as an artistic medium, presumably graphic design has one. Something like: arranged imagery in two dimensions. But if graphic design has a medium, can anything *else* that is, basically, arrangement of imagery in two dimensions? Comics and easel painting? Won't these turn out to be *modes* of the medium – graphic design *genres?*

Perhaps we should simply drop the whole concept of a "medium," if it is what is putting us on a slippery slope to pictureless comics. But if we step off, I think we still find ourselves on a slippery slope.

Pictureless comics: McCloud doesn't lay out any case against them in *Understanding Comics*. But he comes closer to saying what he thinks really matters in an interview with Robert Harvey:

> Harvey: Do you think that your definition also includes children's literature – books in which there is a picture on every page and prose beneath each picture?
>
> McCloud: not if the prose is independent of the pictures. Not if the written story could exist without any pictures and still be a continuous whole. That's how it's usually done, whereas the pictures are usually discontinuous ...
>
> Harvey: [That is] the narrative is continuous and independent of the pictures. And the pictures really are illustrating some moment in the prose narrative. There's no necessary narrative strand in the pictures themselves.
>
> McCloud: If you turn that on its head, you have comics. If the pictures, independent of the words, are telling the whole story and the words are supplementing that, then that is comics.[29]

I'm not going to pick on McCloud's words, which are off-the-cuff, but will address the spirit, which is intuitive yet, I think, unworkable.

Consider a range of cases in which pictures (images) might be inessential to an "independent" text.

(1) Windsor McCay's *Little Nemo in Slumberland* without the pictures.
(2) Dickens without illustrations by "Phiz," Cruikshank, *et al.*
(3) Lewis Carroll without illustrations by John Tenniel.
(4) Jane Austen without illustrations by Hugh Thomson.
(5) William Blake's illuminated works, without the illuminations.
(6) William Morris' Kelmscott Chaucer without the illustrations, illuminations and Morris-designed typefaces.
(7) Lewis Carroll's "The Mouse's Tale," minus the tail-shape.
(8) Any classic German text set using roman type rather than fraktur (blackletter).
(9) *Where the Wild Things Are* without Maurice Sendak's illustrations.

If McCloud is right, in case 1 we are losing something essential, hence we have comics; in 2–9, something inessential, hence we do not. I do not think it is so clear.

1   Winsor McCay often captions *Nemo* in ways that redundantly redescribe what the eye can see in the picture. So if we take seriously McCloud's suggestion that a verbal narrative that is whole, intact, apart from any pictures, indicates non-comics-hood, *Little Nemo* often isn't comics – which is absurd. The source of this odd result is significant: McCloud knows better than to define "comics," narrowly, as story-telling instruments. But once you admit that there might be other functions for juxtaposed images than carrying the story, it's hard to say *not* carrying the story proves some set of continuous pictures *can't* be comics.

2   Dickens collaborated closely with his illustrators, even dictating place-ment of wood engravings in page layouts.[30] Sometimes Dickens suited words to pictures.[31] Dickens' novels were, famously, serialized. Monthly installments were unified by their wrappers (rich "visual confections," to employ Tufte's term).[32] Each opened with two plates.[33] Indeed, each contained as many pic-tures as could be produced under deadline constraint.[34] Jane Cohen writes:

> The illustrations were invaluable even to Dickens' sophisticated readers for other reasons [than those applying to illiterate or semi-literate audiences]. Few could wait to read the novels until they were complete, yet the part-issues protracted the story beyond ready recall. The illustrations provide continuity between the numbers. By internal structure, symbolic detail, parallels, and contrasts, the plates helped to establish the identity and mark the development of Dickens's characters, the sequence of his plots, and the nature of his themes. No wonder these illustrations were studied, as du Maurier has put it, "with passionate interest before reading the story, and after, and between." (1997: 9)

If Hogarth is pre-comics, as McCloud allows (1997: 16), post-Hogarthian Dickens is para-comics, perhaps. In general, to change the form is to change the function; to change the process is to change the product. For Dickens, pictures were part of the process, and integral to the form.[35]

3–4   Lewis Carroll and John Tenniel go together to such a beloved degree that one contributor to the present volume, Thomas Wartenberg, suggests Tenniel's illustrations are semi-constitutive of these works that bear Carroll's name as author. This is plausible but problematic. I do not consider my Mervyn Peake and Tove Jansson-illustrated *Alice* editions "abridged" – a point McCloud would no doubt seize upon as evidence these are not comics. But consider a less canonical case: an edition of an Austen novel that lacks Hugh Thomson's illustrations (very popular circa 1900) lacks nothing essential – unless, of course, the thing you are trying to lay hands on is *that*: a Thomson-illustrated Austen. Some readers want a particular *novel*. Some a particular *book* (or edition). If it is the latter that is wanted, not the former, then the pictures *are* essential. Are all illustrated book collectors *comics* collectors, by McCloud's definition? All book collectors?

5–6   The case for publishing facsimiles of William Blake's illuminated works is obvious. Blake is not just a poet but a consummate book artist. All the same, one *can* cleanly separate the text. It "stands alone." So it isn't comics? But we would hardly conclude that, say, the Grand Inquisitor scene is not "really" a section of a novel, just because it happens to be a section of a novel written in such a way that it is amenable to being anthologized as stand-alone existentialist allegory. That an artistic element is discrete, hence extractable, does not prove that the larger work bears no "essential" relation to it. But why stop with pictures? William Morris' Kelmscott edition of Chaucer is another paradigm of *book* art, such that alteration of the least design element – say, substitution of alternate letterforms for Morris' custom type – would be as aesthetically unacceptable as a moustache on Mona Lisa. Should one regard the Kelmscott Chaucer as comics, in McCloud's sense?

7–8   Regarding Carroll's "The Mouse's Tale," minus the tail-shape: there is no point publishing unshaped "shape poetry." But, again, we are on a slippery slope. Epistolary novels are, in effect "shape prose": laid out, typographically, so as to contain visual "pictures" of letters. Are all epistolary novels "graphic" novels? Shifting to a different sense of "letter": letterforms are an odd case because they are images independent of text (we can change them without altering text) without being non-text (an "*e*" on the page is not a *picture* of an *e*). Georg Lichtenberg: "When I read a German book printed in roman type, I feel as if I should first translate it."[36] Edgar Allen Poe lamented that he had "never written a book," because he felt his handwriting was essential to his works.[37] Readers, too, have been particular. In the late fifteenth century, the Duke of Urbino took pride in the fact that in all his magnificent library there was not a single printed book to be found.[38]

"Text reads as image," as Will Eisner says. The history of the book is really a footnote to the issues Eisner discusses in *his* book. A traditional novel will not go much better, in virtue of good typography, than it can go in virtue of mediocre typography. But any novel, however well-written, can be made to go badly through bad graphic design. Any *printed* novel has become, by nurture, if it wasn't by nature, a *graphic* novel.

It is a truth universally acknowledged, that a single man in possession of a good fortune must be in want of a wife.

Figure 1.7 Created by John Holbo using quote from *Pride and Prejudice*, by Jane Austen a.

Or:

IT IS A TRUTH UNIVERSALLY ACKNOWLEDGED, THAT A SINGLE MAN IN POSSESSION OF A GOOD FORTUNE MUST BE IN WANT OF A WIFE.

Figure 1.8 Created by John Holbo using quote from *Pride and Prejudice*, by Jane Austen b.

Or even:[39]

Figure 1.9 Created by John Holbo using quote from *Pride and Prejudice*, by Jane Austen c.

"Let the wild rumpus start!" But no rumpus *pictures*? Do we have enough rumpus, in a pictureless edition of Sendak, to count as *proper* rumpus? Let's try a different angle – or lack thereof. Perry Nodelman remarks:

> My shot analysis of *Where The Wild Things Are* repeats the words "long shot at eye level" seventeen times – once for every picture in the book. In point of fact, the sequences created by picture-book artists do not take advantage of the variety of shots common in films; they tend to express the significance of the actions they depict by other means, and they have quite a different sort of rhythm.[40]

Building on this, McCloud might try to re-articulate his intuition about "continuous" pictures, as the mark of comics. Isn't it remarkable that so many of Wally Wood's famous "22 Panels That Always Work!!"[41] didn't work before the first decades of the twentieth century, and still don't work in children's books, because so few illustrators offer them employment? The reason they work in comics is that panels are page elements. Even though he is producing a continuous series of pictures, Sendak is seeing like an easel painter, not like a comics artist.

All the same, as Nodelman's comment makes clear, it would be hard for comics to pull clear of "picture books" without backing into film (or a "snapshot" aesthetic). Formerly, sequential juxtaposed "visual confections" (e.g., emblematic book covers with numerous panels) took design inspiration from architecture (every panel a faux niche). Now they tend to emulate operations of the camera eye. Which does not reassure us that we have *one* thing – comics – first looking to buildings, then going to the movies; rather than two things – illustration and comics; or one thing that is neither of the two – graphic design – which can look in many different directions.

Comic Books and Ideal Books

Most authors have not been "book artists" – not in the sense that Blake and Morris were: authors whose intentions extended to every aspect of an envisioned, idealized, graphic design product. Why not? No doubt the likes of Jane Austen have preferred nice paper and readable type. But the general run of authors has soon enough run against the dull but heavy consideration that you cannot intend what you cannot expect to *do*. Authoring and typesetting, layout (rubrication/illumination/illustration) have been separate practical spheres. You can make a virtue of necessity, retrenching intentions to the citadel of such aspects of the work as you *can* control. But this is not the same as "being true to the medium." If there is to be a page, there is something arbitrary about *not* treating it as a canvas. Admitting as much does not oblige artists to achieve *auteur*-ish mastery of all elements of book-making. The book artist-as-auteur is an admirable figure (Blake). So is the author who can't draw but can instruct those who can (Dickens).

Let me make a modest proposal. *Understanding Comics* is not about comics – not as traditionally understood. McCloud has, in effect, written an eloquent, insightful treatise on "the graphical work," presumptively consisting of a mix of image types; intended for visual "reading." Furthermore, McCloud has produced his treatise in a period in which the impulse to produce such works is widely and deeply felt; and in which this impulse is predominantly (though by no means exclusively) fueled by *love of comics* in Meskin's sense; by sensitivity to the history of, by appreciation of – by nostalgia for; attraction/repulsion to/from standard forms and contents of comics.

Understanding Comics is to comics as William Morris' "The Ideal Book" is to medieval literature.

If we imagine an argument about whether Morris is "really" a modern graphic designer or a medievalist – and why that argument must result in some degree of conceptual stalemate – we see why approaches like Meskin's and definitions like McCloud's should be regarded as complementary. We also see why the latter may be deemed to enjoy an insightful edge, despite the fact that it is productive of more counter-examples than confirmatory instances. If you want to *understand comics*, it is quite crucial to see that "comics" has expanded to the point of being a veritable synecdoche for graphic design *and* at the same time become more deeply interested in its own historic, generic roots.

Notes

1 Nabokov (2002: 3).
2 Quoted secondhand by Dylan Horrocks: (http://www.hicksville.co.nz/ Inventing%20Comics%206.htm). Ware has said similar things about drawing-as-typography in interviews. See, for example, Andrea Juno (1997: 53). See also: Gene Kannenberg Jr. (2001), Daniel Raeburn, (2004), and several contributions to David M. Ball and Martha B. Kuhlman (2010).
3 McCloud (1994: 9).
4 Meskin (2007: 377).
5 It is commonly argued that *manga* derives from the American comics tradition, emerging only in the post-World War II period. If we see it this way, *manga* will not be a counter-example to the historicist definition. I myself find *One Thousand Years of Manga* (2008), by Brigitte Koyama-Richard, as plausible a periodization as *Manga: 60 Years of Japanese Comics* (2004), by Paul Gravett. But a weaker point will do: the mere *possibility* that the longer view could make sense – the world *could* contain two genealogically distinct comics traditions – shows the strain on the historicist approach.
6 Philosophers will understand if I say these terms are grue-like. "Grue": *green before time t, otherwise blue.* The example is due to Nelson Goodman. Let "grue-like" mean: any definition that stipulates the (apparently) inessential to be essential. It is perhaps worth noting that the Japanese themselves don't use 'manga' in the grue-ish way Westerners do. Brigitte Koyama-Richards: "In our time, the word *manga* has changed to the point that it is hardly used in Japan other than by people born before World War II, who generally would use the word to refer to satirical or critical political comic strips published in the press. For succeeding generations, the word might call to mind Edo-era prints – and not cartoons at all. For these younger generations of Japanese, publishers and booksellers employ the term *comic*, which covers mangas of all kinds" (2008: 7).
7 Venturi (2002: 13).
8 David Kunzle does so in *The Early Comic Strip: Narrative Strips and Picture Stories in the European Broadsheet from c. 1450 to 1825* (1973, 2). I don't mean to dismiss this approach as absurd, although I do not favor it. My point, rather, is that if one takes this path, one cannot also propose anything so appealingly simple as: it's comics if it works like comics.
9 See Nanay (2009).

10   This is related to points made in Robert C. Harvey's essay, "How Comics Came To Be: Through the Juncture of Word and Image from Magazine Gag Cartoons to Newspaper Strips, Tools for Critical Appreciation plus Rare Seldom Witnessed Historical Facts" (2009).

11   This point should not be misunderstood. If we went through the museum, replacing title plaques with gag-strip punch-lines, that would have a "fundamental" effect on the museum-going experience, of course. Suppose Caravaggio's plaque now reads, simply, "Psych!" It goes from being serious to silly. But not from being non-narrative to narrative, or vice versa, or even from being narrative in one way to narrative in a different way. Serious or silly, the viewer sees not just what is happening but what happened/will happen.

12   It is not common to juxtapose comics panels by *nesting* them, but at least one famous comics artist – Filippo Lippi – employed this technique in his *tondo, Madonna and Child with Stories from the Life of St. Anne*. I borrow the example from Dominic Lopes.

13   As William Empson might say, "the sort of joke you find in hymns." But minus the joke.

14   Wollheim (2003: 10).

15   When you gaze at Laocoön, do you see a man struggling with writhing snakes? If so, you should agree with Wollheim. Because struggling and writhing are actions and events in time. If, on the hand, you see a frozen, purely spatial form, you may be more of Lessing's school. But even Lessing was not strict about it. You see *both*. That seems reasonable.

16   Apparently Dylan Horrocks has being playing this as a party trick for years (http://www.hicksville.co.nz/Inventing%20Comics%205.htm). Also, one of his characters makes the point in his book, *Hicksville* (2010).

17   Strictly, this is one of the "other poems." It has no accompanying picture. The point stands.

18   Beronä (2008: 158).

19   In fact, there is no doubt whatsoever that writing *is* an extension of speech, hence reading must be, and remain, semi-parasitic on the human capacity for speech, even on the human organs of speech. See Liberman (1999). What I argue in this essay is consistent with Liberman's results, because I do not claim that "visual reading" can ever be visually *pure*. I need only claim that it affords, in certain respects, a distinctive mode of linguistic engagement.

20   Levenston (1992: 18–19). Quoted from William Beattie's introduction, *Border Ballads* (1954: 16).

21   Saenger, 2000, 11. Historical details and debates exceed the scope of the present paper. In the sixth century, separated script was approximately nowhere (in Europe). By the twelfth century, approximately everywhere. It appears earliest in Irish (Hiberno-Saxon) manuscripts, whence it spreads. There are complications: the Byzantine tradition of book illumination, older than the Irish; the distinction between illustration (of texts) and decoration (of artifacts, including books); the consideration that word separation has always been mandatory in Semitic language writings (such as Hebrew and Arabic). It was only the Greek addition of vowels to the borrowed Phoenician alphabet that allowed dropping of word

space in what came to be known as the Roman alphabet. It is plausible the Irish monks I say "invented" comics had the great good fortune of access to Byzantine books and Semitic writings. Perhaps, then, books like Simcha Weinstein, *Up, Up, and Oy Vey: How Jewish History, Culture, and Values Shaped the Comic Book Superhero* (2006) should start the story a bit earlier.

22   Saenger makes a compelling case. He points out, for example, that Irish monks used *videre – to see* – to mean *to read*. Continental readers of *scriptura continua* did not (2001: 39).

23   Cut and paste a stretch of text into your word processor. Globally find and delete all spaces and punctuation. Read silently, like Ambrose. You will find yourself pronouncing, inwardly, to determine where words end and begin – intelligence your eyes would normally provide, via saccadic glances ahead. You can actively suppress movement of your lips, but doing so does not speed the process, or make it less an affair of inner voice and ear.

24   Lupton (2004: 53).

25   Lopes (2007: 57).

26   Bringhurst (2004: 19).

27   Quoted in Martin Harrison and Bill Waters, *Edward Burns* (London, 1973: 164). I take the quote from Ashbrook (1992: 291).

28   Morris and Peterson (1982: 293).

29   From *The Comics Journal*, 179. I get the quote from Dylan Horrocks (http://www.hicksville.co.nz/Inventing%20Comics%205.htm).

30   See Stevens (1967: 113–123). After launching *Master Humphrey's Clock*, as a graphic magazine of sorts, and shifting from etched steel plates to wood engravings, whose blocks could be set alongside type, Dickens seized on new page design possibilities. I take the reference from Cohen (1970: 73–74).

31   Dickens' first novel, *The Pickwick Papers*, was a commission to provide text to accompany illustrations by Robert Seymour, who committed suicide before the work took shape, whose widow sued Dickens on the grounds that it was originally her husband's work; which seems not to have been a just charge, but it says something that there has been a lawsuit, alleging that *Pickwick* is comics, by McCloudian standards: text "writing up to" pictures.

32   Tufte (1997: 122–139). Dickens' wrappers had to juxtapose text and sufficient pictorial matter to emblematize episodes and still-unfolding story arc. Various devices characteristic of comics (panel dividers; text that "reads as image") are employed to these ends. Tufte discusses (among other confections: from mnemonic devices to Cornell boxes) how this is an old tradition. See Corbett and Lightbrown (1979).

33   For discussion of the potentialities of two-plate juxtapositions, see Steig (1972: 55–67).

34   "O woodman, spare that block/ O gash not anyhow./ It took ten days by clock/ I'd fain protect it now. CHORUS: *Wild laughter from Dalziel's workshop.*" This mock-George Pope Morris-esque lament is due to Dante Gabriel Rossetti, but the sentiment was shared by Dickens' hard-pressed illustrators (I take the quote from Cohen 1970). Dickens would never have permitted pictures to proliferate to the point of dominating Dickensian prose. He had his moments of doubt

about the appropriateness of illustration at all, as did many of his critics and reviewers. But on the whole his tendency was to press for as much as he could get, which argues against reprinting his works in ways that omit what he got.

35　The only comics artist I have seen make the case for Dickens, as para-comics artist, is Gene Deitch, in passing, in his "word about the format of this book" – that is, the "pictofictional" form of *Pictorama* (2008). The book consists of heavily illustrated stories, by Deitch and his brothers, some hand-lettered, some not. Historians of the illustrated Victorian novel have tended to have a curious blind-spot for comics. Here is Jane Cohen, on why the illustrated novel has no clear future: "Illustrations may appear on dust jackets or paperback covers to attract buyers, as illustrations posted in booksellers' windows used to do, but they rarely appear in the text itself, exceptions, of course, are comic strips for the near illiterate, which Gabriel Garcia Márquez, for example, has termed "the apotheosis of the novel" (the illustrated novel, one might add)" (Cohen 1970: 228). It is a hard to see why *only* illiterates would be interested in the spectacle of an illustrated novel, raised to a divine or semi-divine plane. But there will always be mysteries. John Harvey's excellent *Victorian Novelists And Their Illustrators* (Sidgwick & Jackson, 1970) concludes on a similar note. On the one hand, it is acknowledged that one key to Dickens' success is his post-Hogarthian, Gillray-esque, graphic-satiric sensibility, which suits his prose to illustration. But it is regarded as a mystery where one might find such stuff today. "In respect of illustration, the modern novel has a withered limb, and while with many novelists it may just as well be withered, since they have no need of it, one cannot say who might have used it with the strength, suppleness and sensitivity of a hand" (Cohen 1970: 181). Yet Cohen and Harvey make all the arguments partisans of comics tend to make. They do so on behalf of the likes of Cruikshank and "Phiz" – who, of course, were denounced as fit only for illiterates in their day.

36　Quoted in Shaw and Bain (1998: 18). Germany has a history of *Kulturkampf* over fraktur (blackletter) versus roman, hence Lichtenberg's sensitivity.

37　See Jackson (2001). Poe was a fervent champion of anastatic printing (hand-printed sheets washed with acid, then pressed against copper plates) over and against "comparatively frivolous" lithography. He envisioned a utopian future in which every author could be his or her own self-publishing William Blake, producing hand-lettered, hand-designed plates, for a "print on demand" publishing industry (to apply, very aptly, our contemporary term).

38　The Duke's agent proclaimed: "In that library the books are all beautiful in a superlative degree, and all written by the pen. There is not a single one of them printed, for it would have been a shame to have one of that sort." Quoted in Orcutt (1926: 12).

39　David Carson set a *Ray Gun* interview with Brian Ferry in Zapf Dingbats because he found the interview "boring" (anecdote from *Helvetica* (2007), the Gary Hustwit film). Also, the Introduction to *Abstract Comics* (Molotiu 2009) is set in some abstract, symbol font.

40　Nodelman (1990: 183).

41　See the famous page here, courtesy of its current owner (http://joeljohnson. com/archives/2006/08/wally_woods_22.html).

References

Ashbrook, S. "William Morris and the Ideal Book," in L. De Girolami Cheney, (ed.). *Pre-Raphaelitism and Medievalism in the Arts*, New York: Edwin Mellon, 1992.

Ball, D.M and M.B. Kuhlman (eds), *The Comics of Chris Ware, Drawing Is A Way of Thinking*, Jackson, MS: University Press of Mississippi, 2010.

Beattie W. (ed.), *Border Ballads*, New York: Penguin, 1954.

Beronä, D., *Wordless Books: The Original Graphic Novels*, New York: Abrams, 2008.

Bringhurst, R. *The Elements of Typographic Style*, 3rd ed., New York: Hartley and Marks, 2004.

Cohen, J. *Charles Dickens and His Original Illustrators*, Columbus, OH: Ohio State University Press, 1970.

Corbett, M. and R. Lightbrown, *The Comely Frontispiece: The Emblematic Title-Page in England 1550–1660*, London: Routledge, 1979.

Deitch, K., S. Deitch, S. Deitch, G. Deitch, *Deitch's Pictorama*, Seattle, WA: Fantagraphics, 2008.

Groensteen, T. *The System of Comics*, Jackson, MS: University Press of Mississippi, 2008.

Gravett, P. *Manga: 60 Years of Japanese Comics*, New York: Harper Collins, 2004.

Harvey, J. *Victorian Novelists And Their Illustrators*, London: Sidgwick & Jackson, 1970.

Harvey, R.C. "How Comics Came To Be: Through the Juncture of Word and Image from Magazine Gag Cartoons to Newspaper Strips, Tools for Critical Appreciation plus Rare Seldom Witnessed Historical Facts," in J. Heer and K. Worcester, (eds), *A Comics Studies Reader*, Jackson, MS: University Press of Mississippi, 2009: 24–45.

Jackson, L. "The Italics Are Mine': Edgar Allen Poe and the Semiotics of Print," in P.C. Gutjahr and M.L. Benton, (eds), *Illuminating Letters: Typography and Literary Interpretation*. Cambridge, MA: University of Massachusetts Press, 2001: 139–162.

Juno, A. *et al.*, *Dangerous Drawings: Interviews With Comix and Graphix Artists*. New York: PowerHouse Books, 1997.

Kannenberg, G. "The Comics of Chris Ware: Text, Image, and Visual narrative Strategies," in R. Varnum and C.T. Gibbons, (eds), *The Language of Comics: Word and Imag*. Jackson, MS: University Press of Misssippi, 2001: 174–197.

Koyama-Richard, B. *One Thousand Years of Manga*, New York: Flammarion, 2008.

Kunzle, D. *The Early Comic Strip: Narrative Strips and Picture Stories in the European Broadsheet from c. 1450 to 1825*, Los Angeles: University of California Press, 1973.

Levenston, E.A. *The Stuff of Literature: Physical Aspects of Texts And Their Relation to Literary Meaning*, New York: State University of New York Press, 1992.

Liberman, A.M. "The Reading Researcher and the Reading Teacher Need the Right Theory of Speech," *Scientific Studies of Reading*, 3:2, April 1999, 95–111.

Lopes, D. *Sight and Sensibility: Evaluating Pictures*, 1st ed., Oxford: Oxford University Press, 2007.

Lupton, E. *Thinking with Type: A Critical Guide for Designers, Writers, Editors, and Students*, Princeton, NJ: Princeton Architectural Press, 2004.

McCloud, S. *Understanding Comics: The Invisible Art*, New York: Harper Paperbacks, 1994.

Meskin, A. "Defining Comics?," *Journal of Aesthetics and Art Criticism*, 65 (1), 2007: 369–379.

Molotiu, A. (ed.), *Abstract Comics*, Seattle, WA: Fantagraphics, 2009.

Morris, W and W.S. Peterson, (eds), *The Ideal Book: Essays and Lectures on the Art of the Book*, Berkeley, CA: University of California Press, 1982.

Nabokov, V. *Lectures on Literature*, New York: Mariner Books, 2002.

Nanay, B. "Narrative Pictures," *Journal of Aesthetics and Art Criticism* 67:1, 2009: 119–129.

Nodelman, P. *Words About Pictures: The Narrative Art of Children's Picture Books* Athens, GA: University of Georgia Press, 1990.

Orcutt, W.D. *In Quest of the Perfect Book*. New York: Little, Brown & Company, 1926.

Raeburn, D. *Chris Ware*, New Haven, CT: Yale University Press, 2004.

Saenger, P. *Space Between Words: The Origins of Silent Reading*, 1st ed., Palo Alto, CA: Stanford University Press, 2001.

Shaw P. and P. Bain, (eds). *Blackletter: Type and National Identity*, Princeton, NJ: Princeton University Press, 1998.

Steig, M. "The Critic and the Illustrated Novel: Mr. Turveydrop from Gillroy to *Bleak House*," *Huntington Library Quarterly* 36 (1), 1972: 55–67.

Stevens, J. "Woodcuts Dropped Into the Text: The Illustrations in *The Old Curiosity Shop* and *Barnaby Rudge*," *Studies in Bibliography* 20, 1967: 113–123.

Tufte, E. *Visual Explanations: Images and Quantities, Evidence and Narrative*, Cheshire, CT: Graphics Press, 1997.

Venturi, R. *Complexity and Contradiction in Architecture*, New York: MOMA, 2002.

Weinstein, S. *Up, Up, and Oy Vey: How Jewish History, Culture, and Values Shaped the Comic Book Superhero*. New York: Leviathan Press, 2006.

Wollheim, R. "In Defense of Seeing In," in H. Hecht, R. Schwartz, and M. Atherton (eds), *Looking into Pictures: An Interdisciplinary Approach to Pictorial Spaec: Illustrated Edition*, Cambridge MA, MIT Press, 2003: 3–16.

2

The Ontology of Comics

Aaron Meskin

Introduction

What sort of thing is a comic? Is *Action Comics* #1 an ordinary physical object, a collection of physical objects (e.g., all extant copies of the issue), an abstract object such as a type (like the Union Jack) or a kind (like the Grizzly), or something different altogether?[1] This is the central ontological question about comics, and it is distinct from the definitional question about which much has been written in the last few years.[2] Rather than asking what – if any – are the necessary and sufficient conditions for being a comic, those theorists interested in the ontological question look to locate comics in the broad metaphysical category to which they belong. It is plausible that this amounts to providing a necessary condition for being a comic which must, therefore, be *consistent* with any adequate definition,[3] but it is noticeable that this ontological question has not tended to be of much interest to those pursuing the definitional project.

I shall not focus on the central ontological question about comics in this chapter. A wide range of views about the ontology of art that have been developed in the last sixty years (Platonism, creationism, fictionalism, perdurantism, and action or event-based theories, to name just a few),[4] and comics do not seem to raise any distinctive issues here. Most of these theories look as if they would just as easily apply to comics as to other forms of art, and I suspect a discussion of which theory best fits comics would end up recapitulating extant debates. Moreover, it is not clear what of critical or practical importance hangs on *this* issue.

The Art of Comics: A Philosophical Approach, First Edition.
Edited by Aaron Meskin and Roy T. Cook.
© 2012 Blackwell Publishing Ltd. Published 2012 by Blackwell Publishing Ltd.

My focus in this chapter is on a range of other ontological issues about comics which both appear to raise distinctive questions about the art form and have critical or practical importance. Are comics necessarily – or merely typically – multiples that admit of instances? How are comics created and instanced? What counts as an authentic instance of a comic, and when do we have forgery of one?

A note about my approach to these questions is in order. Sometimes ontology is concerned with the nature of basic or fundamental things. If we are concerned with the fundamental structure and constituents of reality, then our ordinary intuitions about reality, our linguistic and cultural practices, and our goals or interests may be largely, or perhaps completely, irrelevant. But there are cases of non-basic ontology, where we are concerned with the nature and existence of the dependent or non-fundamental. In such cases, careful attention to practice (both linguistic and non-linguistic) and goals or purposes appears to be warranted. It should be obvious that a concern for the ontology of comics falls into the latter category. An exploration of the ontology of comics does not involve an attempt to describe fundamental entities; rather, it is an attempt to describe the most general features of a particular class of artifacts. These artifacts – traditional comics, graphic novels, webcomics, and so on – are richly embedded in social and cultural practices. Answering ontological questions about comics will require attending to those practices as well as the purposes that underwrite them. Of course this isn't likely to be the whole story since practices may be misguided, and the ontology of comics cannot afford to ignore what we know about ontology in general, but surely it is much of the story.

Multiplicity

Like literature and printmaking, the primary art forms from which it is descended (Meskin 2009: 233–238), the hybrid art of comics is typically an art of multiples. That is, comics and graphic novels are typically multiple works of art rather than singular: they are repeatable, admit of instances or occurrences rather than mere copies, and in virtue of this they allow for simultaneous but spatially-distinct and unconnected reception points. In other words, different people can experience them at the same time and in significantly different locations.[5] *Maus*, Amazing Spider–Man #50, *Watchmen*, and so on, are then not ordinary singular concrete individuals.[6] In addition, the comics that we buy in ordinary shops are not like posters made from famous paintings – mere reproductions that allow us to see what those works of art are like without actually seeing them. This is reflected in the fact that those store-bought artifacts are not treated as in some way *artistically* secondary to, or dependent on, the original art from which they are made. They are, of course, *causally* dependent on that original art, but that is all. Although we may have historical or perhaps even distinct artistic interest in the original drawings made by an illustrator, complete access to a comic (that is, experience which allows for full appreciation of it) does not require experience of original art. In this way, comics are much like standard fine art prints. One does not need access to its matrix (the marked object that is used to generate the impression) to properly appreciate an engraving or etching.

In fact, it is plausible that multiplicity is not merely typical of comics; it is a *standard* feature as well. That is, being a multiple is a feature "among those in virtue of which works in the category belong to that category" (Walton 1970: 339). But are comics essentially multiples? Put more precisely, is multiplicity a necessary condition for being a comic? Certainly not, if the question is about actual multiplicity. There might be singly instantiated comics (i.e., ones with only one extant copy). Perhaps uninstantiated comics – ones with no instances (or "tokens" as they are commonly called) – are possible too, since it is arguable that a comic might come into existence before any copies of it are printed and remain in existence even after all its copies are destroyed (in virtue of the creation and continued existence of the original art or plates from which those copies could be made). But this is clearly not the notion of multiplicity at issue. To be a multiple is to have a modal or, better yet, a dispositional property: it is to be *capable* of having instances rather than mere copies. Could there be a comic that does not have this capacity? The fact that most comics are multiples and have this capacity does not entail that all comics do or must, since there is no compelling reason to think that media or art forms must be unified in this way. Hypothetical examples of printing plates that disintegrate after a single copy is made do not settle the issue although they may clarify it.[7] A printing plate that disintegrates after a single use may still dispositionally underwrite multiplicity or repeatability in virtue of its intrinsic nature and our ordinary art-reception practices.[8]

It is plausible that printmaking, which is also standardly thought of as an art form of multiples, is *not* essentially multiple. Stephen Davies suggests that woodblocks and lino-cuts "for which the method of production involves the alteration of the original template at each new stage of the printing process" are not multiples (Davies 2003: 156). These presumably differ from accidentally disintegrating printing plates in that they are both *designed* to alter after the first printing and *embedded* within a practice in which this design is the norm. That is, in normal conditions only a single instance can be made from such matrices. Relevant members of the art world (printmakers, print collectors, curators, print historians) would not count a second impression as a token of the same print type. Clearer still, monotyping is widely recognized to be a non-multiple medium since the ink that is applied to a featureless plate is removed almost entirely during printing. So not all fine art prints are multiples although the vast majority are.

What about comics then? Are they merely standardly multiple or are they necessarily multiple? The issue has not been seriously addressed in the discussion of the definition of comics, but it has important implications for that debate. In an earlier paper, I argued that extant definitions of comics are inappropriately ahistorical and, hence, have anachronistic implications (Meskin 2007: 372–374). So, for example, Scott McCloud argues that comics are "juxtaposed pictorial and other images in deliberate sequence, intended to convey information and/or produce an aesthetic response in the viewer" (McCloud 1993: 9). Greg Hayman and Henry Pratt claim that something is a comic just in case it is "a sequence of discrete, juxtaposed pictures that comprise a narrative, either in their own right or when combined with text" (Hayman and Pratt 2005: 423). Both accounts are extremely broad: they imply that Hogarth's narrative painting sequences, the Bayeux Tapestry, certain Japanese scrolls and arguably some very ancient Sumerian sculptural relief all count as comics.[9] But counting these as comics rather than as mere sequential pictorial narrative seems to make the former category so wide as to make it unfit for most critical purposes. So, for example, while speech balloons are not necessary features of comics, proper appreciation of a comic as a comic requires that speech balloons are recognized as standard in the aforementioned Waltonian sense. The lack of speech balloons in a contemporary comic is aesthetically significant precisely because it is atypical. But the wide category of sequential pictorial narrative fails to underwrite this, since speech balloons are not standard for that category.

Modern and contemporary art generate similar difficulties for the aforementioned definitions of comics. Roy Lichtenstein is known for copying (or, better yet, transforming) single images from comics in his famous pop art paintings, but he also produced sequences of juxtaposed images based on comics (e.g., *Eddie Diptych* and the multi-panel *Live Ammo*). Do these works, and the clearly narrative triptych *As I Opened Fire!* (which is based on panels from an issue of DC's *All-American Men of War*), then count as comics? I do not believe so, even though the McCloud and Hayman-Pratt definitions seem to imply that at least some do. A photographic copy (or transformation) of a painting is not a painting, and a painted copy of a photograph is not properly categorized as a photograph. The multi-panel Lichtensteins should be thought of the same way: they are copies of comics (or, more precisely, parts of comics) done in a different medium. Although they look like comics and share some formal features with works in that medium, they are part of the distinct art form of painting. More recently, the painter Archie Rand has used some of the formal features of comics (e.g., panels, speech balloons, text, etc.) in large-scale multi-panel non-narrative works (*The 613*) as well as narrative series of paintings (*The Nineteen*). Are these comics? The definitions discussed above would seem committed to counting at least some of Rand's paintings as comics. Again, this seems implausible. Rand's works borrow from, and are influenced by, comics (among other things), but borrowing from or being influenced by an art form is not enough to make something belong to that art form.

Treating comics as necessarily multiple would block the unpalatable consequences of accepting the McCloud-Hayman-Pratt definition of comics. If something is a comic only if it is a multiple then neither the Bayeux Tapestry nor the paintings by Lichtenstein and Rand are comics since none of these are plausibly multiples.[10] Perhaps comics are not essentially a mass art in Noël Carroll's sense (since they need not be designed for "accessibility with minimum effort" (Carroll 1998: 196)), but there is a case to be made for the view that they are necessarily repeatable. Or, better yet, we appear to have good reason to use a concept of comics which underwrites such a claim since failure to do so would distort criticism (as I have suggested above).

Such a reason (even if it is more than apparent) is not indefeasible. There might be a reason to allow for the possibility of non-multiple comics. The non-multiple nature of monotypes may point in that direction since it points toward the possibility of monotyped comic. Here is a more basic reason. Every art form allows for an avant-garde. A standard avant-garde strategy involves the attempt to show that some proposed essential condition of that art form is not, in fact, essential. Such attempts often succeed: they are especially likely to succeed when the primary basis for the proposed essential condition is induction on past cases. (Hence the successful production of paintings that are non-figurative and not flat.) Proper appreciation of such works typically requires that we recognize them as atypical examples of their categories rather than merely typical examples of some new category. We have then some reason to leave it open that an avant-garde comics artist could make a non-multiple comic by means of monotyping or some other strategy. This certainly *seems* possible, and I think there may be actual examples to be found among what are sometimes called "gallery comics." For example, Mark Staff Brandl's comics-painting-installation *Panels* series (which consists of large installation pieces in which oil and acrylic paintings are surrounded by additional wall painting to form sequential "pages") appears to count,[11] although the question of whether installations are singular or multiple is a tricky one.[12]

Does this imply that I think a comics artist can make it the case that her work is a non-repeatable work of art by merely intending this to be the case? No – I've said nothing about what would be required in order for an artist to succeed in making a singular comic. But here is a suggestion: it is plausible that for an ontologically singular entity to count as a comic it would have to involve the conscious rejection of multiplicity. That is, in order for such a creation to count as a comic it would have to be a self-conscious anti-multiple rather than a mere non-multiple.[13] If so, neither the Bayeux Tapestry nor Rand's paintings would count as comics since neither is presumably a self-conscious anti-multiple. Producers of gallery comics, on the other hand, appear to be self-consciously exploring the limits of the comics form.

Note that this line of reasoning suggests that there is a problem with extant definitions of comics which (contra McCloud and Hayman-Pratt) *do* include a mass reproduction condition. Consider David Kunzle's account which holds that "the medium in which the strip appears and for which it was originally intended must be reproductive, that is, in printed form, a mass medium" (1973: 2). Kunzle's account blocks the aforementioned unpalatable consequences of "sequential image" approaches (since neither the Bayeux Tapestry nor Archie Rand's paintings are produced in a reproductive medium), but it fails to make room for avant-garde comics that self-consciously reject use of the ordinary reproductive media in which comics are made.[14]

Perhaps, then, something is a comic only if it is a multiple or a self-conscious anti-multiple. This is an attractive view – not least of all because it neatly coheres with the thought that the development of comics is linked with the invention of printing. As McCloud himself suggests, this "is one event which looms as large in comics history as it does in the history of the written word" (1993: 15). Of course, McCloud himself does not think that the invention of printing made comics possible (remember his categorization of the Bayeux Tapestry as a comic), but the view currently on offer does underwrite the claim that its invention is singularly important since it is arguably this event that makes both the production of print-based multiples and self-conscious anti-multiples possible. Nevertheless, the view faces significant challenges; for example, it must make some sense of the following two putative cases of comics: (1) site-specific "comics" etched or painted onto a cave wall or the side of a building (or in sand on a desert floor, etc.), (2) hand-drawn "comics" made by children (or other naïfs) that are not designed to have multiple instances. The worry is that these cases seem to describe single-instance comics that are not self-consciously anti-multiples.

With respect to the latter case the view on offer faces little problem. A child may have no idea of the nature of the medium in which he or she is working. Perhaps in response to seeing the Sunday funnies, such a child makes a drawing that has the formal features of a standard comic (e.g., speech balloons, panels and gutters). I believe that we would properly count the child as having produced a multiple, since the artifact produced would *allow* for repeatability and multiple instances even if its creator had no intention of making a multiple (nor, perhaps, even a grasp of multiplicity). That is, the child's output *has what it takes* to be a multiple and would plausibly be treated as such by viewers. (To be clear: it is plausible that we would not treat any reproductions as instances of the *drawing* – they would be mere copies of the drawing – but I think that we would be tempted to treat them as instances or occurrences of the comic; that is, as providing us access to the work they made. What this shows is that the ontology of drawings is not identical to that of comics. But we know that already. Homemade comics produced by photocopying may produce instances of the comic, but they do not produce instances of the drawing from which that comic is made.) In the extreme case – where we might be tempted to resist attributing the concept COMIC to the child or naïf – we might also be tempted to resist categorizing the drawing as a comic for that very reason.

Cave-located and site-specific comics are a more complicated case; we would need to know more about individual cases in order to determine how to properly categorize them. Some site-specific comics would be paradig-matically self-conscious anti-multiples (and, hence, may count as true comics), others may not belong to the category of comic at all but instead belong to a hybrid category whose ancestors include traditional comics as well as cave paintings and site-specific installation. (For some examples of site-specific comics see http://blog.anthonyfontana.com/artworks/comics/) And certain cave or wall-located comics *might* – like some graffiti tags – count as multiples. Finally, no matter what we want to say about their status as comics, it is likely that all of these cases are instances of sequential pictorial narrative.

The upshot is that it seems likely that comics are not necessarily multiples. But the claim that they are either multiples or self-consciously anti-multiple is an attractive one and appears to be defensible. That being said, I will not worry much about whether that claim is true or not.[15] Multiplicity is clearly a standard condition of comics. And the generic sentence "Comics are multiples" – whatever its ultimate logical form – looks to be just as true and informative as "Dogs bark," "Birds fly" and "Bees sting", even if it – like those other sentences – does not express complete generality. So comics are multiples. What sorts of multiples are they? In the remainder of the chapter I shall explore this question.

How Are Instances of Comics Created?

Stephen Davies has argued that there are three important kinds of multiples; that is, that there are three distinct ways in which multiple works of art are "created and communicated" (2003: 159). There are "exemplar"-based multiples such as novels and poems in which one instance of the work (e.g., a manuscript or a recitation) is used to set a normative standard for what will count as a proper instance that work. That is, nothing will count as an instance unless it matches the exemplar in certain respects (and to some degree). Significantly, Davies argues that exemplars count as instances of the work for which they serve as a model. Manuscripts of standard novels are a nice example of this: we typically count the manuscript of a novel as an instance of that very novel. And so, as Davies puts it, "novels and poems must have at least one instance" (2006: 91).[16] Other multiples such as performances are made by generating "a set of instructions for the production of its instances addressed to their performers or executants" (2003: 161). Finally, there are cases that are propagated by means of what Davies calls an "encoding" (e.g., digital photographs, sounds recordings, films, prints). In such cases, instances are made by decoding the relevant encoding by means of some specified process. Davies argues that such works (like works for performance) "can exist with no instances" (2006: 91) since an encoding does not count as an instance of the work it encodes (and, presumably, such a work comes into existence when it is encoded).

Despite the attraction of performance locutions in the discussion of both the production and reception of comics (see, for example, Worth 2007 and Ware 2004: 11–12), the art of comics is not plausibly a performing art. Performance is a social activity, but the standard experience of comics is not social. Interaction between performer and audience is standard in the experience of performance but non-standard in the experience of comics. The appreciation of a performance focuses on events while the appreciation of comics focuses on objects. And so on. We may, then, dismiss the possibility that comics are reproduced by means of a set of instructions directed to performers. So what kind of multiple is a comic? As mentioned above, the art form of comics is a hybrid: it is descended from art forms that fall into distinct categories of multiples (since printmaking is an encoded multiple and literature is an exemplar-based multiple). Are comics, then, like prints or novels?

Comics (both traditional and web-based) are encoded rather than exemplar-based. Instances of traditional comics are produced mechanically by various means of printing (the transfer of ink from engraved plate to paper). The engraved plates from which comics are printed are, then, encodings and the production of prints is their decoding. Webcomics are literally digitally encoded and decoded by software on you home computer. Moreover, neither the original art (Bristol Board, proofs, etc.) nor the plates made from that art that are used in the reproduction of a standard comic are *typically* counted as instances of that comic. The drawings from which *Action Comics* #1 was made do not constitute an instance of the comic. So, too, for the digital file that serves as the encoding for a webcomic. So comics do not seem to be like novels, poems, and other exemplar-based multiples which have models that are instances of the work itself. To be clear, collectors do show interest in the original art from which traditional comics are made. But that there is interest in original art does not show that this art falls into the category of comics. I think it typically does not; for example, original art is collected and displayed very differently than the comics which are made from it. And while it may be the case that not *every* feature of the original comic art, proofs or plate is determinative of identity (e.g., proper instances of a comic may vary in size and, perhaps color), it is certainly the case that they fix many more features than are fixed by ordinary literary manuscripts (which do not determine such things as font and pagination). So comics are, I suggest, encoded multiples. In this, the ontology of this hybrid art form reflects the ontology of its dominant ancestor – satirical printmaking.

Here is a complication. I said above that original art does not typically count as an instance of the comic which is made from it. But I do not think that this is always the case; it would be overly rigid to insist that the original art from which a comic is produced *never* counts as an instance of that very comic. Consider, for example, penciled comics made by amateurs (children or adults) which are not intended to be duplicated. (I made many of these when I was going through the first few chapters of the excellent textbook, *Drawing Words and Writing Pictures* by Jessica Abel and Matt Madden.) As I have argued above, these are still plausibly multiples since we would count copies of the drawings as instances of the relevant comic. But no copies of these drawings were ever made, and I never intended to make any. If we followed Davies' account of encoding strictly, we would have to say that the drawings we made were not instances of the comics they encoded (and, hence, that the comics were never instantiated). But I do not think many would be tempted to say this. Rather, what such cases seem to show is that there is only a contingent connection between the way in which instances of multiples are produced and the conditions under which we have an instance of those multiples. Some encoded multiples only have instances when they are decoded. Films are like this. But other encoded multiples may have instances prior to decoding since their very encodings may count as instances of the works they encode. Certain comics are like this.

Relatedly, the art of comics is generally a "two-stage" art in Nelson Goodman's sense (Goodman 1976: 113–114). A comics artist's work (qua comics artist) is typically done when he or she has produced the original art even though that art is not the artistic end-product. So comics are – once again – akin to their dominant ancestor. For, as Goodman puts it, in printmaking "the etcher … makes a print from which impressions are then taken on paper. These prints are the end product" (1976: 114). And print-making is, therefore, a two-stage art. But in the traditional literary case "what the writer produces is ultimate" (1976: 114) so literature is one-stage. But all this is only generally true. In some cases (consider self-consciously anti-multiples or my aforementioned amateur productions) comics are made in a one-stage fashion – they are simply drawn and those drawings are treated as the artistic end product in their own right. These are non-standard cases, though, and we can remain confident that the following generic is true: comics are (like fine art prints) encoded two-stage multiples.

Autographic and Allographic

When is a bit of printed matter an authentic instance of a comic? To answer this question, it is useful to consider the distinction between the autographic and allographic arts as introduced by Nelson Goodman in *Languages of Art*. *Pace* Peter Kivy's recent invocation of the distinction his *The Performance of Reading* (Kivy 2006: 2) this is not the distinction between the singular and multiple arts; rather, it is a distinction that has to do with the possibility of a certain kind of forgery. Here's how Goodman first presents it:

> Let us speak of a work of art as *autographic* if and only if the distinction between original and forgery of it is significant; or better, if and only if even the most exact duplication of it does not thereby count as genuine. If a work of art is autographic, we may also call that art autographic. Thus painting is autographic, music nonautographic or *allographic*. (Goodman 1976: 113)

Goodman ultimately characterizes the autographic/allographic distinction in terms of whether or not a work of art is "amenable to notation"[17] That is, on Goodman's view, a work is allographic if its identity is completely determined by notation (e.g., spelling and punctuation) and autographic if not. But this cannot be quite right. As Jerrold Levinson has argued, it is plausible that no actual works of art are such that the identity conditions for genuine instances are completely specifiable in terms of a notation since context of production matters to identity (Levinson 1990: 100–101). In addition, some art forms (e.g., literature and, arguably, music) allow for both allographic and autographic examples so the inference from "a work of art is autographic" to "that art [is] autographic" is questionable.[18] Still, Goodman seems to have been on to something. There does seem to be a distinction (or perhaps a number of distinctions) between works that straightforwardly admit of what Levinson calls "referential forgery" (i.e., the possibility that something might "falsely purport to be the or an original of a particular *actually existing* work of art" (Levinson 1990: 103)) and works that do not.[19] Paintings, cast sculptures, normal photographs and – most importantly – printmaking fall into the former category. It is easy to imagine "perfect" referential forgeries of works in such media; that is, ones which are perceptually indistinguishable from the actually existing works they purport to be. Most – but not all – literature as well as dance and traditional Western music fall into the latter category. I would suggest that comics fall into the former category too: they are autographic works of art that admit of referential forgery (i.e., that allow for the possibility of something that falsely purports to be an original of an actually existing comic even as it is perceptually indistinguishable from an original).

To see this, we should consider two of Jerrold Levinson's reconstructions of Goodman's autographic/allographic distinction:

(1a) A work of art (and the art form it belongs to) is autographic (a) *iff* even the most exact duplication of the work or its genuine instances which does not employ the *appropriate arch form* does not count as genuine. (Levinson 1990: 91)

(An arch form is "some unique physical object ... essentially involved in the process of production for genuine instances and which imparts to those instances a common structure." (91))

(1b) A work of art (and the art form it belongs to) is autographic(b) *iff* even the most exact duplication of the work or its genuine instances by *direct transcription* does not count as genuine." (92)

(Direct transcription involves the attempt to copy a work by means of observation and the use of standard tools. (92))

Traditional comics are autographic on both of these accounts. An exact duplicate of a comic does not count as authentic unless it was mechanically copied from the original plate or art or some other genuine copy.[20] It is in virtue of this, that referential forgery is possible (i.e., something falsely purporting to be mechanically copied from the original plate or art or other genuine copy.) Direct transcription of a comic (i.e., redrawing it exactly) cannot make a genuine instance. Note, however, that webcomics need not be autographic in sense (1a) since no unique physical object need be involved in the production of a genuine instance. But it is plausible that webcomics are autographic in sense (1b) since direct transcription of the manifest image (or even the underlying code) would not be enough to give you a proper instance of the comic. And one must note that Levinson's account was offered prior to the serious development of web-art and that he inclines to formulation (1b) (Levinson 1990, 94). I think this gives us reason to think that the result of (1b) gives the right answer about webcomics.[21]

Levinson suggests two other accounts of the autographic and allographic distinction. Account (2) is Goodman's account (viz., allographicity as amenability to notation and autographicity as resistance to notation) and, as mentioned above, Levinson argues that this will not capture any robust distinction among the arts since no works of art are autographic in this sense.

More intriguingly, most comics do not turn out to be autographic on account (3) offered by Levinson (and alleged to carve up the art forms in just the same way that account (1) does):

> (3) A work of art (and the artform it belongs to) is autographic (3) *iff* the identity of genuine instances of the work is *not at all* determined by identity of character in a notation or compliance with a character in a notation. (Levinson 1990: 101)

This account falls short because the identity of almost all genuine instances of comic – all with text, that is – is surely partly determined by notation. That is, notation – more specifically, the text – is *relevant* to whether something is a genuine instance of the comic in question even if it is not solely determinative. But this is true of just about any non-improvisational art works that contains text (e.g., silent films) even when such works are intuitively forgeable. It follows that Levinson's account (3) is not adequate for making sense of authenticity in certain hybrid and multi-media arts (and thus that autographic (1) and autographic(3) do not "effect only one division of the pie" (Levinson 1990: 102)).

Comics, at least those that are standardly produced, are autographic in the most plausible of the Levinsonian senses (viz., (1a) and (1b)), and they would have been characterized as such by Goodman.[22] The production of an authentic instance of a traditional comic requires mechanical reproduction from a template. In the case of most traditionally- produced comics the particular template is the collection of printing plates that are used to print the token comics. No token comic is an authentic instance of a relevant comic type unless it was produced mechanically by means of those printing plates or, *perhaps*, by mechanically copying another genuine instance (or another set of plates made from the original art) which may serve as a surrogate template.[23] It is because of this that the distinction between original and (referential) forgery in the case of comics is significant.

Perhaps more intriguingly, comics are – at least typically – *wholly* autographic; that is, they contain no aesthetically relevant spatial parts that are allographic.[24] In particular, it is not the case that comics combine autographic images with allographic text as do some works of literature in which images are an essential part. The lettering in comics is at least standardly aesthetically significant and the physically embodied text in a comic functions more than merely linguistically. The words as they appear on page must then be produced by means of the relevant template or they are not genuine. Re-lettering a comic by hand produces something that does not count as a genuine instance of the original.[25] In fact, the same is true of the other features of the standard comic book page: the panel borders and speech balloons also appear to be autographic elements. Even the footnotes in old Marvel comics that refer readers back to events that took place in earlier issues were handwritten and are plausibly autographic elements!

Occasionally comics contain straightforward bits of typeset text. There are, for example, the "source" documents printed at the end of chapters of Alan Moore's *Watchmen* and the prose story "A Wolf in the Fold" published Bill Willingham's *Fables: Legends in Exile*. But the text in Moore's work clearly functions as image: we are directed by, among other things, drawings of fictional paperclips and their shadows, to interpret what looks like ordinary printed text as copies (i.e., pictures) of original source materials. I believe that even these elements are, then, autographic. And Willingham's story is plausibly not a comic at all, nor even part of one, although it is presented inside the covers of the first trade edition of his excellent ongoing series. A harder case is found in comics like Posy Simmonds recent *Tamara Drewe* where much narrative text is straightforwardly typeset and seems allographic.

But even though there are exceptions, the relevant generic statements are true: comics are an autographic art and they are a wholly or completely autographic art. Put differently, being autographic (and being wholly autographic) are standard features of comics. Once again, they share this distinctive ontological feature with their dominant ancestor – satirical printmaking.

Conclusion

In this chapter, I have made an attempt to answer some of the intriguing ontological questions raised by the art form of comics. Must comics be multiples? I have argued that they need not be, although the generic statement "comics are multiples" is true. How are instances of comics produced? I suggest that the art form of comics is typically a two-stage art in which instances are produced by means of what Stephen Davies calls encoding and decoding. In normal cases, decoding (i.e., printing) is required to produce an authentic instance of a comic. But this is only in normal cases; in some cases no decoding is needed to produce an authentic instance of the comic since the encoding is itself a proper instance of the comic. And in some of these cases comics are produced by means of a one-stage process (i.e., they are finished when the artist's work is complete). Finally, when do we have an authentic instance of a comic? I argue that comics (even digital comics) are best understood as autographic – they admit of referential forgery and direct transcription will not suffice to produce an authentic instance of a comic.[26]

Notes

1 For the notion of types in the context of the ontology of art see Wollheim (1968). For kinds see Wolterstorff (1975).
2 For discussion of the definition of comics see McCloud (1993), Carrier (2000), Hayman and Pratt (2005) and Meskin (2007).
3 I assume that comics belong to their basic metaphysical category (or categories) essentially. Note that if the ontology of comics is disjunctive, then this will amount to a disjunctively necessary condition for being a comic.
4 For an example of Platonism about musical works see Kivy (1983). For creationism about music see Levinson (1990). For fictionalism see Kania (2008). For perdurantism see Caplan and Mattheson (2006). For '"action"' or event-based theories about art ontology in general see Currie (1989) and Davies (2004).
5 Cf. Carroll (1998: 188) on mass art and mass consumption.
6 And if they are some other kind of individual – that is, if recent theorists (such as Caplan and Mattheson) are right and works of art are '"continuants"' – then they are still repeatable and have occurrence (though perhaps not instances).
7 Compare Mag Uidhir (2007) on the repeatability of sound recordings.
8 See Kania (2009) for relevant discussion.
9 Will Eisner's definition (1985, 5) has the same result.
10 But see Currie (1988) for – to my mind unconvincing – arguments that all works of art are potentially multiple.
11 See http://www.markstaffbrandl.com/images.html for some images of Brandl's work. Brandl has told me (in personal correspondence) that he considers his *Panels* works to be comics.
12 About which surprisingly little has been written. My guess is that there is no univocal answer to the question about the ontology of installations. But I think a good case can be made for treating Brandl's works as singular rather than multiple. Brandl has told me that the *Panels* installations are "singular" art works that "can be shown in many places" (personal correspondence).
13 Compare Zangwill (2002) on anti-aesthetic art.
14 Thanks to Roy Cook for reminding me of Kunzle's definition. See also Anne Elizabeth Moore's definition of comics in her preface to *The Best American Comics 2006*: "comics are a published medium – created to be mechanically reproduced, either in print or on the Web" (Moore 2006: x).
15 Here is an even more concessive view: nothing is a comic unless it is a multiple or a self-conscious anti-multiple or a naïve comic (that is, made by someone who doesn't fully grasp the nature of comics). Whether or not the simple disjunctive view is adequate, this slightly more complex one is eminently plausible.
16 Surely Davies does not mean they must have one *extant* instance since a novel does not cease to exist merely if all instances are destroyed – as '"print on demand"' shows; rather, it must be that they must have, *or have had*, at least one instance.
17 "Since an art seems to be allographic just insofar as it is amenable to notation" (Goodman 1976: 121).

18 See my "'Comics as Literature'" (Meskin 2009) for arguments to the effect that
some works of literature are autographic (although most are allographic).
19 Referential forgeries also presumably have to be indiscernibles. If not, every art
work admits of the possibility of referential forgery.
20 It is debatable whether a mechanically produced copy of an authentic copy
counts as an instance of the original comic. I do not have a settled view of
this.
21 Levinson offers a related but distinct account (1c), but he sees these three
definitions of the autographic (i.e., 1a, 1b and 1c) as "definitive of roughly a
single notion of autographicity" (Levinson 1990: 94). And, as mentioned above,
(1b) is his preferred formulation of this family of definitions.
22 David Carrier claims that "comics are an autographic art with, potentially, an
indefinite number of copies of the original image'" (Carrier 2000: 63).
23 Thanks to Roy Cook for pointing out the last possibility.
24 I assume here that it makes sense to talk of comics having spatial parts.
25 And so, letterers count as among the artists who make a comic. This is reflected
in the credits that appear in standard commercial comics.
26 An earlier draft of this chapter was presented at the 2008 Annual Meeting of the
American Society for Aesthetics in Northampton, Massachusetts. I thank that
audience – and especially my commentator at that session (my co-editor Roy
Cook) – for useful feedback. Jon Robson and Roy Cook (again!) gave me very
helpful comments on a penultimate draft. Thanks also to Kathleen Stock for a
helpful discussion about the paper.

References

Caplan, B. and C. Mattheson "Defending Musical Perdurantism," *British Journal of Aesthetics* 46, 2006: 59–69.

Carroll, N. *A Philosophy of Mass Art*, Oxford: Oxford University Press, 1998.

Carrier, D. *The Aesthetics of Comics*, University Park, PA: The Pennsylvania State University Press, 2000.

Currie, G. *An Ontology of Art*, London: Macmillan, 1988.

Davies, D. *Art as Performance*. Oxford: Blackwell, 2004.

Davies, S. "Ontology of art," in Jerrold Levinson (ed.), *The Oxford Handbook of Aesthetics*, Oxford: Oxford University Press, 2003: 155–180.

Davies, S. *The Philosophy of Art*, Oxford: Blackwell, 2006.

Eisner, W. *Comics and Sequential Art*, Tamarac, FL: Poorhouse Press, 1985.

Goodman, G. *Languages of Art*, Indianapolis, IN: Hackett Publishing Company, Inc., 1976.

Hayman, G. and H. Pratt, "What are Comics?" in D. Goldblatt and L. Brown (eds), *Aesthetics: A Reader in Philosophy of the Arts*, 2nd ed., Upper Saddle River, NJ: Prentice Hall, 2005: 419–424.

Kania, A. "The Methodology of Musical Ontology: Descriptivism and Its Implications," *British Journal of Aesthetics* 48(4), 2008: 426–444.

Kania, A. "Musical recordings," *Philosophy Compass* 4(1), 2009. Available online at http://philosophy-compass.com/aesthetics-and-philosophy-of-art/ (accessed October 11, 2011).

Kivy, P. "Platonism in Music: A Kind of Defense," *Grazer Philosophische Studien* 19, 1983: 109–129.

Kivy, P. *The Performance of Reading, An Essay in the Philosophy of Literature* Oxford: Blackwell, 2006.

Kunzle, D. *The Early Comic Strip: Narrative Strips and Picture Stories in the European Broadsheet from c. 1450 to 1825.* Berkeley and Los Angeles: University of California Press, 1973.

Levinson, J. "What a Musical Work Is" *Journal of Philosophy* 77, 1980: 15–28.

Levinson, J. "Autographic and Allographic Art Revisited," in *Music, Art, and Metaphysics: Essays in Philosophical Aesthetics* Ithaca, NY and London: Cornell University Press, 1990: 89–106.

Mag Uidhir, C. "Recordings as Performances," *British Journal of Aesthetics* 47(3), 2007: 289–314.

McCloud, S. *Understanding Comics,* Northampton, MA: Kitchen Sink Press Inc., 1993.

Meskin, A. "Defining Comics?" *Journal of Aesthetics and Art Criticism* 65(4), 2007: 369–379.

Meskin, A. "From Defining Art to Defining the Individual Arts: The Role of Theory in the Philosophies of Arts," in K. Stock and K. Thomson-Jones (eds), *New Waves in Aesthetics.* New York: Palgrave-Macmillan, 2008: 125–149.

Meskin, A. "Comics as Literature?" *British Journal of Aesthetics* 49(3), 2009: 219–239.

Moore, A.E. "Preface," in H. Pekar (ed.), *The Best American Comics 2006,* Boston and New York: Houghton Mifflin, 2006: ix–xiv.

Walton, K. "Categories of Art," *Philosophical Review* 79, 1970: 334–367.

Ware, C. "Introduction," *McSweeney's Quarterly Concern* No. 13. San Francisco, CA: McSweeny's, Ltd., 2004: 8-12.

Wollheim, R. *Art and Its Objects,* 2nd ed., Cambridge: Cambridge University Press, 1980.

Wolterstorff, N. *Works and Worlds of Art.* Oxford: Oxford University Press, 1980.

Worth, J. "Unveiling: *Persepolis* as Embodied Performance," *Theatre Research International* 32, 2007: 143–160.

Zangwill, N. "Are There Counterexamples to Aesthetic Theories of Art?" *Journal of Aesthetics and Art Criticism* 60(2), 2002: 111–118.

Comics and Collective Authorship

Christy Mag Uidhir

I've always been more interested in what's possible in the future than what's happened in the past. I've never been very nostalgic and have never been much of a collector. You're never going to hear me moaning about how much better comics were when I was a kid, because they weren't! Comics are much better now ... There are more diverse genres, more diverse creators, more gender-balanced (not as much as they should be, but we're on our way), they're more substantial in terms of literate content, they are more adventurous in terms of design, there's more virtuosity in a variety of styles, there's more exchange of ideas across national boundaries, there's more personal work being promoted, there's increased public perception for a variety of comics for a variety of different applications. Comics are being used for more things, read by more people, and have more of an essential importance to the culture, relevance to the culture, and effect on the culture than they ever have.

Scott McCloud, from an interview
with Christopher Irving (2010)

Introduction

Most mass-art comics (e.g., "superhero" comics) are collectively produced, that is, different people are responsible for different production elements. Although this collectivity largely defines the history of mass-art comic production throughout, the nature of that collectivity has shifted from the

The Art of Comics: A Philosophical Approach, First Edition.
Edited by Aaron Meskin and Roy T. Cook.
© 2012 Blackwell Publishing Ltd. Published 2012 by Blackwell Publishing Ltd.

discrete, assembly-line model of the Golden Age to the comparatively more nuanced and inclusive contemporary model of the Modern Age. Moreover, this shift appears reflected in (or at least is in step with) the changing interests of comic readership. That is, while content (stories, pictures, characters) remains the primary object of interest, readers have also developed production-oriented interests both broad and narrow, ranging from loyalty to certain titles (e.g., *The Spectacular Spider-man, Detective Comics*) or publishers (e.g., Dark Horse Comics, Top Shelf Productions) to devotion to (or rancor for) certain writers (e.g., Alan Moore, Pat Mills), line artists (e.g., Rags Morales, Lee Bermejo), inkers (e.g., Joe Sinnott, George Roussos), colorists (e.g., Laura Martin, Lynn Varley), or team-ups (e.g., Jeph Loeb and Tim Sale, Grant Morrison and Frank Quitely). Of course, comic readers, regardless of Age, recognize and value well-constructed narratives, well-written scripts, and well-drawn panels. What appears to set contemporary comic readership apart from its predecessors, however, is a shift in the value of, preferences for, expectations about, and attention paid towards the purely visual elements of comics,[1] helping to spark a largely heretofore absent visual, if not art historical, interest in comics from previous eras and the figures involved in their production (many of whom were largely ignored during their own lifetime).[2]

As consumers of comic books see themselves less as "readers" and more as "viewers," so too do they see visual elements of comics as being on a level with non-visual elements not just in terms of stylistic variety (and the complexities and subtleties therein) but, more importantly, in terms of contributory significance such that illustrators can be just as important as writers (if not more so). Adding to this, technological innovations in certain production processes have created an environment in which the contributions of colorists, inkers, and even letterers can become just as significant as those of writers and line artists (e.g., Dave Stewart's coloring in *The Umbrella Academy*, John Severin's inking run on *Sgt. Fury and his Howling Commandos*, and Todd Klein's work as letterer in *Sandman*). As a result, production roles previously thought merely workman-like are now regarded in some cases as being (or as having all along been) significantly or even uniquely contributory (e.g., since the early 1990s, Best Colorist, Best Inker, and Best Letterer have been included as principal categories of industry achievement by both the Eisner Awards and the Harvey Awards). As the comic medium comes into its own, not only does authorship of a comic become all the more difficult to determine but the issue of comic authorship itself becomes all the more pressing.

Here's the worry. Common sense tells us that comics (comic books, comic strips, graphic novels, etc.) are the sorts of things that have authors. Commonsense intuitions about authorship, however, are largely (if not exhaustively) informed by cases involving standardly individually-produced works, specifically the standard sorts of works in the literary and visual arts (e.g., novels, poems, paintings, sculpture). Comics, however, at least of the sort under discussion, are standardly *collectively*-produced. So, the mere fact that commonsense intuitions may reliably track authorship for standard literary works doesn't mean that we should expect them to likewise reliably track authorship for comics.[3] Moreover, common sense quickly abandons us in cases involving numerous agents collectively engaging in highly complex production processes, of which *the standard mass-market comic is just such a case*. Given this, one might understandably be tempted to inform comic authorship by looking to other media with similarly collective and complex production processes (e.g., cinema) and the models of authorship at play therein (e.g., *auteur* theory – the director as principal, if not sole, cinematic author).[4]

The problem is that intuitions about authorship are themselves informed by intuitions or implicit background assumptions about production and its principal constitution – to import the former from other media is also to import the latter. For instance, *auteur* theory construes authorship as being largely a matter of a singular individual exerting sufficiently substantial control over production of a work such that the work is seen as executing that individual's singular vision, being in that individual's singular style, employing that individual's singular technique (e.g., Robert Bresson, Alfred Hitchcock, Akira Kurosawa, Stanley Kubrick, Orson Welles are all *auteurs* of cinema). To be sure, importing *auteur* theory (or some translation thereof) from cinema may well capture authorship in analogously *auteur* cases in comics (e.g., Jack Kirby, Carl Barks, Harvey Kurtzman, Daniel Clowes, Chris Ware). However, assuming *auteur* theory to provide a standard let alone exhaustive account for comic authorship requires endorsing a demonstrably false view of comic production, namely one predicated substantively if not entirely on a single individual (the putative *auteur*) exclusively occupying or substantially controlling any and all production roles potentially relevant to ascriptions of comic authorship (writer, inker, penciller, colorist, letterer, editor, etc.).[5] Of course, this all assumes that the *auteur* theory provides a productive and coherent account of cinematic authorship – a view for which currently almost no philosopher would argue let alone readily assume to be the case. As such, the appeal to *auteur* theory seems capable of nothing more than translating what is a bankrupt theory of cinematic authorship into an equally bankrupt theory of comic authorship.[6]

I take the lesson here to be that if we are to take the comic seriously as a medium, then we shouldn't be looking to other media either implicitly or explicitly to inform comic authorship – *what it is to author a comic* should have everything to do with *what it is to be a comic*. Given the collective-production of comics, the more disparate comic production roles we begin to regard as significantly or uniquely contributory, the more difficult questions of comic authorship become, and the more we view various distinct production roles as potentially constitutive is the more we must view comic authorship as potentially *collective authorship*. Given the general unreliability of intuitions with respect to collective authorship (coupled with our general unfamiliarity with the medium), we must look to find a principle of comic authorship out of which authorship questions can be settled for comics *simpliciter*. Furthermore, any such principle found must also be capable of grounding a principled distinction between collective *production* and collective *authorship*; should this distinction be absent, any proper manner of framing the central descriptive and evaluative questions for comics must likewise be absent. Quite obviously we need a theory of comic authorship. No doubt less obvious is how we should proceed and exactly what such a theory should look like.

A Cautious Set-Up

Given that philosophical analysis of comics is rather recent a development, at least when compared to that of other media, the philosophy of comics looks impoverished and its terrain appears little mapped. Accordingly, we should take care not to make any unnecessary claims, entail any unnecessary commitments, or form any unnecessary allegiances. To this end, I propose the following initial (*prima facie*) constraints on theory of comic authorship.

> (1) Comics needn't have authors but comics must be the kinds of things that can have authors.

For instance, if an account of comic authorship entails that if *w* has no author then *w* is not a comic, then that account of comic authorship selects for a theory of comics of a certain sort and not others – this is precisely the sort of unnecessary commitment we at least initially ought to be avoiding. Given the background assumption that comics are the sorts of things that can have authors, we should take the relationship between theory of authorship and theory of comics to entail only the following:

> (2) Any responsible theory of authorship must be able to account for comics being the kinds of things that can have authors.
>
> (3) Any theory of comics must predicate comic authorship on a responsible theory of authorship.

This ensures both that authored comics must be no different *qua* comic than un-authored comics and also that comic authors must be no different *qua* author than authors of non-comics (e.g., poems, novels, paintings, songs, etc.). Any theory of authorship unable to account for comics being the sorts of things that can have authors should come off as exceedingly strange and strike one as being motivated by concerns well outside the domain of authorship as standardly conceived; so too for any theory of comics entailing that comics cannot be the sorts of things that have authors as standardly conceived. Accordingly, merely to claim in philosophical earnest that (*comics cannot have authors*) requires employing either a radically revisionary notion of *comic* or a wildly irresponsible notion of *authorship*.

(4) Comic authorship itself should not depend on the endorsement of (or the allegiance to) any particular definition of comics.

The mere fact that theory of comics T_1 (comic iff Θ) competes with theory of comics T_2 (comic iff Φ) should *itself* entail only that the corresponding accounts of comic authorship differ in specification, and not a difference in comic authorship *itself* (i.e., its minimal structure). That is, where **R** is the minimally specified relation holding between an author of a thing and that thing so authored, it should be the case that an agent standing in (minimally specified) relation **R** to Θ is an author of a comic (according to T_1) if and only if an agent standing in relation **R** to Φ is an author of a comic (according to T_2). Failure for this to be the case entails that either according to T_1 or according to T_2, a comic is not the kind of thing that can have an author.

(5) Comic conventions and practices are in the main (more or less) responsible and coherent but needn't be regarded as absolute.

For instance, if comic convention and practice suggests that the inker, colorist, letterer, and breakdown artist are candidates for authorship, then any theory of comic authorship ought to allow for that (but needn't entail that).

Of course, one might object that this is *too* cautious, that is, no account of comic authorship could plausibly satisfy the above constraints while also remaining a well-specified and robust account. I agree entirely; in fact, as I soon show, *that's entirely the point*. Having to sketch and defend any well-specified, robust theory of comic authorship ought to first require having to sketch and defend a well-specified, robust theory of comics. As to the robust, well-specified nature of *being a comic*, I simply haven't a clue; however, I do have an idea about what it is to be an author.[7] Instead of offering a theory of comic authorship, my goal here is to provide the framework for determining comic authorship, that is, to provide a responsible theory of authorship that when taken in concert with a theory of comics says exactly what it is to author a comic (collectively or otherwise). Moreover, I take my theory of authorship to act as a constraint for a theory of comics. That is, should any theory of comics, when taken with my theory of authorship, yield an incoherent account of comic authorship, then that theory of comics is itself incoherent or itself entails that comics cannot even in principle be authored (collectively or otherwise), such that, any (non-empirical) difficulties had by a theory of comics with respect to *comic authorship* are simply difficulties had by that theory of comics with respect to *comic*.

Minimal Authorship (of Sorts)

According to most theories of authorship, what it is to be an author is to stand in such-and-such relation to a work; furthermore, all authors stand in the same relation to the works they author regardless of the varieties of disparate media descriptions under which those works may appear (e.g., poems, novels, paintings, sculptures, films, comics). On this view, what it is to be the author of a work of one sort (e.g., a poem) is just what it is to be the author of a work of any other sort (e.g., a comic) – what it is to be the author of a work is independent of what it is for a work to be a certain sort (e.g., *poem, painting, film*, or *comic*). This of course ignores the very real and very substantial differences in the nature of production of works under those various descriptions. The result of this is a tendency to force-fit challenging sorts of works (i.e., those involving highly complex and collective production processes) into models of a standard, more familiar sort (i.e., those typically involving a single agent carrying out or fully controlling all relevant aspects of production). The more unfamiliar and challenging the medium, the more attributing authorship to works under that description requires doing violence to that medium; the more complexly collective the production, the more distinctions between collective production and collective authorship reduce to games of blind intuition.

I provide an alternative to the above view, but in doing so I do not claim merely that a work being of a certain sort or under a certain description matters for what it is to be an author of that work. Rather, I claim that *authorship itself must be work-description relative*, that is, we must abandon the two-place relation xAw – *authorship-of-a-work* – in favor of the three-place relation $xA(Fw)$ – *authorship-of-a-work-as-an-F* (where F is some work-description). Only authorship as a three-place relation between agents, works, and work-descriptions can underpin crucial and productive distinctions between singularly-authored collectively-produced works and collectively-authored collectively-produced works.

On my view, *authorship-of-a-work-as-an-F* minimally entails the following for an agent (*A*), a work (*w*), and a work-description (*F*):

> *A* is an author of *w* as an *F* if and only if *A* is directly responsible, at least in part, for *w* as an *F*.

To be an author of a work under a description is to be directly responsible, at least in part, for that work being under that description, that is, to be directly responsible for the way in which that work satisfies the conditions for being under that description (e.g., to be an author of a work as a *poem* is to be directly responsible for the way in which that work satisfies the conditions for being a *poem*). To help illustrate this, assume for the sake of argument and simplicity the following. Let *C* be the set of all and only those features essential for work-description *F*. So:

> Work *w* is an *F* if and only if *w* possesses the features in *C*.

From this, the following:

> *A* is the author of *w* as an *F* if and only if *A* is directly responsible, at least in part, for *w*'s possession of the features in *C*.

Further specified with the following:

> For *A* to be directly responsible, at least in part, for *w*'s possession of the features in *C* is for *A*'s intentions to figure substantively in *w*'s possession of at least one of the features in *C*.[8]

For instance, if *w* is a poem, then if *A* is the author of *w* as a *poem*, then *A*'s intentions must substantively figure in that work being a poem (the way in which that work satisfies the conditions for being a *poem*). For *w* to be the particular poem that it is, is for *w* to be a poem in a particular sort of way (to satisfy the conditions for being a *poem* in virtue of the particular features it possesses). Authorless poems, if there can be such things, then are works that satisfy the conditions for being a *poem* but works for which no one is directly responsible, at least in part, for the particular way in which the work satisfies those conditions. If *A* is an author of *w* as a *poem*, then it cannot be the case that *A* is directly responsible for *w* being a poem but not directly responsible for the particular way in which *w* is a poem. So, being the author of *w* as a *poem* entails being the author of that particular poem.

Additionally, I take there to be two broad classes of authorship: singular and collective (assume A≠B):

> **Singular Authorship**: Only *A* is an author of *w* as an *F*.

A subspecies of which is:

> **Conjunctive Authorship**: Only [*A* and *B* ...] is an author of *w* as an *F*, but neither *A* nor *B*... taken alone is an author of *w* as an *F*.[9]

The other broad, distinct class is:

> **Collective Authorship**: *A* and *B* ... are authors of *w* as an *F*.

Prima facie, collective authorship entails collective production – to be collectively produced just is to be the product of activities with multiple, distinct intentional sources. For my purposes, I do not count as collectively produced works produced by a single intentional source where that source is some group or collective agent (collective intentions). Collective production, however, should neither entail nor suggest collective authorship.

For instance, most mass-market films are collectively produced, but while I suppose that key grips fulfill crucial production roles, key grips are not thereby authors of films. Likewise, many prints are collectively produced, and while I suppose that print technicians and master printmakers play critical production roles for prints, they are not (at least not obviously) thereby authors of the prints they help produce. We don't discount key grips and print technicians as authors because they don't fill significant production roles – they obviously do. Rather, we regard the activities in which key grips and print technicians engage, though they be however complex and highly skilled, as being (at least in standard cases) broadly directed by – or facilitating those activities directed by – the intentions of others (e.g., film directors, cinematographers, graphic designers, print artists). Of course, while collective production doesn't entail collective authorship, many collectively produced works under certain work-descriptions are collectively authored. The operative question then to which we can now turn is whether *comic* is just such a work description.

Minimal Authorship (of the *Comic* Sort)

Assume *comic* to be an author-relevant work-description. From this, we get the following:

> A work *w* is a comic if and only if *w* possesses the features in *C* where *C* is the set of all and only those features essential for being a comic.

And from this:

Someone is the author of *w* as a comic if and only if that someone is directly responsible, at least in part, for *w*'s possession of the features in *C*.

Further specified by the following:

For someone to be directly responsible, at least in part, for *w*'s possession of the features in *C* is for the intentions of that someone to substantively figure in *w*'s possession of at least one of the features in *C*.

Note I am not assuming that any theory of comics must be an essentialist account; I merely employ one for the sake of simplicity.[10] My view should perform equally well for more pluralist or open-ended accounts.[11] I claim only that for a thing that is a comic, someone is an author of that comic just in case that someone is directly responsible at least in part for whatever makes that thing a comic, and this itself doesn't require that what makes that thing a comic must be the same as what makes another thing a comic (or make any other thing a comic). Of course, theories of comics with nebulous or variable satisfaction conditions for *being a comic* unsurprisingly ought to result in equally nebulous or variable satisfaction conditions for *being an author of a comic*.

Also note that I do not target trivially essential/necessary features, for example, being an object, being a non-minotaur, being (a comic or a marmoset). Likewise trivial and so excluded from *C* are redundant or non-constitutive essential/necessary features, that is, a feature for which *w* satisfying the conditions for being an *F* (necessarily) entails *w* possessing that feature, but possessing that feature is not itself constitutive of being an *F*, that is, not itself a distinct condition that *w* must satisfy in order to be an *F*. For instance, I consider *being an artifact* to be a non-constitutively (and so trivially) essential feature for *being a chair*; however, while a thing satisfying the conditions for being a chair (necessarily) entails the thing being an artifact, being an artifact is not itself constitutive of the thing being a chair, that is, a distinct condition a thing must satisfy in order to be a chair. For example, suppose a thing to be a chair just in case that thing (i) is made with the purpose of being sat upon and (ii) is able to be sat upon as the result of being successfully so made. Clearly, the extra condition ((iii) *is an artifact*) adds nothing of any substance – anything satisfying i) and ii) *ipso facto* satisfies iii). Accordingly, the assumption that comics must be artifacts need entail only that any *w* possessing all features in *C* must thereby be an artifact; it needn't (and I assume doesn't and shouldn't) entail that being an artifact is *itself* constitutive of being a comic, that is, itself a distinct feature in *C*. As such, we shouldn't expect someone to be an author of a comic merely in virtue of being directly responsible for its *bare artifactuality* and nothing else (e.g., writer, line artist, letterer, *artifactualist*).[12]

Finally, note that this allows both for the possibility of authorless comics and for the possibility of conjunctive but single authorship. That is, it allows there to be no such single person who satisfies the conditions of authorship. This is consistent both with the view that comics needn't have authors and the view that comics can have only singular authorship (i.e., the author must be either a single person or a conjunction of persons such that no conjunct taken by itself is an author and only the conjunction is itself sufficient).[13] Of course, this makes an account of comic authorship only as good as the account of comics upon which it is based, but this is what we ought to expect.

Some Work for a Theory of Comic Authorship

Motivating interest in comic authorship and its corollaries (especially the method of its determination) ought to be relatively straightforward; clearly authorship matters for a variety of reasons (e.g., legal, moral, social, artistic) germane for a host of concerns (e.g., ownership, authenticity, interpretation, aesthetic value). Additionally, some philosophers claim authorship to play a foundational if not also essential metaphysical role for works (of a certain sort), especially with respect to work identity and work individuation. (For example, if a work has an author, could it have had a different author (or no author) and still be that work, are two works identical in all respects save authorship the same work or are they nevertheless different works, and is it even possible for a work to be identical in all respects save authorship?)[14]

To help illustrate this, consider *Batman: The Killing Joke*. Most consider this widely influential comic to be (at least in a pretheoretic sense) collectively authored by Alan Moore, the writer, and Brian Bolland, the line artist. In addition to the line art, Brian Bolland had intended to also do the coloring for the comic's 1988 release, but due to time constraints, John Higgins was employed instead as the colorist. For the 2008 "re-release" of *The Killing Joke*, Bolland made good on his decades-old intentions by re-coloring the entire comic, the result of which was a coloring substantially different from that had by *The Killing Joke* released in 1988. For instance, 1988 release featured the iconic Batman chest emblem – yellow oval surrounding the bat symbol – while the 2008 release removed both the oval and the yellow. In the 1988 release, the flashback scenes (the Joker's pre-Joker past) were fully colored; in the 2008 release, however, those scenes were entirely colored in sepia tones save things traditionally considered or implied to be red were actually colored red (e.g., cooked crawfish, Red Hood's hood and cape). Further still, the 1988 release looks like a comic from the 1980s largely because of its coloring; likewise, and perhaps problematically, the coloring in the 2008 release reflects its time – it looks like a comic from 2008. Given all this, it seems legitimate to ask whether *Batman: The Killing Joke* (1988) is the same comic as *Batman: The Killing Joke* (2008).[15]

One way to answer the above is to assume that authorship matters for work identity. If colorists ought to be counted as authors (at least in these specific cases), then John Higgins is an author of *The Killing Joke* (1988) but not of *The Killing Joke* (2008). If authorship must be preserved, then *The Killing Joke* (1988) is not the same comic as *The Killing Joke* (2008), and this would hold even were they otherwise qualitatively identical. Of course, to employ this individuation method requires support from a theory of comics according to which colorists can count as authors. If knowing the specific conditions under which a colorist counts as an author of a comic entails knowing the specific conditions under which something counts as a comic, then so too must knowing the specific conditions under which something counts as *that* comic. However, in the absence of further argument, we should take authorship itself to be more or less metaphysically neutral, e.g., absent further argument, one shouldn't conflate comic authorship with comic individuation. While determining the specifics of comic individuation is certainly an interesting project, it certainly isn't mine. That said, my view of comic authorship remains well-suited for employ in some further metaphysical view should one choose to do so (e.g., author essentialist view of works of certain sorts).

At this point, one might cry foul, claiming that I have yet to offer any insights into comic authorship or that I cannot provide any such insights given the strikingly uninformative account of what it is to be a comic heretofore employed. This clearly misses the point; the strength of my view is precisely that authorship doesn't vary according to work-descriptions (e.g., if we know exactly what it is to be an author, then our not knowing what it is to be an author of a comic just is our not knowing what it is to be a comic). Most importantly, authorship shouldn't be tested against theories of comics; rather, any theory of what it is to be a comic ought to be tested against authorship (at least as I have described it). If we assume *comic* to be an author-relevant work-description, then we must also assume that any theory of comics must entail a coherent account of comic authorship. Notice, however, that entailing a coherent account of comic authorship *should not* be viewed as a mark for a theory of comics; rather, entailing a coherent account of comic authorship should be seen as necessary condition on any theory of comics' *prima facie* viability. That is, if a theory of comics is such that no one even *in principle* could be directly responsible for the manner in which something satisfies the conditions for being a comic, then according to that theory, comics cannot even in principle have authors. To even seriously entertain such a claim requires such a radically revisionary notion of *comic* that we ought to regard any theory entailing that comics cannot even *in principle* have authors *ipso facto* unable to be even *prima facie* viable as a theory of comics.[16]

Illustrating Robust Comic Authorship

An account of comic authorship is only as robust as the theory of comics out of which it falls. So, for purely illustrative purposes, I adopt Scott McCloud's (1993) definition of comics.[17] According to McCloud, comics are juxtaposed images in deliberate sequence intended to convey information and/or produce an aesthetic response in the reader. The principal constituent of comics are images; the images are juxtaposed with one another; this juxtaposition results from the images' position in the sequence; the sequencing itself gets determined according to the information such sequencing is intended to convey and/or the aesthetic response intended to be produced in the reader. So, while a particular comic must have images, what images are had depends upon the juxtaposition, which in turn depends on the sequencing, which in turn depends on what particular purpose the sequencing is intended to serve.

First, notice the above when combined with the progression and development of the techniques typically employed in comic production looks to ground contemporary comic conventions and practices. Contemporary comic practice isn't, compared to its Golden Age forebearer, more pluralistic with regard to comic authorship because of some new found, deep commitment to egalitarianism or labor rights. Colorists, inkers, and letterers are considered candidates for comic authorship largely because the techniques, technologies, and styles involved in coloring, inking, and lettering have evolved in such a way as to now offer substantial contributions both to content and the aesthetic reception. Moreover, this underpins why one might consider comics produced under the old, assembly-line, studio system of production to be, in a sense, "authorless" comics. Under this system, colorists, inkers, and letterers often weren't entirely aware of exactly what they were coloring, inking, and lettering (often even writers and pencillers had little to no contact with one another). As this changed, so too did attitudes regarding coloring, inking, and lettering, both professionally and in terms of how comics were received.

Consider again *Batman: The Killing Joke*. Higgins' coloring, like the coloring of many superhero comics from the 1980s and earlier, fails to be a constitutive component of the narrative. Coloring for much of the history of mass-art comics functions like background music; it makes the experience more pleasant but doesn't demand attention to its particulars (it need only be musical/colored within a broad range rather than be any particular music/color) – the same holds for the history of inking and lettering. So, one could plausibly contend that Higgins' coloring is such that Higgins fails to be an author for *The Killing Joke* (1988) (i.e., either that the coloring itself is not constitutive of *The Killing Joke* (1988) as a comic or that the intentions directing the production activities of coloring, of which Higgins is the source, failing to substantively figure even in part for whatever makes *The Killing Joke* (1988) a comic). Bolland's coloring, however, is nuanced and complex, complimenting and deepening both narrative and theme. So, perhaps Bolland's coloring (and Bolland's intentions directing his coloring) is such that Bolland *qua* colorist is an author for *The Killing Joke* (2008). Just as two people may share a destination but differ as to arrival method, I suppose that *The Killing Joke* (1988) and *The Killing Joke* (2008) share purpose *P* but differ with respect to the elements employed to fulfill *P*. Moreover, imagine that *The Killing Joke* (1988) and (2008) are visually indistinguishable. We might nevertheless count Bolland but not Higgins as author *qua* colorist. In this case, Higgins would *fail to be an author* and Bolland would be *an author who failed*.[18]

While authorship is intention-dependent, presumably, in many cases, exactly whose intentions matter won't be clear. Often authorship of a comic gets attributed to that comic's creative director. For example, *Watchmen* was created by Alan Moore, though Moore contributed no artwork (*Watchmen* was illustrated by Dave Gibbons and colored by John Higgins).[19] That comics can have a sole author that does not draw, ink, color, or letter isn't the problem. Determining when the creator is *the* author, *an* author (one among others), or not an author at all looks to be the problem. For example, Alan Moore is infamously known for being controlling – Moore not only creates the story, he also writes the script, which he then turns into a panel by panel breakdown, describing each panel, what objects it contains, where they are located, how they should look, and how that panel fits in with those before it and those after it.[20] Recall that, at least according to McCloud's definition, being an author entails not just being responsible for a thing possessing images, image juxtaposition, and image sequencing but also being responsible for that thing's possession of those elements with respect to some purpose. Presumably, Alan Moore at least gets to be an author of *Watchmen* in virtue of determining the purpose those relevant features are supposed to serve, but what further distinctions can and must be made?

Comic Authorship of the McCloudian Sort

Again, assuming Scott McCloud's (1994) definition of comics:[21]

> A work w is a comic if and only if w possesses some $C\,[C_w]$ and some $P\,[P_w]$ such that C_w is constituted largely with respect to P_w.

Being a comic isn't simply (i) being a sequence of images and (ii) being intended to fulfill some narrative or aesthetic purpose; rather, being a comic requires image sequencing in service to some narrative or aesthetic purpose.[22] This must be reflected in what it is to be an author of a comic. So:

> *A* is an author of *w* as a comic if and only if *A* is directly responsible, at least in part, for C_w being constituted with respect to P_w.

Comics with single authors are comics for which only one person is directly responsible for *C*'s constitution with respect to *P*. Collectively authored comics must then be not just collectively produced comics but comics for which multiple people or agents are directly responsible for *C*'s being constituted with respect *P*, each author bearing the same type of relation to the work and therefore to one another. The above framework for comic authorship allows us to ground the following crucial distinctions between *singularly-authored* collectively-produced comics (either an appropriation case or a commission case) and *collectively-authored* collectively-produced comics (either collaborative or non-collaborative). Of course, one needn't endorse McCloud's definition (or at least my reading of it) to make the above informative and productive distinctions. In fact, any *prima facie* viable theory of comics must entail an account of comic authorship able to coherently support the above distinctions, and any theory of comics out of which such distinctions cannot coherently emerge or emerge as neither productive nor informative *ipso facto* can itself be neither coherent nor informative and productive as a theory of comics.

Before I address collective authorship in comics (collaborative or non-collaborative), I must first discuss how best to characterize collectively produced but singularly authored works, namely as either appropriation cases or as commission cases.

Appropriation Cases

Consider Dan Walsh's comic strip *Garfield Minus Garfield*. To create his work, Walsh selects certain *Garfield* comics (authored by Jim Davis), then removes the images of the character Garfield from those *Garfield* comics.[23] To be a *Garfield Minus Garfield* comic is to have a *Garfield* comic as a proper part, but *Garfield Minus Garfield* comics are not *Garfield* comics. Although Walsh's work is a comic in virtue of his appropriation of Davis's comic, Davis, while directly responsible for *Garfield* being a comic, is in no way responsible for *Garfield Minus Garfield* being a comic. That is, Davis's intentions substantively figure only for *Garfield* being a comic, and do not figure at all for *Garfield Minus Garfield* being a comic. *Garfield Minus Garfield* may loosely be described as collectively produced in that *Garfield*

Minus Garfield contains images that when considered alone were produced by someone other than Dan Walsh.[24] Clearly though, *Garfield Minus Garfield* has nothing to do with Jim Davis's intentions and everything to do with Dan Walsh's intentions, so *Garfield Minus Garfield* has but one author.

Commission Cases

Imagine that I want to make a comic with a certain narrative content. Rather than appropriating panel images from pre-existing *Garfield* comics, I instead hire Jim Davis to create some images for me. I send him a set of detailed instructions for each image but deliberately do so in such a way that he never comes to believe that these images bear (or are intended to bear) any relation to one another. Davis doesn't think he is creating *panel* images, only discrete, stand-alone images. The juxtaposition of these drawings according to a sequence, let alone with respect to a particular purpose, simply doesn't figure for Davis. So, Davis's intentions cannot substantively figure in any relevant relations the images bear to one another. Even though every panel in the comic features an image, for which, considered alone, Jim Davis is the sole author, I am nevertheless the sole author of the comic featuring those images. My intentions and my intentions alone substantively figure in the work possessing the relevant comic properties, and images, considered discretely, aren't relevant for being a comic – images are relevant for being a comic only when considered *relationally* (e.g., image paneling). That the work possesses these images and how these images, in virtue of their sequencing, serve the narrative and thematic content has absolutely nothing to do with Jim Davis's intentions and everything to do with mine. The comic may have been collectively produced but the comic isn't collectively authored; I am the sole author of the comic.

Consider the graphic novel *The Filth*, for which the salient production credits are as follows: Grant Morrison (writer), Chris Weston (penciller), Gary Erskine (inker), Matt Hollingsworth (colorist), and Clem Robins (letterer).[25] Most people's intuitions about comic authorship point toward the writer and penciller (though often not to the same degree), that is, if anyone is an author of *The Filth*, then it must be Morrison if not also Weston. Other contributory roles fair considerably less well, that is, some view inkers as glorified tracers, colorists as glorified computer operators, and letterers as, well, unglorified letterers. We shouldn't simply dismiss letterers out of hand as potential comic authors; rather, being so dismissed should result from systematically showing that no agent can be a comic author merely *qua* letterer. Similarly, we shouldn't just assume, as many of us do implicitly if not explicitly, that writers have the greatest claim to comic authorship; rather, we should see if these intuitions could be supported in terms of the nature of the relation (symmetric or asymmetric) between authors in cases of collective authorship.

Collaborative Cases

Suppose that I hire Jim Davis to illustrate the work. I have written the script and have broken that script down into meticulously detailed panel-descriptions, which I then provide as instructions to Davis. Notice that in this case Davis draws the image in the panel-description as just that, *a paneled image*. That is, in this case, Davis is not only aware of the intended narrative and thematic content but also aware of how the images described in the detailed panel descriptions relate to that narrative and thematic content in virtue of how those images relate to the other images described in other panel-descriptions. Davis then draws the images with this in mind. So, the activities from which the images substantively result are not merely directed by the intention that they conform to the detailed sketches I provided (merely following instructions) but by the intention that they look a certain way in virtue of how looking that way relates to the narrative and thematic content – how looking a certain way relates to other images, their juxtaposition and sequencing, and how this relates to the narrative and thematic content. Notice that if Davis fails to be aware of this or fails to have this inform the intentions directing his activities, then this collapses into a commission case.[26] That the work possesses these images and how these images relate to the narrative and thematic content, in this case, has everything to do with Davis's intentions. Therefore, the comic has two authors. Of course, we might further claim that since my intentions govern the conditions under which Davis's intentions are allowed to figure, though Davis is an author, I am the primary author – *Davis's intentions substantively figure only if my intentions substantively figure*. After all, not all collaborations must be equal. For this to be a truly equal collaboration requires the way in which I am directly responsible for the work being a comic to *inform/affect and be informed/affected by* the way in which Davis is directly responsible for the work being a comic.

Non-Collaborative Cases

McCloud's definition appears at least *prima facie* to exclude non-collaborative collective authorship.[27] The features required for a work's being a comic (image, juxtaposition, sequence, purpose) depend on one another; no feature counts as constitutive non-relationally, independent of the others. *A*'s intentions may figure substantively in *w* possessing a particular discrete image, but this doesn't entail that *A*'s intentions substantively figure in *w as a comic* – discrete images aren't constitutive components of McCloudian comics. Crudely put, *A* and *B* cannot simply divvy up comic production (e.g., *A* produces the image sequencing and *B* produces the narrative content), complete their assigned roles, and have a comic result. In fact, such cases, when coherent, appear to be *commission* or *appropriation* cases rather than *collective authorship* cases (i.e., a comic, of which *A* is not an author, that nevertheless has components produced by *A* that are constitutive of the comic only as a substantive result of *B*'s intentions). Of course, to object to the rejection of non-collaboratively collectively-authored comics just is to object to McCloud's definition of comics (or at least to my reading of McCloud's definition of comics). The important point is that, at least as I have described it, *authorship* is easy, so *comic authorship* can only be as complicated as *comic*.

Final Thoughts

Using the preceding analysis, perhaps the history of mass-market comics can instructively be seen in terms of moving from commission cases to collaborative cases. When writers or artists get employed only in virtue of being able to write stories or produce images in a standard (conventional) style, commission cases should be common. When writing and artistry begin to become more nuanced and complex, as in contemporary comics, we begin to see more collaborative cases. Mechanical skill or stock storytelling isn't enough anymore. Writers and creators want artists who can understand the complexities and nuances of their scripts or creative visions, and create images in virtue of that understanding (e.g., Moore and Gibbons on *Watchmen*). Likewise, artists seek writers or creators with nuanced and complex scripts or projects that they can make more complex or nuanced in virtue of their artistry (e.g., Tim Sale's illustration of Jeph Loeb's story in *Batman: The Long Halloween*). Of course, the best sort of collaboration results when the authors creatively compliment each other (e.g., Grant Morrison's story and Dave McKean's paintings in *Arkham Asylum* or Frank Miller's frantic line art and Lynn Varley's wild, garish coloring in *The Dark Knight Strikes Again*). Note that being a writer of a comic doesn't entail being an author of that comic, or if an author, being the "primary" author. Just as images can be appropriated and artists commissioned, so too for scripts, stories, and writers.

Finally, whether or not one finds McCloud's definition of comics persuasive, questions of comic authorship, collective or otherwise, can be properly answered only by first specifying the work-description *comic*. Determining the work-description *comic* then allows for determining who, if anyone, is directly responsible, at least in part, for the work being under that description. Subsequently, the presence of any (or at least a preponderance of any) non-empirical difficulties in determining comic authorship suggests that the source of the difficulty firmly rests with that operative theory of comics, revealing either that the work-description *comic* itself is *in principle* resistant to authorship or that the account of comics under consideration is *itself* unworkable. For if it turns out that *comic* is an elusive or fractious work-description, then comics are *ipso facto* works for which authorship is elusive or fractious.[28] Most importantly, comic authorship is no queerer a thing than authorship of any other sort. The sort *comic*, however, may well be a queer thing indeed.

Notes

1   Of course, the fact that contemporary comics may be visually more sophisticated than comics were half a century ago doesn't mean that contemporary comics are thereby better (either visually or *simpliciter*) than their Golden Age brethren.
2   The increased attention to, study of, and value placed upon comics from earlier Ages largely concerns their purely visual elements, often having little to do with (or even in spite of) their narrative content (e.g., we value classic Graham Ingels *Tales from the Crypt* comics and Burne Hogarth *Tarzan* Sunday strips not for narratives but for their visuals).
3   At least to the extent we take the medium of comics itself to be outside literature (either as a fully stand-alone medium or as a hybrid medium related to but distinct from other literary media). For a discussion of this, see (Meskin 2009).
4   Though perhaps in terms of production, a more apt comparison for comics would be serial works for television. For the most famous example of the origins, defense, and employ of cinematic auteur theory, see (Sarris 1996).
5   For a discussion of auteur theory in comics, see (Ault 2004).
6   With respect to authorship concerns, the medium of cinema is certainly no better, and likely much worse, off than that of comics.
7   My view of authorship is fully fleshed out and explained in depth in (Mag Uidhir 2011).
8   I use the term "substantively" to mean at least non-trivially and non-accidentally and at most exhaustively or essentially.
9   For example, consider the painting *United States: Most Wanted*. There are seemingly only two candidates for authorship of the painting, Vitaly Komar and Alex Melamid. Both Komar and Melamid claim, however, that neither authors the painting; instead, they claim that there is but one author of *Most Wanted*, which is (Komar and Melamid), the artist team made up of Vitaly Komar and Alex Melamid – the team, not its members taken alone, is the source of the substantively figuring intentions. I want to allow at least in principle for such claims to be true.

10 For an essentialist definition of comics, see (Hayman and Pratt 2005). For a response to essentialist definitions of comics, see (Meskin 2007).

11 For example, theories involving some open-ended and ever-expanding set of relevant features $\{f_1, f_2, ...\}$ such that for a work to be a comic just is for that work to have some combination of those features with no particular combination itself being necessary.

12 For example, suppose that a comic must be a *print*. While the printer may be directly responsible for a comic being a print (*simpliciter*), this doesn't entail that the printer is thereby directly responsible for the comic being the particular print that it is. While the former may warrant production credit, only the latter warrants ascription of authorship. In what follows, I discuss such distinctions in terms of production being either commissioned or appropriated. For a detailed discussion of this, see (Mag Uidhir 2011).

13 It should also appeal both to those in favor of actual intentionalism and to those opposed to it (e.g., perhaps intentions need only be rationally reconstructed instead of psychologically real, or perhaps authors are constructs rather than actual agents).

14 For examples, see (Levinson 1990; Rohrbaugh 2005).

15 This question and how I form answers to it ought to be regarded in an ontologically neutral way; the question could easily be reformulated to reflect type-token relations (to be the same comic is to token the same type) or plate-process-print relations (to be the same comic is to be printed from the same template).

16 I do think investigating comic authorship may well turn out to be broadly informative at least with respect to authorship for works of certain other sorts (namely film). Comics (i) intuitively have authors (i.e., *comic* is an author-relevant work-description), (ii) are often collectively produced but in a manner far less complex than that of film, and (iii) involve elements of other work-descriptions (visual and literary components). Furthermore, comic *qua* work-description is not obviously or traditionally considered an artform, and so perhaps less likely than other work-descriptions to be muddled by art-theoretic issues. For related issues in film, see (Gaut 1997; Livingston 1997; Sellors 2007; Meskin 2008).

17 McCloud's I think is the most instructive in virtue of being one of the earliest and still best- known definitions of comics as well as developed from an "insider's" point of view – McCloud is the author of the comic *Zot!*

18 For an in-depth analysis of failure in art, see (Mag Uidhir 2010).

19 Furthermore, consider that for many mass-market comics, the cover art is done by yet another party (one not involved with the comic's "interior"), and as such we can also legitimately ask whether the cover artist ought to count as an author.

20 DC Comics is also notorious for this kind of control over its artists, while Marvel is known for being much freer (e.g., Marvel may tell the artist that on page 1, Wolverine walks into a room and spots the Hulk, while DC may tell the artist "Page 1, Panel 1: close up of Wolverine in the doorway, he is chomping a stubby cigar, looking twenty degrees to the left ...").

21 Note that I do not make claims about what it is to be a comic, what it is to be the author of a comic, or the particular merits or demerits of McCloud's

definition – for that see (Meskin 2007); (Hayman and Pratt 2005). My account of authorship merely shows what it is to be an author of a *McCloudian* comic, that is, how to determine comic authorship given a McCloudian definition of comics.

22 Suppose an analogous account of poetry. I take it that on such an account being a poem isn't simply (i) being a verse composition in a natural language and (ii) being intended to fulfill some narrative or aesthetic purpose; rather, I take that being a poem requires being a verse composition in service to some narrative or aesthetic purpose.

23 In the *Garfield* comic, Garfield's owner Jon converses and regularly interacts in humorous ways with the titular cat. In *Garfield Minus Garfield*, there is no Garfield, only the character Jon. *Garfield* portrays Jon as a hapless but well-meaning character who attempts to control the antics of his mischievous cat, Garfield. In *Garfield Minus Garfield*, however, Jon is clearly both emotionally and mentally disturbed, terribly lonely and depressed, and perhaps even psychotic (e.g., he always appears to talk to himself, is prone to outbursts for no apparent reason, or simply stares at the wall). *Garfield* is typically light-hearted and humorous; *Garfield Minus Garfield* is typically poignantly sad and darkly humorous. The strip *Arbuckle* does much the same; it leaves Garfield in the strip but removes Garfield's thought bubbles so as to represent Jon's experience of non-verbally "communicating" with his cat. Also *Garfield Randomizer* randomly selects and juxtaposes three panels from Garfield strips so as to create a new three-paneled comic.

24 While Davis still writes and develops stories for *Garfield*, his assistants carry out most of the comic's physical production (drawing according to Davis's famous style).

25 Often only the color studio (e.g., Hi-Fi) rather than an actual person will be listed as the colorist. While one could make the case that studios count as a collective agents and as such are *prima facie* candidates for comic authors (at least inasmuch as actual, single-agented colorists).

26 Davis *strictly* following my meticulously detailed instructions doesn't entail that Davis is *merely* following my meticulously detailed instructions.

27 Assume that $[F$ iff f_1 and $f_2]$ and that both f_1 and f_2 can be satisfied independently from the other, and let A's production contribution (AP) satisfy f_1 and B's production contribution (BP) satisfy f_2. From this it follows that w as an F is a case of non-collaborative collective-authorship just in case: (i) only AP and BP are constitutive of w as an F (*Collective Production*), (ii) only A's intentions substantively figure in AP being constitutive of w as an F, (iii) only B's intentions substantively figure in BP being constitutive of w as an F, (iv) it is not the case that $[AP$ if or only if $BP]$, and (v) A is an author of w as an F and B is an author of w as an F (*Non-Collaborative Collective Authorship*).

28 Should *comic* be a hybrid work-description (Meskin 2009) comic authorship must also be hybrid.

References

Ault, D. "Preludium: Crumb, Barks, and Noomin: Re-considering the Aesthetics of Underground Comics." *ImageTexT: Interdisciplinary Comics Studies* 29, July 2010. Available online at http://www.english.ufl.edu/imagetext/archives/v1_2/intro.shtml (accessed August 6, 2011).

Gaut, B. "Film Authorship and Collaboration." in R. Allen and M. Smith (eds), *Film Theory and Philosophy*, Oxford: Oxford University Press, 1997: 149–172.

Hyman, G. and Pratt, H. "What Are Comics?" in D. Goldblatt and L. Brown (eds), *A Reader in the Philosophy of the Arts*, Upper Saddle River, NJ: Pearson Education, Inc., 2005: 419–424.

Irving, C. "Talking Comics with Scott McCloud." *NYC Graphic*. March 1, 2010. Available online at http://www.nycgraphicnovelists.com/2010/03/talking-comics-with-scott-mccloud.html (accessed August 6, 2011).

Levinson, J. *Music, Art, and Metaphysics*. Ithaca, NY: Cornell University Press, 1990.

Livingston, P. "Cinematic Authorship." in R. Allen and M. Smith (eds), *Film Theory and Philosophy*, Oxford: Oxford University Press, 1997: 132–148.

Mag Uidhir, C. "Failed-Art and Failed Art-theory." *Australasian Journal of Philosophy* 88(3), 2010: 381–400.

Mag Uidhir, C. "Minimal Authorship (of Sorts)." *Philosophical Studies*, 154(3), 2011: 373–387.

McCloud, S. *Understanding Comics*, Northampton, MA: Kitchen Sink Press Inc., 1993.

Meskin, A. "Defining Comics?." *Journal of Aesthetics and Art Criticism*, 65, 2007: 369–379.

Meskin, A. "Authorship." in P. Livingston and C. Plantinga (eds), *Routledge Companion to Philosophy and Film*, London: Routledge, 2008: 12–28.

Meskin, A. "Comics as Literature?" *British Journal of Aesthetics* 49(3), 2009: 219–239.

Rohrbaugh, G. "I Could Have Done That." *British Journal of Aesthetics*, 45(3), 2005: 209–228.

Sarris, A. *The American Cinema: Directors and Directions 1929–1968*, New York: De Capo Press, 1996.

Sellors, C.P. "Collective Authorship in Film." *Journal of Aesthetics and Art Criticism*, 65, 2007: 263–271.

Comics and Genre

Catharine Abell

Introduction

As comics develop as a medium and as an art form, more and more comics genres emerge. My aim in this chapter is to explain what comics genres are and what it is for a comic to belong to a particular genre. An adequate account of comics genres should illuminate the nature of genres more generally. Nevertheless, it will be fruitful to focus on the particular case of comics genres. Both film and literary practice and the philosophy and criticism of film and literature have advanced to a point at which it is reasonably clear what the main genres of movies and literary works are, and what features distinguish them. By contrast, comics are a relatively young art form, and the philosophy and criticism of comics are in their infancy. Past discussion of comics has even confused the art form of comics with particularly popular and influential genres, with the result that comics have been dismissed as artistically unimportant, because they have been equated with superhero escapism for adolescents (McCloud 1993).

Comics fall into a broad array of categories, including funny animal comics, romance comics, superhero comics, Tijuana bibles, alternative comics, autobiographical comics, mini-comics, graphic novels, comix, adult comics and fumetti (also known as photo-comics). While some of these categories seem clearly to be genres, it is not obvious that all are. Funny animal comics, romance comics, and superhero comics are comics genres, but it is not obvious whether or not graphic novels or fumetti comprise genres. Comics categories therefore provide a good test case for an account of genre.

The Art of Comics: A Philosophical Approach, First Edition.
Edited by Aaron Meskin and Roy T. Cook.
© 2012 Blackwell Publishing Ltd. Published 2012 by Blackwell Publishing Ltd.

An adequate account of genre should provide a plausible way of distinguishing between comics categories that are genres and those that are not, and should provide principled reasons for this distinction. In doing so, it will help inform our understanding of comics, by elucidating the significance of the various categories of comics.

I begin, in the next section, by outlining some desiderata for an adequate account of genre. In the following section, I assess existing accounts of genre, and argue that none can adequately distinguish those comics categories that are genres from those that are not. In the final section, I provide an alternative account of genre and of the conditions for genre membership. I then use this account to distinguish those categories of comics that are genres from those that are not, by identifying features in virtue of which they either fall within the scope of the account, or fail to do so.

Desiderata for an Account of Genre

An adequate philosophical account of genre should provide solutions to the various philosophical problems that genres pose. To clarify what this requires, I will now outline some of these problems.

First, it is not clear what makes a certain feature of a work relevant to determining its genre. There is no single type of feature that determines the genre to which a work belongs. Rather, a variety of different types of features of comics may be relevant to determining their genre. Their genre may be determined, not just by their content – their setting, characters, themes and subjects – but also by their structure, and the effects they have on an audience. Whether or not a comic is a science-fiction comic depends, amongst other things, on its setting; whether or not it is a romance comic depends both on its subject and on its structure (a comic about a boy's love for a girl, in which the boy has already got the girl, and does not lose her, may not qualify as a romance comic despite its subject); and whether or not it is a horror comic is determined partly by its capacity to induce fear in an audience. If fumetti comprise a comics genre, a comic's genre membership may also depend on its format (if a comic does not include photographs, it is unlikely to be a fumetti). Some types of features seem to be relevant to determining a work's genre in some cases, but not in others. While a comic's emotional effects on an audience are clearly relevant to determining whether or not it is a horror comic, they are not obviously relevant to determining whether or not it is a science-fiction comic. An adequate account of genre should explain both which features of a work are potentially relevant to determining its genre membership, and under what conditions they do so.

A second problem concerns, not what features determine a work's genre membership, but the manner in which they do so. It does not seem possible to specify individually necessary and jointly sufficient conditions for membership of a specific genre. Rather, certain features are *standard* for works in a specific genre, such that a work's possessing one of those features counts towards its belonging to the genre at issue, and other features are *contra-standard* for works in a specific genre, such that a work's possessing one of those features counts against its belonging to the genre at issue (see Walton 1970). A work may belong to some genre despite its lacking features standard for that genre (for example, a comic about a boy's love for a girl that fails to meet the boy meets girl, boy gets girl, boy loses girl structural format may nonetheless qualify as a romance). It may also belong to some genre despite possessing features contra-standard for that genre (for example, a comic may qualify as a horror comic despite not being capable of frightening an audience). A work's possessing a feature standard for some genre is a *pro tanto* reason for classifying it as belonging to that genre, and its possessing a feature contra-standard for that genre is a *pro tanto* reason for not classifying it as belonging to that genre. An adequate account of genre should provide an account of the manner in which those of a work's features that are relevant to determining its genre help to determine the genre to which a work belongs, and this account should accommodate the fact that such features provide only *pro tanto* reasons for genre classifications.

An adequate explanation of what determines genre membership and how it does so should also accommodate the fact that a single work may belong to more than one genre. For example, one can imagine a comic that is a funny animal romance comic, belonging both to the genre of funny animal comics and to that of romance comics. Such an explanation should also accommodate the fact that some genres incorporate works in a variety of different media. For example, superhero comics and romance comics comprise sub-genres of the broader superhero and romance genres, which include not only comics, but also works in other narrative media, such as novels and films.

Furthermore, as I suggested in the introduction, an adequate account of genre needs to distinguish genre categories from the various other categories into which works can be classified. These other categories include categories based solely on history of production, such as Canadian comics produced between 1950 and 1965, or comics produced by Charles Schulz, as well as arbitrarily specified categories, such as comics produced using more than five colors of ink. More importantly, an adequate account of genre should distinguish genre categories from style categories. The notion of genre is closely related to that of style: so closely related that it is often unclear whether a category is a genre or a style category. For example, is realism a genre or a style? What about pop art? This lack of clarity is due not just to philosophical uncertainty about the nature of genre, but also about the nature of style. In the absence of an adequate philosophical account of style, one should not expect an account of genre to provide a definitive explanation of the distinction between a genre and a style. Nevertheless, it is reasonable to expect an account of genre to identify some features of genres that, *prima facie*, distinguish them from styles, and also to identify features that, *prima facie*, genres share with styles, and that account for the close relationship between genres and styles.

A final philosophical problem posed by genres – and one of the most interesting – concerns the relationship between a work's genre and its content. A work's genre membership appears to affect its content. We can see this by focusing on *narrative content*: the content that works of fiction have, considered as such. The narrative content of a work of fiction incorporates everything that is true *according to the story that the work recounts*. A work's narrative content generally incorporates a lot more than the work explicitly represents. For example, it is part of the narrative content of the *Peanuts* comics that Charlie Brown is insecure, although they do not explicitly represent him as insecure. A work's narrative content must therefore have additional determinants, besides its explicit representational content. It seems pretty clear that a work's genre is one such determinant. For example, it would not be true according to a funny animal comic that explicitly represented an animal as talking that anything unusual had taken place. By contrast, it would be true according to a war comic that explicitly represented an animal as talking that something extremely unusual had taken place. In war comics it is unusual for animals to talk, but in funny animal comics it is not.

An adequate account of genre should help us to understand the relation between a work's genre and its narrative content. The nature of this relation depends, not just on the nature of genre, but also on that of narrative content. One influential thought is that a work's narrative content incorporates what would be the case, were things as the work explicitly represents them as being (Lewis 1978).

On this understanding, what makes it part of the *Peanuts* comics that Charlie Brown is insecure is the fact that any child who did and said the things that *Peanuts* explicitly represents Charlie Brown as doing and saying would be insecure. However, such considerations will not always yield a satisfactory explanation of a work's narrative content. Consider, for example, a superhero comic that represents a masked and caped man but does not explicitly represent him as employing any special powers or abilities.[1] It seems plausible that it is nonetheless part of the comic's narrative content that the man has special powers or abilities, but this cannot be because anyone who was attired as that man is represented as being attired would have special powers or abilities. This seems patently false. David Lewis considers the analogous case of a story that represents a dragon, Scrulch, a princess and a knight, but does not explicitly represent Scrulch either as breathing fire or as not breathing fire. It nevertheless seems plausible that it is part of the story's narrative content that Scrulch breathes fire. However, this cannot be because any creature with the features Scrulch is explicitly represented as possessing would breathe fire. He argues that it is part of the story's narrative content that the dragon breathes fire "because dragons in that sort of story do breathe fire" (Lewis 1978: 45). He writes, "If Scrulch does breathe fire in my story, it is by inter-fictional carry-over from what is true of dragons in other stories" (45). Lewis can thus be interpreted as claiming that it is in virtue of the story's genre membership that the dragon breathes fire in the story he considers.

Similarly, one might think that it is part of the narrative content of the superhero comic that the masked and caped man possesses special powers or abilities because in superhero comics masked and caped men possess such powers or abilities. On Lewis's view, therefore, a work's genre can affect its narrative content by making it include things in addition to those that would be the case were things really as the work explicitly represents them as being. Let us call such effects *positive* effects of genre on narrative content.

Andrea Bonomi and Sandro Zucchi claim that a work's genre membership can also have *negative* effects on its narrative content. That is, it can affect its narrative content by preventing it from incorporating certain of those things that would be the case were things as it explicitly represents them as being. They consider *Othello*, in which Shakespeare represents the character Othello as uttering lines that would ordinarily indicate eloquence of an order of which only a great poet is capable. Nonetheless, as Kendall Walton points out, Othello is supposed to be a rough military man whose first language is not English. It is not part of the narrative content of the play that Othello is especially eloquent (Walton 1990: 175). Bonomi and Zucchi claim that Othello is not to be credited with astonishing eloquence since *Othello* belongs to the genre of Elizabethan plays and "by the conventions of Elizabethan plays a man who expresses himself like Othello need not be a first rank poet" (Bonomi and Zucchi 2003: 114).[2] If this explanation is correct, it is not true in funny animal cartoons that talking animals are unusual because, although it would be extremely unusual were an animal to talk, it is a convention of the funny animal genre that talking animals are not unusual.

Neither Lewis nor Bonomi and Zucchi offer any explanation of how genres affect narrative content in the ways they describe. An adequate account of genre should explain why genre membership can have these effects. With this, and the other desiderata just outlined in mind, let us now examine how existing philosophical accounts of genre fare in relation to them.

Existing Accounts of Genre

There is little discussion of the nature of genre in the philosophical literature. Two discussions, by Gregory Currie and by Brian Laetz and Dominic Lopes, are the only recent exceptions. To begin with, let us consider the account of movie genres proposed by Laetz and Lopes. On their view:

> Category K is a movie genre if and only if K [is a type of movie which] has multiple members, which are made by more than one artist (for any given artist role), from any background, and K has features in virtue of which K figures into the appreciations or interpretations of K's audience. (2008: 156)[3]

This account suffers from several problems. First, it is unable to distinguish genre categories from the various other types of categories into which works can be classified. The stipulation that, for a type of movie to comprise a genre, it must be made by more than one artist, from any background is supposed to distinguish genre categories from categories based solely on works' histories of production. Laetz and Lopes claim that genres are distinct from traditions, such that a work's genre does not depend on social facts about its maker (Laetz and Lopes 2008: 156). They may also have insisted on the irrelevancy of history of production to genre membership because they want to distinguish genres from styles. Because the work of an individual artist may be distinguished from the work of others by its distinctive style, as with the case of Seaurat's pointillism, for example, it is not always the case that more than one artist can produce works in any given style.

However, a work's genre does seem sometimes to depend on its history of production. Like the genres of Dutch realist painting, Texas country music, and Asian extreme, the comics genre Manga seems to be partly geographic in nature.[4] Arguably, a comic must have been produced in Japan in order to belong to the Manga genre, just as a painting must have been produced in the Netherlands in order to belong to the genre of Dutch realist painting, and a musical work must have been produced in Texas to be an instance of the genre of Texas country music. Thus, one might think that Amerimanga or, more generally, original English-language manga (like Chinese manhua and Korean manhwa) are distinct genres from Manga proper. Certainly, someone who produces something that looks like an instance of Manga, but is unaware of and unconnected to the Manga tradition has not made an instance of Manga. Bonomi and Zucchi clearly think that Elizabethan plays comprise a genre, but Elizabethan plays can only be produced by playwrights living in England in the Elizabethan era. Laetz's and Lopes's overt denial that history of production has any role to play in determining genre membership seems too strong.

Genres are therefore not distinguished from styles by the irrelevance of works' histories of production to genre membership. Furthermore, the requirement that a genre have features that figure in appreciation or interpretation also fails to distinguish genre categories from styles. Laetz's and Lopes's comments suggest that, by the requirement that genres have features that enter into appreciations or evaluations they intend to impose a fairly narrow condition. In particular, they seem to mean that genres must have features that generate interpretative and evaluative *expectations* (Laetz and Lopes 2008: 156). The fact that a comic belongs to the superhero genre will generate in someone who likes that genre the expectation that they will enjoy the comic at issue. Similarly, the fact that a comic belongs to the funny animal genre will generate the expectation that it will represent talking animals. However, like genres, styles have features which generate interpretative and evaluative expectations. The fact that a comic is in Dan Clowes's distinctive style may generate such expectations in an audience, but his style is not a genre. The fact that their account fails to distinguish genres from the various other categories into which works may fall prevents Laetz and Lopes from resolving the issue of whether or not fumetti and graphic novels are genres.

Their account is also unable to explain how genre membership affects narrative content. Laetz and Lopes are aware of the role of genre in determining narrative content, and propose to accommodate it by the following *genre principle*:

A story belonging to genre K represents that q [i.e. incorporates q in its narrative content] if it explicitly represents that $p_1 \ldots p_n$ and it is a feature of K that it would be the case that q, were it the case that $p_1 \ldots p_n$ (2008: 153)[5]

However, this principle seems inadequate as a description of how genre affects narrative content. While it accommodates the positive effects that Lewis notes, it does not accommodate the negative effects noted by Bonomi and Zucchi. Moreover, it raises the question of which features of a genre determine that, if it were the case that $p_1 \ldots p_n$, it would be the case that q. What sorts of things are genres that they have these features? Perhaps Laetz and Lopes would claim that genres have these features because of the interpretative expectations to which they give rise. To see how such an explanation might proceed, let us now turn to Currie's account, which purports to explain the role that expectations play in producing the effects that genre has on narrative content.

Currie claims that genres are simply sets of features or properties that works can have (2004: 47). He holds that any set of features a work can have constitutes a genre. Consequently, on his view, there is an infinite number of genres. However, on his account, genre membership is not simply a matter of possessing the features constitutive of a given genre. If this were the case, every work would belong to some genre because every work has some set of features. Rather, Currie argues, a work belongs to a genre to the extent that it possesses the relevant features *and* this creates an expectation among the members of the community in which it was produced that it will possess the others (2004: 49). Thus, while there is an indefinite number of genres, the number of genres to which works actually belong is much more limited, because not every genre is such that a work's possessing some of its constitutive features will create the expectation among community members that it will possess the others. Currie claims that these expectations are created by prior experience of certain features being co-instantiated, and perhaps also by such other factors as innate expectations about narrative form (2004: 54).

On Currie's account, a work's causal and temporal relations to other works can help to determine its genre (2004: 43). This is so because these causal and temporal relations help to create the expectations that determine genre membership. It is because a work is causally and/or temporally related to other works with which it shares some features that we expect it to share further features with them. Unlike Laetz's and Lopes's account, therefore, Currie's can accommodate genres membership of which depends partly on a work's history of production.

Nevertheless, there are problems with Currie's account. First, it fails to distinguish genre categories from other types of categories. Like Laetz's and Lopes's account, it fails to distinguish genres from styles. Like genres, styles are associated with sets of features works can have and, like genres, the fact that a work possesses some of the features constitutive of a style leads interpreters to expect that it will possess the others. For example, when we watch a film with features of Robert Altman's distinctive style, such as that of representing a series of apparently unrelated episodes, we expect that it will exhibit other features of his style, such as revealing unexpected relations between those episodes.

It also fails to distinguish genres from media, such as photography or watercolor. Different media are associated with different sets of features. Moreover, the fact that a work possesses some of the features associated with a given medium leads interpreters to expect that it will possess the others. For example, the fact that a work possesses some of the features of photography, such as a high degree of realism and a glossy surface will lead interpreters to expect that it will possess the other features we associate with photographs, such as representing actual objects and states of affairs. Currie's account therefore cannot help to solve the problem of which comics categories are genres and which are not. Graphic novels and fumetti are conceivably media rather than genres. It is the task of an adequate account of genre to determine whether or not this is the case. However, because Currie's account fails to distinguish genres from media, it cannot illuminate the nature of these comics categories.

Second, Currie's account does not provide a satisfactory explanation of the effects of genre membership on narrative content. He claims that these effects are a consequence of the expectations that help to determine a work's genre membership. These expectations, he claims, affect narrative content by enabling *genre-based implicatures* (2004: 45–46).

Implicatures are pragmatically – as opposed to semantically – determined aspects of content. The paradigmatic form of implicature is a *conversational implicature*. According to Grice's influential theory, what a speaker conversationally implicates by producing an utterance is determined by her intentions (Grice 1975). Conversational implicatures arise when what speakers intend to communicate by an utterance differs from the semantic content of that utterance. Although interpreters do not generally have any access to a speaker's intentions independently of the utterances she produces, Grice argues that they are nonetheless able to identify her intentions because, in communicating with interpreters, speakers conform to the *cooperative principle*: "Make your conversational contribution such as is required, at the stage at which it occurs, by the accepted purpose or direction of the talk exchange in which you are engaged" (Grice: 45–46). When the semantic content of a speaker's utterance does not conform to the cooperative principle, interpreters work out what the speaker intended to communicate by ascribing an alternative content to the utterance that does conform to the principle.

Interpreters' expectations play an important role in their ability to identify conversational implicatures, because those expectations determine what they take to be required in order for an utterance to conform to the cooperative principle. However, Currie denies that genre-based implicatures are conversational implicatures, on the basis that they do not exploit apparent violations of the cooperative principle (Currie 2004: 46). On his account, therefore, expectations cannot play the same role in enabling genre-based implicatures as they do in enabling interpreters to identify conversational implicatures.

Conventional implicatures depend, not on speakers' intentions, but on conventions associating certain types of utterances with certain implicatures. For example, utterances of "but" between coordinate clauses conventionally implicate a contrast between the relevant clauses. When I say "Tom is rich but unattractive," I cannot help but indicate a contrast between being rich and being unattractive, whether or not I intend to indicate such a contrast. Conventional implicatures cannot be canceled. By contrast, Currie argues, genre-based implicatures are cancellable and thus cannot be Gricean conventional implicatures (Currie 2004: 46).

Currie is right to claim that the effects of genre on narrative content are cancellable. For example, when we read a comic strip in the funny animal genre, we will assume that there is nothing abnormal about an animal talking in the context of the cartoon. However, this expectation can be undermined – for example, because the comic explicitly represents a human character as reacting with incredulity to a talking animal. Kaz undermines this very expectation to humorous effect in his cartoon *Lumberger* (Brunetti 2006: 18). If the expectation is canceled in such a way, we *will* take it to be part of the narrative content of that work that the talking animal it represents has unusual capacities.

However, Currie's account of genre does not explain how genre affects narrative content in ways that are cancelable. First, because he characterizes genre-based implicatures predominantly negatively (they are neither conventional implicatures nor conversational implicatures), it remains unclear exactly what genre-based implicatures are. Second, his account fails to explain exactly how audience expectations generate genre-based implicatures and what distinguishes those expectations that do so from those that do not. Not all the expectations that accompany genre membership affect our ascriptions of narrative content. For example, when we read romance comics, we expect the romances they represent to end happily. This expectation may be met, or may be explicitly violated. Alternatively, it may be neither met nor violated, as when a comic ends before it is evident whether or not the romance it represents will end happily. In the latter case, although our expectation has not been violated or canceled, we do not take it to be part of the comic's narrative content that the romance ends happily. Rather, we take it to be unclear whether or not it does so. Similarly, our expectation, on encountering a funny animal cartoon, that it will contain animals that can talk need not be either met or undermined. For example, a funny animal cartoon may represent a group of animals going silently about their lives, without making it clear whether they are simply refraining from speaking, or whether they are not speaking because they cannot do so. In this case, although our expectation is not undermined, it does not lead us to ascribe the ability to talk to the animals it represents. Expectations such as these do not generate genre-based implicatures.

Despite these problems, I think there's something right about Currie's claim that genre membership affects narrative content by enabling implicatures. In the next section, I propose an account of genre that explains the sense in which the effects of genre on narrative content are implicatures, and explains the role that interpreters' expectations play in enabling them to identify these implicatures.

An Account of Genre

I propose that genres are sets of conventions that have developed as means of addressing particular interpretative and/or evaluative problems, and have a history of co-instantiation within a community, such that a work's belonging to some genre generates interpretative and evaluative expectations among the members of that community. To belong to some genre, a work must be produced in a community in which its constitutive conventions have a history of co-instantiation and must be produced in accordance with some subset of those conventions that is sufficient to distinguish the set of conventions at issue from all other sets of conventions that have developed as means of addressing interpretative and/or evaluative concerns and have a history of co-instantiation within the community in which the work was produced. A work is produced in accordance with a convention if and only if it both has features of the type picked out by the convention at issue and its maker gave the work those features so that the convention would apply to it.

On this account, a work's history of production is relevant to determining its genre membership. One cannot produce a work in a given genre unless one belongs to a community in which its constitutive conventions have a history of co-instantiation. Nevertheless, the notion of a community at issue is not narrowly geographic. A community is a group of people who interact through the production, interpretation, and evaluation of works. On this account, therefore, manga comics are not necessarily Japanese, but one must be familiar with comics conventions that originated in Japan in order to produce a manga comic. Someone who produced a comic perceptually indistinguishable from a manga comic in total ignorance of those conventions would not thereby produce a manga comic. Genres that are partly geographically identified, such as Dutch realist painting, arise when the community in which their constitutive conventions have a history of co-instantiation happens to be relatively geographically isolated.

New interpretative and/or evaluative concerns, not addressed by the conventions of existing genres, may lead to the emergence of new genres, comprising new conventions that have arisen in response to those concerns. Alternatively, they may lead to the emergence of hybrid genres, which are created when the conventions of different existing genres are combined to address new combinations of interpretative and/or evaluative concerns. Finally, new concerns may lead to the emergence of subgenres, which are created when a set of conventions distinctive of an existing genre is supplemented with new conventions, which modify the existing genre to enable it to meet those concerns. Artists can help to create new genres, hybrid genres or subgenres that do not have a history within a given community by producing works that solve new interpretative and/or evaluative problems or address old problems in novel ways. If the works they create lead others to adopt those solutions, such that new sets of conventions emerge and develop a history of co-instantiation within a community, those works may be responsible for initiating new genres. Nevertheless, the works themselves do not belong to the genres they may help to create, because the conventions constitutive of those genres, hybrid genres or subgenres do not exist at the time of their creation.

This account explains why a variety of different types of features is relevant to determining a work's genre. Different types of conventions may develop as means of addressing interpretative and evaluative concerns, including conventions of content, structure, format, narrative content and effects, since a work's content, structure, format, narrative content and effects are all of potential interpretative and/or evaluative significance. Moreover, it explains why these features are not generally individually necessary for genre membership, but instead provide *pro tanto* reasons for classifying a work as belonging to a certain genre. To belong to some genre, a work need only be produced in accordance with a distinctive subset of the conventions of that genre. It is possible that a specific member of the set of conventions comprising a certain genre will be essential to distinguishing that genre from all other genres with a history of co-instantiation in the community in which it was produced, and thus that there is some feature, or set of features possession of which is necessary for membership of some genres. Nevertheless, this will not generally be the case. Often, there will be no single convention in accordance with which a work must have been produced in order to belong to a given genre. Moreover, most of the constitutive conventions comprising any given genre will not be individually necessary to genre membership. Consequently, the features that determine genre membership are generally only *pro tanto* determinants of genre membership.

A work may have features with conventional significance according to a set of conventions that are jointly distinctive of one genre, and also have features with conventional significance according to a set of conventions that are jointly distinctive of another genre. This account of genre membership is therefore consistent with a work belonging to more than one genre. It is also consistent with the existence of genres that incorporate works in a variety of different media, such as the fantasy genre, which incorporates not just fantasy comics, but also fantasy novels and films. The fantasy genre incorporates works in a variety of different media because works in different media may each be produced in accordance with a distinctive subset of its constitutive conventions.

The fact that genres are sets of *conventions* distinguishes them from categories based solely on works' histories of production, such as the category of comics produced by Charles Schulz. It also distinguishes genres from styles. Genre categories are distinct from style categories because style categories are not comprised of conventions. As I noted earlier, a style can be unique to the work of an individual artist. However, it is a necessary condition for something's being conventional that it be widely adopted among the members of a community (Lewis 1969). Nevertheless, style categories are like genre categories in being responses to evaluative and/or interpretative concerns. My account of genre thus explains how genres differ from styles, and also why the notions of genre and of style are nonetheless closely related.

Genres are distinct from media such as watercolor and photography because, although media are often developed as means of addressing interpretative and/or evaluative concerns, a medium consists in a set of tools and techniques, rather than of conventions. Although certain of the techniques constitutive of a medium may become conventionalized, such conventions are not constitutive of media themselves. For this reason, a work's being a watercolor or a photograph does not generate interpretative and/or evaluative expectations among the members of the community in which it was produced. People do not generally like photographs or watercolors in general, or have general expectations about the sorts of things they will represent. The account's appeal to conventions and to interpretative and evaluative expectations therefore distinguishes genres from media.

We are now in a position to understand why it is so difficult to decide whether graphic novels and fumetti comprise genres or media. On the one hand, the category of graphic novels has a claim to be considered a medium, since graphic novels may be used to address a very wide range of interpretative and/or evaluative problems and consequently the fact that a work is a graphic novel need not generate interpretative and/or evaluative expectations in an audience. On the other hand, graphic novels also have some claim to being considered a genre. As a matter of historical fact, graphic novels have been used to address a fairly restricted range of interpretative and evaluative problems, such that the fact that a comic is a graphic novel may in fact generate interpretative and/or evaluative expectations in an audience. Nevertheless, the interpretative and/or evaluative expectations that a comic's being a graphic novel generates are an accident of the way in which graphic novels have evolved, and are not essential to the category. Consequently, graphic novels comprise a medium, rather than a genre. Likewise, the comics category of fumetti identifies a medium, not a genre. Although fumetti happen to have been used to address a limited range of interpretative and evaluative concerns, such that fumetti are associated with a set of conventions that generate interpretative and evaluative expectations, it is not essential to a comic's being a fumetti that it instantiate a distinctive subset of those conventions.

Genre membership can affect narrative content because the conventions constitutive of a genre may include *generalized conversational implicatures* (Grice 1975: 56). Such implicatures are the result of conventions associating specific features of sentences (or of works, in the present case) with specific kinds of conversational implicatures. Consequently, unlike ordinary conversational implicatures, they depend on conventions rather than on makers' intentions, and hence are carried by *sentences* (works), rather than by *speakers* (work makers) (Davis 2008). Nevertheless, unlike conventional implicatures, they are cancelable. For example, "some frogs are green" carries the generalized conversational implicature that not all frogs are green.

However, it is intelligible to say "some frogs are green, indeed all are" in which case the sentence one utters does not implicate that not all frogs are green. If one produces a work that carries a generalized conversational implicature, one's work will have that implicature, so long as it is not canceled, irrespective of whether or not one intends the implicature in question. My utterance of "some frogs are green" carries the generalized conversational implicature that not all frogs are green, even if I do not mean by my utterance that not all frogs are green.

Currie is wrong to claim that genre implicatures cannot be conversational implicatures because they do not depend on our perceiving an apparent violation of the cooperative principle (Currie 2004: 46). First, Grice is clear that not all conversational implicatures need involve the violation of maxims (Grice 1975: 51). More importantly, however, because generalized conversational implicatures are determined by conventions rather than by intentions, our ability to identify what generalized conversational implicatures a work carries depends on knowledge of conventions, rather than on an appeal to the cooperative principle.

Both the positive and negative effects of genre membership on narrative content can be construed as generalized conversational implicatures. It may be part of the narrative content of a superhero comic that represents a masked and caped character but does not explicitly represent her as employing special powers or abilities that she possesses extraordinary powers or abilities because the constitutive conventions of superhero comics include the generalized conversational implicature that masked and caped characters possess extraordinary powers or abilities. This implicature may be canceled, for example by explicitly representing the character as lacking any such powers or abilities, but unless it is canceled, it will be part of the comic's narrative content that the character has special powers or abilities. Likewise, it may be part of the narrative content of a funny animal comic that represents an animal as talking that there is nothing unusual about the animal's talking because the constitutive conventions of funny animal comics include the generalized conversational implicature that talking animals are not unusual. This implicature may be canceled, as Kaz cancels it in the *Lumberger* strip referred to earlier, but unless it is canceled, it will be part of the comic's narrative content that the animal's talking is not unusual.

A work's genre membership depends on its maker's intentions because, in order for a work to have been produced in accordance with a distinctive subset of a genre's constitutive conventions and thus to belong to that genre, its maker must have deliberately given the work features picked out by a distinctive subset of those conventions so that they would apply to it. By contrast, the effects of a work's genre on its narrative content are independent of its maker's intentions. Given that a work belongs to a certain genre, if it has features that carry generalized conversational implicatures according to the conventions comprising that genre, it will carry those implicatures irrespective of its maker's intentions, unless they are canceled. Makers may sometimes inadvertently produce works with a certain narrative content, by producing works that belong to a genre according to which certain of their features carry generalized conversational implicatures.

We are now in a position to explain the role that interpreters' expectations play both in generating the generalized conversational implicatures by which genre affects narrative content, and in enabling them to identify those implicatures. Interpreters' expectations help to generate these generalized conversational implicatures because conventions associating certain features of works with certain conversational implicatures arise partly as a consequence of interpreters' expectations that works with certain features will carry certain conversational implicatures. To understand the role of interpreters' expectations in enabling them to identify the generalized conversational implicatures a work carries, we need to distinguish between two kinds of expectations that genre membership brings with it. First, interpreters expect a work that employs a distinctive subset of the conventions of some genre to employ the rest of the conventions of that genre. We therefore expect works that have certain features, in virtue of which they belong to certain genres, to have certain further features characteristic of works in that genre. For example, we expect the romance in a romance comic to end happily. However, the expectation that a work which employs conventions distinctive of a genre will possess all the conventions of that genre plays no role in interpreters' ability to identify genre-based implicatures. It is an inductively-based expectation that works' makers may deliberately exploit for purposes such as humor and suspense, but it does not affect the identification of narrative content. Such expectations contrast with the expectation that a work which belongs to some genre and has features to which the generalized conversational implicatures partly constitutive of that genre assign a certain narrative significance will have the narrative significance they assign to it. Interpreters rely on the latter expectation in order to identify a work's narrative content.

Conclusion

An adequate account of the nature of genre and of the criteria for genre membership is essential to understanding the nature of the various categories into which comics can be classified. Because they fail adequately to distinguish genre categories from other ways of categorizing works, including categorizations according to medium or according to style, previous accounts of genre fail to illuminate the nature of comics categories. I have argued that genres are sets of conventions that have developed as means of addressing particular interpretative and/or evaluative concerns, and have a history of co-instantiation within a community, such that a work's belonging to some genre generates interpretative and evaluative expectations among the members of that community. Genres are distinct from styles in consisting of conventions, and are distinct from media both in consisting of conventions and in generating interpretative and evaluative expectations.

This account helps us to understand the interpretative and evaluative significance of the various comics categories. Comics genres, such as manga and funny animal comics are associated with specific interpretative and evaluative expectations. These expectations result from the conventions constitutive of the manga and funny animal genres, which address particular interpretative and evaluative concerns in specific ways. By producing comics according to these conventions, makers can help to ensure that interpreters' expectations are met. New interpretative and/or evaluative concerns, not addressed by the conventions of existing genres, require new solutions, which may in turn lead to the emergence of new genres, comprising new sets of conventions that address those concerns. Existing genres do not themselves incorporate the means of responding to new interpretative or evaluative concerns. By contrast, media such as graphic novels and fumetti consist in tools and techniques that can be applied to a range of different interpretative and evaluative problems. A medium's constitutive tools and techniques impose limitations on which solutions to such problems the resources of the medium can provide. Nevertheless, unlike genres, media incorporate the flexibility to respond to interpretative and evaluative concerns in a variety of different ways. Certain ways of responding to certain such concerns within the confines of a medium may lead to the development of different genres within that medium. As the artistic exploration of the interpretative and evaluative scope of the graphic novel continues, we can expect an array of graphic novel genres to emerge.[6]

Notes

1 Not all superheros have extraordinary powers. Batman, for example, is merely extremely skilled and well-equipped.
2 Gregory Currie proposes something similar (2004: 45, note 5).
3 The text in square brackets is mine.
4 Thanks to Aaron Meskin for the example of Texas country music.
5 The text in square brackets is mine.
6 Thanks to both Aaron Meskin and Roy T. Cook for helpful comments on this chapter.

References

Bonomi, A. and S. Zucchi. "A Pragmatic Framework for Truth in Fiction," *Dialectica*, 57(2), 2003: 103–120.

Brunetti, I. (ed.), *An Anthology of Graphic Fiction, Cartoons and True Stories*, New Haven, CT: Yale University Press, 2006.

Currie, G. *Arts and Minds*, Oxford: Oxford University Press, 2004.

Davis, W. "Implicature," *The Stanford Encyclopedia of Philosophy* (Winter 2008 Edition), Edward N. Zalta (ed.), URL = http://plato.stanford.edu/archives/win2008/entries/implicature/ (accessed October 11, 2011).

Grice, H.P. "Logic and Conversation," *Syntax and Semantics* 3, 1975: 41–58.

Laetz, B. and D. Lopes. "Genre," in Paisley Livingston and Carl Plantinga (eds), *Routledge Companion to Philosophy and Film*, London : Routledge, 2008: 151–161.

Lewis, D. *Convention*, Cambridge, MA: Harvard University Press: 1969.

Lewis, D. "Truth in Fiction" *American Philosophical Quarterly* 15, 1978: 37–46.

McCloud, S. *Understanding Comics: The Invisible Art*, New York: Harper Collins, 1993.

Walton, K. "Categories of Art," *The Philosophical Review* 79, 1970: 334–367.

Walton, K. *Mimesis as Make-Believe*, Cambridge, MA: Harvard University Press, 1990.

Part Two

Comics and Representation

Wordy Pictures: Theorizing the Relationship between Image and Text in Comics

Thomas E. Wartenberg

My aim is this chapter is limited. I present an analysis of the text-image relationship that is characteristic of comics, in order to develop one aspect of the ontological structure of comics. My central claim is that it is characteristic of comics to give equal priority to the text and the pictures. Illustrated books, for example, are different because their texts provide constraints on the illustrations, but not the other way around. But in a comic, neither the text nor the image provides an independent constraint upon the other.

Before moving to a defense of this claim, I need to spend a moment clarifying some issues about the nature of comics. In a remarkable work of what might be called "graphic philosophy," the comic book artist Scott McCloud puts forward the following definition of comics[1]: "juxtaposed pictorial and other images in deliberate sequence, intended to convey information and/or produce an aesthetic response in the viewer." (9). There are a number of features of this proposed definition of comics that call for comment.[2] Perhaps the most evident is the fact that McCloud's definition denies that what I shall call "one-panel comics" such as *Dennis the Menace* (Hank Ketcham) and *The Far Side* (Gary Larson) are comics at all, since, according to the definition, a comic must include a *juxtaposition* of images and so cannot consist of simply a single one.[3] This is highly arbitrary. After all, anyone reading the *comics* page(s) of their favorite daily newspaper is accustomed to the presence of single-panel comics (a.k.a. "cartoons") alongside multiple-panel ones (a.k.a. "strips"). Furthermore, *The Yellow Kid* is generally held to be the first "newspaper comic strip" despite the fact that it is a single-panel comic.[4] This

The Art of Comics: A Philosophical Approach, First Edition.
Edited by Aaron Meskin and Roy T. Cook.
© 2012 Blackwell Publishing Ltd. Published 2012 by Blackwell Publishing Ltd.

suggests that, unless some grounds could be found for excluding one-panel comics, an adequate definition of comics will have to include both single- and multiple-panel comics within a single framework.

But the feature of McCloud's proposed definition to which I want to direct our attention here is that it privileges *image* over *text*. McCloud is quite clear that, in his view, images are an essential element of comics, but text is not. In *Understanding Comics*, McCloud pictures himself giving a lecture and, in response to a question from one of the members of his depicted audience – "What about **words**?" – McCloud's comic *alter ego* responds, "Oh, it doesn't have to contain words to be comics..." (1993: 8). In fact, he goes on to specify that the *images* contained in a comic must be *pictorial* to rule out treating the presence of a written text, which after all is in some sense a visual image of a word, as fulfilling this condition for being a comic.

McCloud is certainly right in claiming that the presence of words or, as I think is more accurate, text is not a necessary feature of a comic. In fact, it makes sense to think of wordless comics as a specific genre of comics. *Biozoic* by Gerry Swanson is but one example of a textless comic, one in which there are no words but merely the juxtaposed pictorial images that McCloud takes to be a necessary feature of comics.[5] *Biozoic* is certainly a comic, albeit a web-based one, and it shows that a comic need not have any text at all. For skeptics, there is a list of textless comics at (http://comics.lib.msu.edu/rhode/wordless.htm) that will convince them that textless comics are an important sub-genre of this artform.[6]

Despite the existence of this sub-genre, as any reader of the comics page of a daily newspaper knows, comics *generally* are characterized by the presence of both images and text. So in what follows I propose to examine this widespread feature of many comics, for it presents us with an interesting ontological question. How are we to understand the structure of a comic that is marked by the co-presence of images – especially pictorial images – and text, for words and pictures signify in very different ways? Not any assemblage of images and text counts as a comic, so our goal will be to find a way of characterize the unique complex of text and image that constitutes the vast majority of comics.

Illustrated Books: A First Step

Our attempt to understand the distinctive relationship between image and text in comics will be assisted if we first consider two other image/text complexes that are similar to, but different from, that typically found in comics. Although many theorists, including McCloud, reference film as an artform that includes words and images and therefore needs to be distinguished from comics, our investigation will take a different path. Because films generally do not include (written) text but rely on sound as the medium through which words are presented, they are not the artform closest to comics ontologically speaking. We shall instead focus upon other visual artforms that involve both (written) text and (visual) images.

The first type of image/text complex we will consider is that found in illustrated books. Take, for example, Barry Moser's illustrated edition of The Holy Bible: King James Version. This edition of the Bible includes 232 relief engravings made by Moser that are presented alongside the text of the King James version of the Bible. While this edition of the Bible is certainly a work of art, there is a clear asymmetry between the text and the images contained in it. This is because the images are *illustrations* and not independent images or pictures.

But what is it that makes an image an illustration? The most obvious feature of an illustration is that it is *directed*, that is, stands in necessary relation to some other thing that it is the illustration *of*. In most cases, what an illustration is an illustration of is a previously existing story. Take the first illustration in Moser's edition of The Holy Bible. It bears the title "Adam and Eve in the Garden of Eden" (1999: 3). The image contains a naked man and woman in the left upper corner of a bucolic scene of lush vegetation with a stream in the center of the page that ends in a waterfall in the bottom center of the page. This engraving would be an impressive work, even if it stood alone. But it doesn't. It is intended to illustrate a scene from the story of Adam and Even, specifically the one described in Chapter 3 of "Genesis." The story concerns God's creation of the Garden of Eden and contains a number of details about the landscape in which God placed the first two human beings. Here is a portion of the text:

> And the Lord God planted a garden eastward in Eden; and there he put the man whom he had formed. And out of the ground made the Lord God to grow every tree that is pleasant to the sight, and good for food; the tree of life also in the midst of the garden, and the tree of knowledge of good and evil. And a river went out of Eden to water the garden; and from thence it was parted, and became into four heads. (Moser 1999: 2)

This text specifies many features that a picture has to have in order for it to be an illustration of the Garden of Eden. For example, the picture would have to be one of a landscape in which there were many trees and there has to be a river flowing through them. If a picture was placed next to this text, but lacked all of the features specified by the text, it would not be an illustration of the Garden of Eden even if it were a wonderful picture. This is because, for an image to succeed as an illustration, it must be a *faithful* representation of what the text says about the scene the image illustrates. In this case, the illustration must include all the elements of the landscape described in Chapter 3 of "Genesis." So, for example, it is important that there be trees, that these trees be pleasant to look at, that a man be represented as inhabiting this place, and that there is a river flowing through the garden. If the illustration lacked most or all of these features, even if such a difference made it an artistically superior engraving to the actual one, it would no longer be an illustration of the place described by the text, for it would not be faithful to what the text says.[7] And *faithfulness* is one important standard by which illustrations are judged.

What conclusions can we draw about the ontological structure of illustrated books from this example? The primary one is that there is an asymmetry between text and image in illustrated books. As the example of Moser's Bible demonstrates, the text is ontologically primary. This is because the text specifies a story-world and the images are to picture that world for us and, as such, must be faithful to what the text says about it. Even when an illustrated book is a genuine work of art, as is the case, I think, with Moser's illustrated Bible, the images remain subordinate to the text, for they are illustrations of the world described by the text, no matter how deeply moving and beautiful they may be. They can only be illustrations if they are faithful to what that text says about that world.

It is worth noting that nothing prevents the illustrations in illustrated books from becoming independent works of art. Especially when a book and its illustrations are hand printed, the illustrations may be separated from the book in which they are found and exhibited as independent works of art. Such is the case, for example, with Pablo Picasso's illustrations of Aristophanes' *Lysistrata* (1934). Nonetheless, the point still remains that the illustrations are ontologically dependent upon the text that they illustrate, even if we choose to ignore the fact that a picture is an illustration.[8]

The second type of image-text complex we need to distinguish from that present in comics involves images that are less subordinate to the text than those I have just described. Many children's books provide examples of this type of image-text relationship. Works having this structure include Lewis Carroll's *Alice in Wonderland* (1865) and A.A. Milne's *Winnie the Pooh* (1926). Even though the images in such books are illustrations of the story whose text they accompany, and thus are bound by the faithfulness constraint, they have a different status than those in books such as Moser's Bible. The reason for this is that they are much more closely associated with the story they illustrate than the images are in Moser's Bible and similar works, a fact whose significance we need to investigate more fully.

In another context, I called this second type of image-text complex one in which the images are *iconic* (Wartenberg 2007: 40–41). I used that term to indicate that we needed to view such images as more than simply illustrations of the story specified by their text, though they are that as well. I now would prefer to use the term *canonical*, for I believe that better indicates the role that such images play in our imagining of a work's fictional world. So, for example, John Tenniel's illustrations of *Alice in Wonderland* are so closely tied to Alice's story that it is plausible to say that when we refer to the work, *Alice in Wonderland*, we are referring not just to Carroll's text but also to Tenniel's drawings. In support of this contention one could point out that Tenniel's drawings are linked so intimately to Carroll's text that they contain features that determine what readers take to be true of the story-world of the work. That is, they take Alice to be a girl who looks like the girl in Tenniel's illustrations, just as centrally as they take her to have undergone the adventures described in Carroll's text. The fictional world of *Alice in Wonderland*, we might say, is *codetermined* by the text and the illustrations. So even though the images in this case are still illustrations, and thus both are ontologically dependent on their texts and must also adhere to the standard of faithfulness we previously articulated, they have a more fundamental role than the illustrations in illustrated books like Moser's The Holy Bible.[9] They, together with the text, determine the nature and structure of the work's fictional world.[10]

This difference can be clarified by means of the following thought experiment. Imagine an illustration of the central character of an imaginary novel that pictures him with a beard. Say that the novel does not specify whether the character has a beard or not. The difference between a *mere* illustration and an *canonical* one is that, in the former case, I do not think that it would necessarily be true that the character had a beard in the story-world of the book, while it would be in the latter case.

Is it possible to specify why some illustrations of books count as canonical while others do not? One might think that an illustration will count as canonical only if it was present in the original edition of the work. But this turns out not to be the case. Consider, for example, Mark Twain's *The Adventures of Huckleberry Finn* (1884). I think most people believe that this is a purely textual work, indeed, one of the classics of nineteenth-century American literature. What most people do not realize, however, is that the original edition of the book, published by Webster and Company in 1884, included 174 illustrations, such as the one seen here.

ON THE RAFT.

Figure 5.1   Huck and Jim "On the Raft," from Twain, M. *The Adventures of Huckleberry Finn*. New York: Charles L. Webster and Company, 1884.

Thus, the written text is ontologically primary in the case of *Huckleberry Finn,* despite the fact that the first edition contained a large number of drawings illustrating Huck's story.[11] Those images are what I have called *mere* illustrations and are not canonical.

On the other hand, illustrations can be canonical even if they did not appear in the original edition of the book. We can see this by considering the case of *Winnie-the-Pooh* (Milne 1926). E.H. Shepard's illustrations were not the ones with which the Pooh story first appeared. When the first Pooh story was published in *The London Evening News* on December 24, 1925, it was accompanied by illustrations made by J.H. Dowd, and not those of Shepherd. Nonetheless, Shepherd's illustrations have become canonical in that, despite their recent Disneyfication, they are taken to specify how things appear in the story-world of Pooh and his friends. Of course, the first edition of the book, *Winnie-the-Pooh*, did have Shepherd's illustrations, but those illustrations were not the first to accompany a Pooh story and thus attempt to picture its story-world.

In light of these facts, I am not sure it is possible to give a general account of what makes an image a canonical illustration. Even though Arthur Conan Doyle never states in his Sherlock Holmes stories and novels that Holmes wore a deerstalker, once Sydney Paget placed one on his head, it became impossible to imagine Holmes without one.[12] Clearly, this canonical illustration (or feature of a set of them) determines how we imagine Sherlock Holmes. Even in films that depart from Doyle's actual stories, Holmes himself is still usually pictured in ways derived from Paget's illustrations. Perhaps all we can say in general is that an illustration that seems uniquely suited to a story, that somehow captures the essence or feel of that story and its characters, is likely to become canonical, to determine features of the story-world described by the text. If this conjecture is true, then we can say that, in addition to the norm of faithfulness, canonical illustrations will conform to the norm of *appropriateness*.

The Image-Text Complex in Comics

Having investigated two different types of image-text complexes that do not have the structure characteristic of comics, we are now ready to turn to the problem of determining the distinctive features of the image-text relationship in comics. One might think that there is a quick and easy answer to the problem of distinguishing comics from all the various different types of illustrated texts we have been discussing. After all, unlike them, the images of comics are not illustrations of a preexisting story specified by a written text. The images of comics are thus free of the faithfulness constraint that governs illustrations.

Attractive as this *simple theory* is, it won't do as it stands. Think about the *Classics Illustrated* comic book series that was published between 1941 and 1971. Each comic book was an illustrated version of a classic literary text, such as James Fenimore Cooper's *Last of the Mohicans* (1919). Clearly, the comic is intended as some type of version of Cooper's novel, so that the images in the book are, in some sense, illustrations of the story presented in the original book. And, if this is so, the simple theory cannot be correct.

Figure 5.2   Image from Kanter, A.L. *Classics Illustrated Last of the Mohicans.* New York: Gilberton Co., Inc., 1942.

But we should not be too quick to reject the simple theory or, at least, the insight upon which it rests. Let's consider a more or less arbitrarily chosen panel from *Last of the Mohicans* comic such as the one reproduced in Figure 5.2. At first blush, we might think that the picture of the man pointing at the figures in the river is simply an illustration of the text that is present in the panel – "Hist! Look there! The risky devils have swum across to our island." – and so is an example of what I have called a "mere illustration."

This is not the case, however. For one thing, the text of this panel is itself derived from Cooper's novel. The passage in the novel runs as follows: "Hist! Look into the water above, just where it breaks over the rocks. I am no mortal, if the risky devils haven't swam down upon the very pitch, and, as bad luck would have it, they have hit the head of the island." (Cooper 1919: 65) Because the comic's text is itself derived from the novel, it does not have ontological priority over the image: Both are derived from the novel and its story-world. In addition, there are many features of the image that are clearly derived from the novel, for they are not mentioned at all in the text of the comic. Take a look, for example, at this passage from Cooper's novel:

> With no other guide than the ripple of the stream where it met the head of the island, a party of their insatiable foes had ventured into the current, and swam down upon this point, knowing the ready access it would give, if successful to their intended victims. As Hawkeye ceased speaking, four human heads could be seen peering above a few logs of driftwood that had lodged on these naked rocks, and which had probably suggested the idea of the practicability of the hazardous undertaking. (Cooper 1919: 65–66)

Although there are some details in the novel's description of the scene that are not clearly present in the illustration, most clearly the driftwood logs, the general description of the location and the characters are very specifically present in the picture. So if the image illustrates anything, it is not the story derived from *the text that appears with it* but rather the story-world specified by the text of the novel. But, in this respect the image is no different from the text in the comic. Both the image *and* the text together illustrate one (part of an) episode in Copper's book specified by *its* text. So the text and images of the *Classics Illustrated* version of *Last of the Mohicans*, both stand in a specific relationship to Cooper's original text, but only together do they tell an illustrated version of Cooper's story. As a result, even though the simple theory is not correct as it stands, we might be able to offer a slight revision of it to handle the case of *Classics Illustrated* comics: the distinctive feature of the (pictorial) images in comics is that they are not illustrations of a story-world determined by *the text with which they appear*.

At this point, it will be useful to introduce some terminology for describing the image-text structure that is characteristic of comics. I have already used the term *panel* to refer to the basic unit of a comic. Panels are generally rectangular in form, like the panel in Figure 5.2, and constitute a basic unit of text and image in a comic. Comics can be composed of just one panel or a number of panels, but the basic unit of a comic is always the panel. When panels are juxtaposed, they constitute the sequence, usually a temporal one in the depicted world of the comic, that McCloud refers to in his attempted definition.

A panel is usually composed of an image or picture, mostly but not always a drawing, and a written text. We will investigate what the text can signify in a moment. For now, we need only note that, in the types of comics we are interested in, there is always a text composed of one or more words. We have already noted that there are even cases in which there are no words in a panel; we now have to add that, although more rarely, there are instances in which the panel is not filled with any image at all. Nonetheless, at a basic level, comics are composed of panels and panels generally involve a complex of (pictorial) images and (written) text.

Seeing comics as composed of panels clarifies some of the ontological issues associated with them as well as providing the unified treatment of one- and multiple-panel comics I earlier claimed was needed. By taking the basic unit of a comic to be the panel, both one-panel comics and multiple-panel sequences can be seen to be two species of the comic.

A second term that will be important for our analysis is *frame*. Generally speaking, each panel of a comic contains a *frame*, that is, a drawn box or other plane figure that designates both the panel's representational space as well as identifies the unity that constitutes a single panel. The line-drawn plane figure resembles the physical frames within which oil paintings are traditionally displayed or the edges of a sheet on which a picture is drawn. These both establish the extent of the physical space upon which the representational image(s) is (are) drawn and that there is a representation at all. In Figure 5.2, you can see the presence of such a frame.

Two quick comments are in order. First, sometimes the frame will be merely implicit, suggested, for example, by the drawn frames on contiguous panels. Generally, though, comics include actually drawn frames that help individuate the different panels or to establish the limits of a single panel comic. Second, the frame can be identical with a panel or else a proper subset of it. That is, although often the frame establishes the boundaries of a panel, both the imagistic and textual features of a panel can extend beyond the frame. Most single-panel comics, for example, include text that is placed outside the frame. But the text in a strip can also transgress a frame's boundary.

Another feature of the pictorial space created by the frame is that it need not be pure in that it can also contain text, often indicating words that are uttered by the comic's characters. However, some comics do have pure pictorial spaces, so that nothing is placed within the frame except for visual elements with a depictive function.[13] *Dennis the Menace* (Hank Ketcham) is an example of such a comic. Its daily comic is a one-panel comic in which the frame contains no non-depictive linguistic elements (other than the copyright by North American Syndicate that we will simply ignore). Below the frame there are usually a couple of lines in quotation marks, often representing a comment that Dennis makes about the scene represented within the frame. Such a rigid separation of image and text occurs mostly in one-panel comics. Multi-panel comics tend to integrate image and text within each frame, although, as I have mentioned, the text sometimes breaks out of the limits established by the frame.

The central point I have been trying to establish here is that a distinctive feature of comics is that the images and text both contribute at an equally basic level to their story-worlds. Neither the text nor the images have a more fundamental role than the other, but they work together to create the story-world of the comic. But before exploring precisely how these two elements work together with one another in the creation of a story-world, let's look a bit more carefully at each of these two features of a comic.

The Image

As we have seen, McCloud characterized comics as having "pictorial images." What I take this to mean is that he sees the frame as characterizing a perceptual space within which images have a pictorial or depictive function. That is, using as our paradigm either newspaper or book-length comics, the frame marks a space on the page that is to be taken as allowing for images that partially characterize the story-world of the comic. Saying that these images are *pictorial* means that they present us with a visual *depiction* of the world they specify.

The pictorial space determined by the frame is not, as we have seen, generally purely pictorial. That is, it can also accommodate text within it without confusing viewers/readers. Generally speaking, the text present within the frame of a comic functions to specify the speech or thought of a character, but there are other uses of text as well. I will discuss them in the next section of this chapter.

Not every other aspect of the image is pictorial. There are various other markers that are used to characterize elements of the story-world. For example, consider speed lines. Comics often indicate that an object or a person is moving quickly by drawing a series of lines emanating from that object or person. These are *speed lines*. Clearly, they are features of the image, but they are not pictorial, although they are representational in that they indicate features of the story-world, namely the speed with which objects move. So even though the frame indicates a pictorial space within a panel, not every feature of the image within that frame must have a pictorial function.

The Text

Generally speaking, there are four different ways in which text functions in a comic: as the representation of the thought or speech of a character; as narration; as a pictorial element; or as the representation of sonic events. I will explore each of these in turn.

The first use of text is within what David Carrier, the first philosopher to write a book about the philosophy of comics, mistakenly takes to be one of the essential features of a comic: the *text-balloon*.[14]

Figure 5.3   A text-balloon.

What exactly is a text-balloon (see Figure 5.3)? First, it is a symbol that occurs within the pictorial space created by the frame of a comic that indicates the presence of a (more or less) enclosed space, generally within the frame of a comic, that is not part of the pictorial representation in that panel. Instead, that space is a linguistic space and its linguistic element can be understood in at least two ways. In both of its basic uses, a text-balloon is attached to a particular character, indicating that the words inside the balloon are either (i) thought or (ii) said by that character. So text-balloons attribute the words written within them to a specific character as either their thoughts or speech, although multiple stems can indicate that these words are uttered or thought simultaneously by more than one character.

As the example of *Dennis the Menace* demonstrated, characters' speech does not have to be rendered via text-balloons in comics. Words indicating Dennis' speech and that of other characters, such as the eternally frustrated Mr Wilson, are always placed *outside* and *beneath* the frame of this comic's panels, thereby indicating that it should not be understood pictorially. Speech rendered in this way is less common than the presence of text within the frame of a comic, at least in multi-panel comics. But there need be no actual text-balloon at all for the words within the frame to be attributed to a character's thought or speech. Given audiences' understanding that comics have an ontological structure in which text often is employed to represent the speech and thoughts of the characters depicted in the image, some comic artists use minimal means to indicate that this is how the text should be interpreted. Although Gary Trudeau often uses text balloons in *Doonesbury*, he frequently just connects a section of text to its speaker with a single line and no plane figure at all. In doing so, he relies on the more explicit rendering that the text-balloon gives to this specific use of text within the frame of a comic.

A second, and quite prominent use of text in comics is for narration or commentary. For example, the *Mark Trail* strip for November 16, 2009, contains two yellow boxes with words in them (one of which is superimposed over the two frames of the comic) that explain what is happening in the strip, namely that the man depicted running in the right hand panel has escaped from the poachers shown shooting in the background of the left hand panel. The running man is trying to rescue the little dog that is being threatened by an alligator in both panels. The text in these boxes provides the narrative needed to understand what is happening. The text in the first box reads: "One of the poachers fires at the big alligator as it comes out of the water to get the pet dog." Although such extensive use of text as a narrating tool is not very common in comics, especially since it tends to subordinate the pictures and thus threaten to render them mere illustrations of the story, many comics do use narrative text, albeit in a more restricted manner. Comic readers are familiar with small text boxes in the first frame of a daily strip that say things like "Meanwhile …" and thereby indicate how one is to understand that day's strip in relation to previous ones.

A third use of text in comics is pictorial. I have already mentioned the use of the word "STOP" within the image of a stop sign. Other examples of such pictorial use of text abound. What characterizes such a use of text is that the text depicts a feature of the story-world in which the text appears. So when, in the Doonesbury strip for August 9, 2010, we see the word "ARMY" on the image of Leo's shirt, that is because Leo's shirt in the story-world depicted by the strip actually has the word "ARMY" on it.

The final use of text that I shall discuss is neither purely linguistic nor simply pictorial. It is rather a translation of (usually) auditory features of the depicted (fictional) world of the comic into visual form as shown in Figure 5.4.

Figure 5.4 Text used to represent a sonic event.

In the example of "POW!" in Figure 5.4, the text is used in a representational way, but not *visually* or *pictorially*. Rather, the text represents *sonic* elements of the scene that is represented pictorially by the images in the other frames in the strip. Roy Lichtenstein has established that this use of text is one of the distinctive features of comics through his paintings of comics such as *Whaam!* (1963). That painting is derived from a large panel in DC Comics' *All American Men of War* (Grandenetti 1962). The use of text in this manner originated in comics, although this use has subsequently been taken up occasionally by television (as in the *Batman* TV series) and films.

This use of text moves beyond a simple representation of a sonic element of the pictured scene. The "Whaam" does not simply provide an onomato-poetic representation of the sound caused by the rocket's striking the plane, the event that is pictured in the panel. Instead, it, together with the "WHOOSH!," provides a means for the static image to indicate the dynamic process that the panel presents, namely that of the shooting down of one plane by another. Although there are pictorial elements that are used to convey the fact that it is a process and not a single, discrete temporal moment that is being depicted in the panel – the multi-colored, diagonal path that the rocket takes being the primary one – it is the two words that most clearly indicate that the panel is presenting a temporally-extended process, while also representing (non-simultaneous) auditory aspects of the process.

When we see a word such as "Pow!" in a comic, it indicates the presence of an event, such as someone hitting someone else. So although comics cannot directly present the passing of time since they lack duration – something that films have the capacity to can do because of their nature as temporally extended objects – they have developed a unique representational scheme for presenting temporal events in a less indirect manner than verbally representing them with a phrase such as "and then ...." Through an interest-ing use of visual signs, but primarily through the use of onomatopoetic words, comics are able to represented temporally-extended processes or events in a way that traditional visual mediums such as painting standardly do not, since they eschew such symbolic means of representation.[15]

How Comics Work

In order to investigate how image and text work together to create the story-world of a comic, I will focus on a one-panel comic from Gary Larson's *The Far Side* that includes two of the different uses of text I have just identified. What we see in the comic's frame is a man, who appears to be in some sort of cave, facing two doors with a devil holding a pitchfork to his back. The doors read, "Damned if you do" and "Damned if you don't." The devil is speaking to the man and his words are rendered in a caption: "C'mon, c'mon – it's either one or the other."

This comic gets its punch from our having to figure out what exactly is being represented. After a bit of reflection, I think it becomes pretty obvious that the poor man with the devil's pitchfork poking in his back is being presented with a fool's choice. Larson has taken the common saying, "Damned if you; damned if you don't," and given it a graphic representation in this comic. But we only realize that as we use the images to interpret the man's situation as one in which he has been brought to Hell, the text below the frame to specify that he is being forced by the devil to make a choice, and, finally, by the text on the doors to realize that there really is no choice in such situations.

I have not spoken at all about the nature of our engagement with comics as an artform and I will not discuss this important question in any great detail or generality here. But in the case of Larson's comic, it is clear that we get pleasure from two sources. First of all, we have to figure out exactly what the pictured situation is, and we get pleasure from our ability to solve this puzzle. But we also get pleasure from the wit that Larson uses in visualizing a situation in which you really are "Damned if you and damned if you don't." Cognitive pleasure is an important source of our engagement with certain comics, such as *The Far Side*.

The point that I wish to emphasize here, however, is that Larson's comic provides us with a clear example of the interplay between image and text in a comic. It is impossible to specify the story-world created by the comic without making reference to both the text and the image. While we might be able to grasp the fact that the man is in Hell simply by referring to the images, we don't fully understand the situation envisioned by the comic without making reference in addition to the text that not only specifies his situation but also gives the comic its punch, its entertainment value. Unlike the case of illustrated books, in which the text is ontologically more basic than the illustrations, comics give images and text equal ontological priority in determining the story-world the comic creates and in providing reader-viewers with the enjoyment they get from the comic.

An Objection

I have claimed that a distinctive feature of the text-image complex in comics is that the images are not illustrations of aspects of the story-world created by the text with which they appear. An objection to my account is that there are other artforms that share this characteristic, so that I have not isolated a feature that is distinctive of comics.

Consider children's picture books. One might argue that the illustrations in such books are not less basic that their texts. After all, picture books give pride of place to their pictures, which are crucial to our appreciation of the books as works of art. Doesn't this mean that the image-text complex in picture books is of the same type as that present in comics?

Even though the story-world created by a picture book depends on both the images and the text, I think that the text has a very specific priority: namely, the images of such books still illustrate the story that the text with which they appear creates. Take even a picture book like *Goodnight, Moon* (Brown 2005). The wonderful pictures by Clement Hurd are still illustrations of the story created by Margaret Wise Brown's spare text. And even though our appreciation of the book depends on the presence of those illustrations perhaps even more than on the text itself, the text maintains its ontological priority over the illustrations. For this reason, a different image-text complex characterizes picture books than the one present in comics.

My response also explains why it is a mistake to claim that the true object of my analysis is graphic design and not comics per se.[16] Picture books are certainly an example of an art form that includes graphic elements, namely the pictures, but, as I have just explained, I do not think that the images and the text in picture books function in precisely the way they do in comics. As a result, I think that my analysis applies to comics and not to a broader category such as graphic design that includes other art forms.

That said, perhaps there are other art forms that share the distinctive image-text relationship I have attributed to comics. All I have tried to argue in this chapter is that the image-text complex present in comics has an ontological structure that is different from that of other traditional art forms like that of the illustrated novel. Although I think this structure is distinctive to comics, I am open to the possibility that there are art forms that share this structure. I simply do not know of any. But I don't think that issue can be settled *a priori*.

Conclusion

My goal in this paper has been to characterize the unique combination of images and text that constitute what I have called the image-text complex characteristic of comics as an art form. I have been careful to acknowledge that not every comic need avail itself of the ontological structure I have described, but it is a unique one that distinguishes comics from other related artforms such as illustrated books. The crucial feature of the comic image-text complex is the mutual interaction of each element in creating the story-world of the comic and providing such satisfaction as possible for its reader-viewer.

Notes

1   McCloud attempts to define "comics." I prefer the locution *a* comic.

2   Both Hyman and Pratt (2005) and Meskin (2007) give more systematic criticisms of McCloud's proffered definition of comics.

3   One-panel comics are sometimes also called "cartoons," as in *The Complete Cartoons of the New Yorker* (Mankoff *et al.*: 2006). Such usage is derived from the art historical use of the term to refer to the full-size drawings some artists made for their oil paintings. However, this terminology is confusing, since the term "cartoon" is also used for short animated films. In addition, I see no systematic reason for denying that one-panel comics are, in fact, comics.

4   http://xroads.virginia.edu/~MA04/wood/ykid/illustrated.htm accessed on 12/10/09. *Wikipedia* makes a similar claim.

5   *Biozoic* can be accessed at http://www.webcomicsnation.com/gerry/biozoic/series.php

6   Parity considerations would lead us to expect the possibility of imageless comics. In fact, I only know of pictureless comics, that is, comics in which the images consist solely of text. See for example, Kenneth Koch (2004).

7   Can there be illustrations that are not faithful to the text they illustrate? This is an interesting question for a theory of illustration that would have to take into account the possibility of what might be called "creative illustrations" of texts that are intentionally unfaithful to the texts they illustrate.

8   Illustrated books do not include a variety of books that include images. There are, for example, illuminated manuscripts that contain beautiful images but those images are not illustrations in the sense I am using that term.

9   Nothing prohibits illustrations like Moser's from becoming canonical. At this point in time, however, it is clear that they are not.

10   In his contribution to this volume, John Holbo questions whether Tenniel's drawings are really canonical for *Alice in Wonderland*. It certainly is true that they might turn out not to be if alternative sets of drawings come to predominate. It may be that we need to relativize the notion of canonicity to a particular time, place, and/or social context. On the other hand, if Tweedledum and Tweedledee are presented as siblings in all other sets of illustrations of *Alice*, that will show that Tenniel's drawings are canonical in that features of the story-world are derived from the drawings rather than Carroll's text.

11   Richard West suggested that the reason for this is that Twain's books were originally published as children's literature, a genre that required the presence of illustrations. Now, however, since we regard his works as great works of American literature, the illustrations are no longer treated as part of the works. This explanation may not be valid, however, since many nineteenth-century books intended for adult readers had illustrations in them.

12   I owe this point to Richard West.

13   We should note that words can be present in what I am calling a purely pictorial space when the words are features of the depicted sign, as when the image includes a stop sign with the word "STOP" in it. For convenience, I refer to such words as *depictive*.

14   Carrier refers to "text-balloons." Since the words need not be spoken and there need be no closed plane figure such as a balloon, I prefer the term "text-balloon." See Carrier (2000: Chapter 2).
15   Text balloons also represent the temporally extended processes of thinking and speaking. I am here only concerned with the relation of text and image.
16   John Holbo suggested a version of this objection to me in private correspondence.

References

Aristophanes. *Lysistrata*, trans. Gilbert Seldes, New York: Limited Editions Club, 1934.

Brown, M.W. *Goodnight, Moon*. New York: Harper Collins, 2005.

Carrier, D. *The Aesthetics of Comics*. University Park, PA: Penn State University Press. 2000.

Carroll, L. *Alice in Wonderland*. London: Macmillan and Company, 1865.

Cooper, J.F. *The Last of the Mohicans*, New York: Charles Scribner's Sons. 1919.

Grandenetti, J. *All American Men of War*, New York: DC Comics, 1962.

Hayman, G. and H. Pratt. "What Are Comics?" in D. Goldblatt and L. Brown. (eds) *A Reader in Philosophy of the Arts*, Upper Saddle River, NJ: Pearson Education Inc., 2005: 419–424.

Kanter, A.L. *Classics Illustrated: Last of the Mohicans*. New York: Gilberton Co., Inc., 1942.

Koch, K. *The Art of the Possible: Comics Mainly Without Pictures*. New York: Soft Skull Press, 2004.

Mankoff, R., A. Gopnik, and D. Remnick. *The Complete Cartoons of the New Yorker*. New York: Black Dog & Leventhal Publishers, 2006.

McCloud, S. *Understanding Comics: The Invisible Art*. Amherst, MA: Kitchen Sink Press, 1993.

Meskin, Aaron "Defining Comics?" *Journal of Aesthetics and Art Criticism* 65(4), 2007: 369–379.

Milne, A.A. *Winnie-the-Pooh*. London: Methuen and Company, 1926.

Moser, B. The Holy Bible. New York, Penguin, 1999.

Twain, M. *The Adventures of Huckleberry Finn*. New York: Charles L. Webster and Company, 1884.

Wartenberg, T. *Thinking on Screen: Film as Philosophy*. London and New York: Routledge, 2007.

What's So Funny? Comic Content in Depiction

Patrick Maynard

Where are the Funnies?

Aesthetics' recent, welcome attention to comics arts has focused on such topics as definition, stylistics, comics' relations to other visual arts and their status among the arts generally. This essay addresses a truly philosophical topic that, while underlying these and others, appears unnoticed. That is the problem of how comic representations can be, in the first place, funny or even light. "Funny" and "light" are just two descriptions with which we ascribe basic comics content, content not in the sense of subject-matter but of the attitudes under which subject-matter is conceived. The generic term "comic" itself, like "light," "funny," "scathing," "ironic," "corny" and many other relevant terms, describes not just situations, but situations as taken in certain ways, with different attitudes of mind. Such terms apply to how things are conceived and presented, and so attribute different mental characteristics to a representation's content. But, ironically, while much is said about how mental content is depicted within comics – speech and thought bubbles being favorite examples – little is said about such mental content as expressed by comics themselves, about the invisible bubbles of conception and attitude that enclose entire strips. Yet this is their appeal. How is such mental content possible, and in what does it consist? Let us approach this topic by following the thread of funniness – or at least lightness – beginning briefly with two of the more commonly discussed topics, comics among the arts and comics' distinctive combinations of word and image.

Perhaps a way to consider what comics are is to think about where they are. The comics with which we may at least begin are those occurring in newspapers

The Art of Comics: A Philosophical Approach, First Edition.
Edited by Aaron Meskin and Roy T. Cook.
© 2012 Blackwell Publishing Ltd. Published 2012 by Blackwell Publishing Ltd.

and magazines, as single-frame or strip, solo or grouped, in what are called "the funny pages," not the longer, more intense productions of the graphic novel. Beginning in the nineteenth century, with, for notable example, *The Katzenjammer Kids*[1] and continuing with classics such as *Nancy, Pogo, Blondie, Family Circus, Garfield, Peanuts, Hagar the Horrible, Calvin and Hobbs, Dilbert*,[2] such comics usually stand separate from the main features, considered serious – and as individual strips become serious, they tend to drift toward the editorial section. That people should turn to the funny pages for relief from the more serious seems important. What kind of relief is it? A lightening of mood. The location of such comics indicates several kinds of lightness, partly by being presented as fiction, partly by their overlap with jokes, also by their connection with drawing.

Many standard comics function as visual jokes. A kind of relief they offer is that of jokes, with the shared rhythm of puzzle and punch-line resolution, usually absurd. Typically, such comics are amusing – mildly, hardly at all, and in various ways, including wry, aggressive, and so on. Like jokes, one of their important features is non-seriousness, not only of content but also of our attitude or "form of attention." Often the main point of telling verbal jokes is not to entertain but to induce a less serious state of mind: thus to affect, even shift, our states of mind. Kant observed something similar in what he called the "agreeable arts," for example, "the art . . . with jokes and laughter, of inducing an air of gaiety," without responsibility, as "only given out for the entertainment of the moment, not as a lasting matter to be made the subject of reflection or repetition."[3]

Normal humans vary utterances. It would be a tiresome person many of whose utterances were intended for "reflection or repetition."[4] Even where privacy is not an issue, most comments are meant to be forgotten. The same holds for many depictions, including comics. That we tend not to place such comics among fine arts is not surprising. "Fine," as applied to visual arts, has the functional, not just honorific, meaning of permanent work for display, notably in the context of galleries and museums. Such "high art" tends to be literally high, up on walls, where it can stay for long periods, to be seen and discussed, not only with interest and admiration but prolonged, repeated and shared attention. It therefore aspires to be virtually inexhaustible, a "lasting matter," "the subject of reflection." Skill, work, material, complexity and beauty are often factors here, but a main factor in representational works is that they "sustain recognition" of subject-matter.[5] There is an old-fashioned term for that, "contemplation," whose quiet connotation may be misleading. In depictive works the recognition process often involves difficulties, complications of subject, as we move back and forth between subject and worked medium, taking cues from each about the other. Perception is then something beyond immediate response: an active, extended, often collaborative process, open to revision, in which aspects of subjects build gradually from their medium. Such works may be called "creative" for their audiences, not just their makers, since their comprehension calls on a wide range of psychic resources, not only to react to them, but actively to meet the challenges into which they draw us.

It would be not only unfair to expect this of an agreeable art, but out of place. Comics are not normally meant for contemplation or even to be kept. Thus the standard function of newsprint comics is the opposite, of providing a place of brief refuge from the challenges of the news pages – which, unlike art, provide scant resource for activities of resolution. Uniformity of simple subjects and manners of presentation are these comics' stock in trade, with slight variations on restricted and predictable themes. Rather than a challenge to mobilize breadth of perceptual, mental and psychic resources, the main aim of such works is relaxing complacency – often depending upon stereotypes of personages, situations, and actions.

There is also lightness of means. The ephemeral in visual arts is often reflected in materials, in modern times by paper – for comics, newsprint. This is because comics, like the news, are for daily printing in multiples and quick destruction, their presses turning with the diurnal motion of the planet, and must be produced through dispensable materials of slight bulk by rapid processes. Their method is drawing transferred to ink – notably in lines, largely contour-bounding, with in-filling, forming two-dimensional regions on a surface, used to depict substances, but typically also working among themselves as shapes and patterns. In so beginning to describe them, we begin to consider their typical appearance; as soon as we attend to appearance we take interest in the process of perceiving it. That is the basis of aesthetic interest, even aside from questions of art. The very look of daily comics' bold screened patterns on smooth, grey, absorbent newsprint surfaces, already admired by artists for working in charcoal, graphite, and ink, becomes an object of aesthetic appreciation. Whatever the representational content of their work, many comics artists have played their shapes and colors against that ground with aesthetic perception. Despite the daily comics fare being different from fine art, as in all human endeavors, given the skills and inventiveness of some of its practitioners – even those working under the closest restrictions of function, time and economics – they provide scope for artistry.[6]

Writing Images, Drawing Words

What one standard comics topic has helped us recognize perhaps a second topic will help us understand. Recent thinking about comics and cartoons has been much in terms of form, where their characteristic integration of visual depiction and speech – notably in speech or thought bubbles, but also in captions – has merited attention. Such discussions occasionally place comics in a wide context of word and image traditions, East and West, notably those that combine drawing and painting with writing.[7] Let us take these assimilations to be more than perfunctory, as indicating neglected matters of significance, related to the theme of mental content.

Language has come to be understood as more than a mode of communication, as also a way of conceiving things, presenting them in the mind. Its study applies not only to propositional joining of subjects and attributes but also to speakers' acts, their attitudes towards what is said, and much more indicating mental content. Considering visual depictions that are closely related to words might help show how they, too, could express mental content beyond just identifying subjects and qualifying them with properties – including the possibility of funny depictions, not just pictures of funny things. Most relevant to comics would be traditions not only of words with images but as combined in reciprocal supplement to one another. Strict interdependence might mean neither's being comprehensible without the other; less strict ranges over many subtle and interesting variations, as we find today in the variety of commercial logos. For example, medieval drawing's well-known close association with writing would commonly be thought to be of the word with image kind: mainly of image illustrating text, or of word as legend to diagrammatic image, or text inscription as forming images. However the

Figure 6.1   Corbie Psalter. Fol. 67v, Initial V of Psalm 76.
Image courtesy of Bibliothèques d'Amiens Metropole.

variety of cases within that tradition shows far closer and subtler interdependencies. A single example may serve to indicate this richness.

A page of the Psalms from the Carolingian Corbie Psalter would have been made for reading (maybe singing) aloud (see Figure 6.1). That means that readers were to look at its painted inscriptions to discern letters, syllables, words, in order to utter the words of the psalm. There the "Vo" in "Voce mea" is the first sounded syllable of the line.[8] Its beginning letter's inscription also depicts its enunciation by the psalmist, with whom the reader identifies, and whose mouth, touched by an angel whose depicted form completes it, sounds the "o," the inscription of which seems to lift the angel's wing, perhaps as breath. But the phrase this open vowel begins to utter, "Voce mea," "my voice," also refers to the reader's voicing those words, mouth moving from the first depicted letter (possibly even depicted by the psalmist's and angel's compressed lips), to the "o," whose image shapes like the exhaling mouth of the reader, who moves on. The result is a complex mental project defying description. Let us try.

First, readers are to understand of their own reading or singing aloud that they are divinely guided by the words of the psalm. Next, the initial sounds they utter they are to imagine seeing uttered by one who is depicted by the shapes forming one of the letters that guide that utterance; also, by identifying with the depicted psalmist, they are to imagine this as led by the angel. But at least those initial sounded words also denote their own voices uttering them. Thus the words they read refer to the very sounds of their reading, and they read them by letters depicting their own forming of those sounds, by multiple guidance. This complexity of sight, sound, touch and bodily sense, actual or imagined, involves an interweaving of language and visual figuration of an intricacy reminiscent of polyphonies as well as visual interlace patterns of the time.

Without Words

We see from a single case how imprecise is the term "illustrated" for the relation of image and word in different traditions, right from the early ninth century. We might then wonder why such rich relations were not developed along a main line of what would become Western fine arts – notably of painting and drawing. Practice might then have shaped theory, as in other cultures that more closely integrate the "arts of the brush." Far from being anomalous, devices we think peculiar to modern comics might then have been mainstream. Out of that, different theories of image content might have developed, closer to those of language while not linguistic.

Despite the fact that potentials for design were far from exhausted, a depictively visual, nonverbal redefinition of drawing and other forms of depiction appeared in the Renaissance, whose benefits may be briefly noted. Regarding the loss of words, we should consider which words. These were not just words, but established texts. European visual arts' gradual parting from them constituted a liberation from authoritative verbal accounts, historical and religious. To be sure, the main function of these increasingly visual arts was to illustrate and elaborate stories assumed already known. That meant finding aspects of familiar verbal narratives to vivify for the illiterate. More slowly came the growth of interest in what we observe around us, including natural situations that do not even involve subjects that could appear as agents in narratives. The gradual discovery of a natural world as natural, with unlimited ranges of effects, is a great step forward in understanding the universe and our place as part of it. Here the visual arts have an important role beside the sciences. From such arts proceeds the modern discovery of a world of visual effects, an appreciation of visual experience itself, thereby of visual intelligence and creativity, eventually freed from even the subject-matter of figuration. For those not always interested in stories as narratives or situations, human or otherwise, that constituted further liberation.[9] In principle, such art might have evolved in combination with words. But, for the West, autonomy seemed to require depictive visual images' going it alone.

This appears to have been achieved at cost to our conceptions of depiction, which have shaped our subsequent enormous development of image technologies. Problems in thinking about these arts that attended their becoming strictly visual involved two levels of mental content. The first is a well-known problem of representing mental attitudes of thought and feeling, absent words. This has been addressed by art history, notably in terms of depicted physical gestures and facial expressions.[10] It remains central for comics, where, in addition, thought bubbles often enclose nonverbal contents, sometimes embedded images. Not all such content is verbal. Obvious are light bulbs, stars, question and punctuation marks, as are "z"s of sleep, but there are more subtle devices. Closer to the second kind of mental content, the enclosed speech and thought bubbles are further modified to show the agent's attitude toward that content, notably by standard shapes of their surrounds, smooth or jagged. A work's thus representing mental content is but an aspect of our larger topic of how depictions themselves can express such content.[11] This includes a problem of how a depiction, not just what it depicts, can be, as remarked above, light or even funny – a problem concerning, as it were, the "shape" of a mental "bubble" enclosing the depiction, which expresses its conception and attitude regarding its contents.

Such questions have been rendered unanswerable by ideas that accompanied the Renaissance redefinition of depiction. From that period, an emphatically stated conception of visual depiction has equated it with the rendering of natural visual effects through mastering nature's perceptual means. This was enforced by the rise of painting over drawing, now redefined as preparation for painting, hence valued for its relative immediacy and informality, rather than as the finished work of medieval times. With the separation of image from word, our understanding of the image surface itself changed, from being a partly reserved, flat ground on which image shapes and calligraphic marks are spread, to being a base for covering, layering, to suggest spatial depth. Not only image without word, but image as "realistic" offshoot of natural perception, became the paradigm for depiction itself, departures from which, as in most comics, are understood as "distortions" of a canon of realism, although most are not themselves experienced as distortions of anything. More specifically, it became the norm to understand pictorial depictions as corresponding to views of actual scenes from positions at some distance, perspective points.[12]

Just Looking

The ensuing mental content problem was not entirely unnoticed. According to Michael Podro, by "the mid-eighteenth century":

> It was thought that there was an inherent limitation to the art of painting because it presented its subject matter only for visual scrutiny; it was experienced as something *external* to the mind – it confronted the mind as opposed to offering, like language, something that could be absorbed within the mind's movement, something in which the mind could actively participate. The problem for the defenders of painting was to show how it could – like language – become *internal*, open to the mind's participation, part of the mind's thought and feeling.

"Thought," because theory has accepted that thought exists in language-like form; "feeling," at least because it contains thought, conception. Such might not have been at issue at the time of the Corbie picture, where image and language were closely intertwined. More relevant to present concerns, this problem, Podro remarks, now reappears as background to most current theory of depiction, beginning with vision sciences.

> A second convergent route was from philosophers who [have] treated depiction as a matter of how the visual array offered by the picture could elicit recognitions as of the visible world. Such philosophers restrict the representational content of a painting to what could be said about the object itself seen face to face, the rest being attributable to style. The implicit argument is that we can only pick out representational content by reference to possible or at least plausible aspects of the real world.[13]

Indeed, such aspects are often referred to as "the actual scene" or "the real world," expressing a correspondence assumption, that depictions are basically portrayals of – that they denote – actual things, while those that do not are to be treated as secondary, marginal. These ways of thinking might not have prevailed with comics subjects in mind. It is not clear what it could mean to encounter most comics figures "face to face." Yet such is the vocabulary by which comics are discussed, remote from the categories by which they are experienced. We need to do better.

The "visual scrutiny" approach has taken different forms, all which may be called "just seeing," since they have in common that depictions are to be understood as Podro says, "externally": as visual stimuli that perceivers receive, needing only the equipment they have for natural or environmental seeing, guided by cultural pointing in the right direction – although typically (until technology takes care of these deficiencies) requiring four kinds of adjustment: for paucity of the stimulus, visual noise and paradox (notably two-dimensionality, but also evidence of physical materials and processes used), distortion (notably in comics) plus supplemental "conventional" matters, for example, speed-lines, feeling-stars, words and such, in comics. This dominant "just looking, just seeing" approach began from a global, space-based, perspective-scene idea, which attended the invention of that technique in the Renaissance, a current version of which states: "A picture is nothing but a more convenient way of arranging matter so that it projects a pattern identical to real objects."[14] Something like this is still widely accepted, albeit not likely with comics and cartoons in mind; no one thinks of Disney's drawings as projecting patterns approximating those of either Mickey Mouse or other "real objects" such as mice.

More recent science has undercut the optical, projection model of perception. The newer approach is psycho-physiological, analyzing vision in terms of discrete systems responding to particular kinds of cues. That optical images are formed according to perspective projection only tells us how information is moved into the shop for work; afterwards it must be taken up in bits and constructed by at least thirty different visual centers in the primate brain. Most recently, brain-imaging through PET scans and fMRI, together with study of localized traumas, has added a second step to a modularized understanding of perception. Such traumas notably include agnosias or "unknowings," cognitive inabilities of quite specific kinds, such as not being able to recognize objects, faces, by sight or touch, or to integrate movements into actions. In general, these results seem to confirm the insight that, far from being an imitation of appearances, depictions work by appealing to separate receptors.[15] For example, modern researchers find that linear perspective in pictures itself works as a concomitance of cues taken from natural vision, including gradients of foreshortening and texture, its characteristic diminution, horizon ratio and occlusion or overlap, and so forth. History proves that any of these may be taken over from environmental perception to be used pictorially, alone or in various combinations, yielding different effects, which are readily comprehended by audiences lacking any sense of incoherence, distortion or impoverishment. Notably, the most effective depth indicator of the group, occlusion, is widely used, without or with various of the others, to order shapes in depth.

A more recent modular approach to vision and depiction, stressing exploitation of various clusters of cues for the working of neural mechanisms, promises to free us from optical, perspective-projective ideas. For example, neuroscientist V. S. Ramachandran, remarking on the complex neural processes of vision, with multiple stages of refinement through many neural brain centers, holds that "this is what makes art possible": the opportunity to "change the image in specific ways, to more optimally titillate the visual centers," thereby "to send signals to the reward centers."[16] "The point of art is not realism," he argues, "but deliberate exaggeration, hyperbole, even distortion of the image to evoke specific moods and sentiments in the human brain." This it achieves by exploiting artistic universals based on perceptual laws. For example, caricatures – and presumably cartoons - provide central examples for application of the "peak shift" principle of changes to stronger response regarding exaggerated aspects of stimuli on which perceivers have been trained. Thus, in well-known ethological studies, gull chicks, biologically programmed to peck energetically at spots on parents' beaks, respond even more vigorously to manufactured "super beaks," which are straight sticks with several painted spots.[17] At issue is not overall resemblance but rather selective exploitation of what is called "receiver bias." Similarly, releasers for our own recognition responses can be exploited through receiver bias – our sensitivity to "seeing" faces in all sorts of things being a familiar case.[18] A related perceptual principle particularly relevant to comics is "isolation," whereby small doodles can be more evocative than elaborate renderings of a subject, given that although the visual system's working ability is impressive it has limited attention capacities, and may be more responsive to stimuli that are free of redundant information. In summary, recent vision theory provides bases for understanding depictive effects independently of norms of naturalism, thereby providing improved ways of understanding how comics work.[19]

But when applying such findings to pictorial experience, we need to avoid reductive over-generalization, long a tendency of perspective-based theory. Showing that depictive representation uses biologically fixed mechanisms, one might again assume that this is all there is to it: that picture perception is a minor branch of vision studies – "just seeing," with the noted qualifications. The earlier "just seeing", optical version involved the fallacy that, since many image-makers use effective systems that approximate perspective, pictures are in principle just projections. The later modular version runs the danger of a similar fallacy, that depiction consists in activating select modules of natural visual response. It is tempting for such researchers to think of it as play on a neural keyboard, making shapes that, like the "super beak," have ours "behaving exactly like a bird brain," as the neuroscientist remarks. But it does not follow that, if one thing is necessary for another, the latter consists in the former and can be comprehended in its terms. Running is necessary to most field sports, but these sports neither consist in running nor can be basically understood in its terms. Rather, we have to know what a sport is in order to understand what the running is doing there, what it is used for: moving toward goals, minimal time, chasing a ball, gaining momentum, evasion, pursuit and so forth.

Similarly, finding perceptual laws that render depiction, including comics, effective illuminates but does not explain it. Nor does it tell us much about depictive mental contents such as being light or funny. Like running, activation of visual responses is of little meaning without context, which requires relating vision to tasks. The challenge for perception theory is to explain how representations of an environment are constructed in those terms. Our challenge is different: better to understand depictive content, for which the recent approaches offer two things. These are freedom from an ancient "imitation of appearances" conception, plus "what makes art possible" – an active, constructive model, on which it is possible to "change the image in specific ways," to work aspects of our visual processing for our own aims – in other words, to use our brains. To be sure, that can involve titillating "reward centers."[20] But, according to anthropologists, ours are not bird brains, entirely. Indeed, the technological invention of depiction is thought by anthropologists to mark the emergence of modern humans and language, as it became possible not only to communicate regarding the present, but "to re-create the world mentally and dream up endless new realities"[21] – to which we may add, presenting attitudes towards things.

By their notorious "impurity," it may be that comics can contribute more to vision sciences than the other way around. Free of projective or even space-based canons, "the comix" – that typical comics remix of appeals to spatial and physiognomic recognition cues, along with limbic probes, language, "conventional" signs, analogy and metaphor, and whatever works – may better reflect recent sciences of the brain and mind, regarding synaesthesia, visual pathway duality,[22] hand to mouth and other neural motor linkages, mimic neurons, and so forth: a less tidy bundling of our hardwires than was supposed by earlier vision science.

Where's the Fun?

Although an improvement, approaching depiction in terms of selective exploitation of biologically evolved responses, even freely combined with a host of other factors, suggests little for understanding mental content in the work. For depiction, such content must include, besides things and situations represented, the ways they are seen. To overlook that would be to treat depiction all over again in terms of "just seeing." But depictions, as things we perceive, themselves express visual conceptions of things – including funny ones. They, as much as profound artworks, are "open to the mind's participation, part of the mind's thought and feeling." That is not true of actual subjects we see. To be sure, when we see persons, things and situations, we perceive them in certain ways, characterized by our mental attitudes: indifferently, attentively, hurriedly, quizzically, affectionately, critically, honestly. Even a neutral gaze is a kind of gaze. But while we look upon a situation dispassionately, the situation is not dispassionate. Seeing something perceptively, with attention, is not seeing something that is perceptive or attentive; seeing maliciously does not mean seeing something malicious; seeing something humorously or in a funny way does not mean seeing something funny, and this holds for affectionately, curiously, scathingly and countless other mental attitudes. Therefore, while we use many of the same mechanisms to look at things and look at depictions of things, a remarkable difference is that depictions, as things we see, already include ways of seeing, characterized by a host of mental descriptions. Also, these mental states may be highly nuanced. Funny depictions are funny of a sort: corny, scathing, whimsical, arch, twisted, wacky, understated. Different comics are savored for their unique sensibilities, their ways of taking things.

Again, our challenge is not just that of stating how comics can be light or funny. Sometimes they are funny mainly because they depict funny things. Many cartoons are funny that way, their drawings not particularly so: jokes illustrated. People amuse themselves by inventing funny captions for serious pictures. Then there are pictures of funny characters, clowns, which may be mistaken for funny pictures. More relevant is that depictions, like any other artifacts, can be joke objects. Just as one can make a joke chair, one can make a joke picture. For example, a joke painting on one side of a fifth-century Greek red-figure pot is a parody of a black-figure work of the previous century, making fun not only of the subject (Odysseus crossing the sea) but also the usurped method of depicting it.[23] Closer to our topic is that many funny comics are drawn by amusing or at least light means, with minimal use of techniques such as perspective, shadow modeling, volume, depth of space, textural difference, which would detract from the effect. Avoidance of more complex "languages" of depiction is sometimes part of comic content; some even suggest technical awkwardness. But we appreciate these better by not assuming that most comics presuppose comparison with non-comic, notably naturalistic, styles. No arguments have been presented for the view that comic depiction presupposes – rests on exaggeration of – any other style.

It may appear that the answer to the question of mental content is "expression." It is usual for aesthetics to supplement approaches to depiction with independent treatment of expression, typically in terms of "association" with the depictive design elements. For example, feeling qualities associated with colors, shapes, and patterns in depiction may be thought to provide the required "internal" aspect. However, lightness and funniness are not plausibly described as sensed qualities independently associated with colors and shapes, which can be brought into depiction. Marks and shapes often have independent qualities of sureness, strength, warmth, incisiveness, tentativeness, of searching or being leisurely and so forth, all of which may be highly relevant to depictions that present their subjects those ways. But it seems highly implausible that this is what depictions presenting their subjects consists in, even more implausible that funny pictures are those made of funny lines, shapes, colors, that satiric or ironic presentation of subjects can be explained in terms of satiric or ironic associations of pictorial elements used to depict them. It may seem funny that no standard approach to depiction can account for funny pictures – more so that none has tried.

"What's That For?" Arts and Artifacts

If we wish to continue thinking in terms of visual perception, an entirely different approach seems required to answer the embarrassingly simple question of how it is possible for comics and other kinds of depictions to be light or funny and in different ways.[24] Such an approach might be found by returning to our beginning, to comics as artworks of a general kind. As the term "artwork" says twice, such things are *artifacts*, rather than natural or accidental occurrences: that is, they are made by people for certain purposes, and we have conjectured what these purposes might be.

We understand artifacts of any sort according to two sorts of purposes, taking their features as present, unlike most nature, *for* purposes, and also present – unlike living nature – *on* purpose, intentionally. It is generally overlooked in discussions of pictorial perception, especially those of the "visual scrutiny" sort, that this is how we look at them, which makes a great difference to how they appear. What the difference is, is something that we can turn to cognitive science of a different sort to explain. Developmental researchers point out that comprehending the useful aspects – the "affordances" – of artifacts in terms of intentions, purposes, goals is an important feature of child development within the first year. In watching adults' uses of artifacts, infants learn to identify their goals, what they are using artifacts for. Then by imitative behavioral learning children join others in affirming what such things, in that social group, are "for": hammers are for pounding, pencils for writing, and so forth. According to primatologist Michael Tomasello, the child then "comes to see some cultural objects and artifacts as having, in addition to their natural sensory-motor affordances, another set of … intentional affordances based on her understanding of the intentional relations that other persons have with that object or artifact,"[25] notably regarding purposes. Then children learn to identify accidents, mistakes, incompletions regarding the goals for which the tools are used; they also playfully "decouple" intentional affordances from objects, mischievously using tools in wrong or funny ways.

Asking what such a thing is, we ask "what's that for?," for us or for them. To perceive something as an artifact is thus to experience it not only in terms of its potential use affordances, but also in terms of others' shared perceptions of that use. The emphasis on others' perceptions is of great importance. It means that the mere taking of something as an artifact is understanding it in terms of a community. In most circumstances, this is a community to which we belong. "What's that for?" means "How do we use it?," with emphasis on a real, historical community, not an ideal one of all people or all rational agents.[26] This is the artifact basis for shared perceptions and communications, including differences and disagreements – notable features of our dealings with art.

We observed earlier how recent science brings to our understanding of depiction findings about distinct mental capacities, sometimes corresponding to distinct neural structures. We noted that study of agnosias – such as inabilities to recognize colors, shapes, objects (notably faces), to produce words of certain sorts, to integrate movements into actions – has revealed a complex modular structure to most of our mental capacities. The familiar experience of opportunistic perception, when we look for something to do an ad hoc job – to seal, prop, cut and so forth – is not like that of perceiving something as an artifact – as a gasket, strut, knife – whether we need one or not. Lack of that perception would seem to constitute a disability.[27] Inability to recognize something as an artifact would presumably constitute an agnosia, a "non-knowing," since the natural/artifact distinction, tied closely to perceiving things in terms of goals, shared goals, is basic to us.

Since depictions have been understood as artifacts apparently as long as modern humans have existed, this applies to them.[28] A specific theoretical "artifact-agnosia" is therefore necessary to the "just seeing" or "visual scrutiny" approaches now prevalent in vision sciences and philosophy of art, in order not to treat them just like shoes, pots, wheels, writing, laws or any other common artifacts of more restricted use, all of which depictions predate by many millennia. Overlooking depiction's artifact nature, these approaches are able to ignore the great differences between looking at things and looking at depictions. Notably, they neglect that we seek out features of depictions, unlike those of real scenes, for their representational affordances, attempting to make sense of them in terms of purposes, of why they were put or left there – which usually includes judging whether they should have been.

Accordingly, any perceptual cue adapted from nature – such as occlusion, gradient change, foreshortening, horizon ratio, shading, highlight – though it work similarly in a picture, also works there differently, since it is experienced as being there on purpose, for purposes, which we seek. Questions why there is or is not a shaded shape at a certain place in a depiction, which guide our visual activities, not just our comments, would make no sense regarding an actual scene.[29] This applies not only to the means by which entities are shown in depictions, but also to represented entities.

Figure 6.2 *Max and Moritz* by Wilhelm Busch, 1865.

Letting comics reply to philosophy, consider a depiction of the philosopher Arthur Schopenhauer by one of the founders of the modern comic strip, Wilhelm Busch (Figure 6.2). Of some of its dark areas the question "what's that doing there?" has a very different meaning from what it could regarding an actual scene, where the answer, "in order to suggest a shadow," has no sense, since dark areas do not occur in inanimate nature for indicating shadows or any other purpose. The indicated shadow is in the picture for a reason: to work as a "Waltzian shadow," chiefly to place the main figure on the ground while, together with two crack or contour lines, relating him to other objects on a common "floor," while also indicating the direction of light. Such differences of experience carry to higher levels of interpretation, beyond the visual, and not just in order to be seen. For example, we reach the light, irreverent content of the picture when we see why the tail of the Pessimist's poodle (Atma or Butz) is raised. The reason would not be what it is in nature. The pictorial alone seems to include satirical intent, related as well to why the main figure is placed on a parallel plane to the dog's and holding his hat at a certain position and angle.

Thus Busch's picture has mental content. Its depiction is pretty clearly irreverent, comic satire of the philosopher "for the entertainment of the moment": no deep interpretation, also nothing trenchant, cutting or nasty, as in some newspaper political cartoons. That is part of its mental content. Its way of seeing, conceiving, being light, so is its style of drawing, and we thus experience the marks and the gestures that made it, partly understanding what they evoke through this awareness, which tells us why they are as they are. For example, besides the cast shadow and crack/contour we noticed, the drawing calls on several spatial perception cues for use similar to nature. As noted, in nature occlusion is the strongest depth indicator. Three occlusions are prominent here for ordinal recession into space: poodle ear barely nips philosopher's hem, philosopher's elbow overlaps potted tree, also interrupts the pavement line. The last not being also broken by the tree's marks, its placement behind is achieved by relative heights of bases in the field, which also help arrange the represented order: poodle, man, pot. Secondary occlusion ordinals include: tail, rump, head; thumb, hat, coat, trousers. That is why Busch put those natural space-perception affordances there, what they are doing in the picture, whereby they are transformed into intentional affordances for our perception. When we look at the picture we understand them as put there by another in order to produce certain mental effects in other viewers, including ourselves, as part of a perceptual community. Once we form a hypothesis about what a picture is doing, we look for like affordances, adjusting our hypotheses.

Our easy acceptance of this artist's use of such cues is complemented by acceptance of his not using others: he avoids color, relief shading, side-plane foreshortening, texture, diminution and other perceptual gradients. Absence of such natural cues is no more usefully described in terms of "conventions" than is our acceptance of any other artifact's possessing certain affordances of use and not others.[30] One picks up from others the intentional affordances of new tools and, if possible, uses them accordingly. Similarly with a great variety of depiction kinds, which we acquire from early childhood. This includes the variety of comics styles.

As earlier argued, essential to this approach to depiction is that in pictorial perception a selection of natural perceptual cues is taken over and mixed with a variety of other factors. Like most cartoonists, Busch relies minimally on cues for spatial layout, heavily on those for facial, physiognomic, and postural attitude recognition. The correspondence of the latter between man and dog are important to the humor. It is typical of depiction, not just in comics, to work by intentional analogies, occurring for definite purposes, which we look for. Again, our understanding of the intent with which cues are used and correspondences made – "getting it" – is crucial to our understanding of the depiction, and to its light satire. Of course, we can see actual situations in a like way. When we do, our view of them is termed "satiric," but the situations we see cannot be satiric. However, the picture that we see here is satiric. It expresses a benignly satiric idea of the philosopher, since it presents effective intentional affordances for experiencing its depiction of him that way. That is the style of the imaginary bubble around Busch's cartoon, which is even suggested by his sheet edge loosely drawn around it. Contrary to "visual scrutiny" views, although itself a visual presentation engaging visual recognition processes, even without its label the picture would contain much "in which the mind could participate": a light, irreverent mental conception presented through its intentional affordances for our seeing it.

Such is a beginning on our important subject of content by one example. Closer comic connoisseurship is needed, to show the many ways in which comics' devices work. But one example may be enough to show how the purposive aspect to our understanding of depictions is more than one more addition to the wide mix of factors that depictive experience may involve, a mix already separating it from natural visual perception. It amounts to more than a further freedom from direct response to environmental stimuli, in order "to re-create the world mentally and dream up endless new realities." Purpose runs across all the factors employed by artists, whether borrowed from nature or not. Since we take them as not only affordances but as intentional ones, and regarding a community of users, purpose directs our experiences of them, making possible the sharing of nonverbal conceptions. These conceptions may be light, humorous or irreverent regarding serious matters. Or they may be profound regarding what we would normally take to be mundane. Matters of high or low art, serious or "agreeable" art seem of less importance than comics' and other depictions' ability to express ways of taking things – their mental content. This freedom to put things before ourselves and others – not just to react – lightly or seriously, even without words, constitutes an important part of our mental life and consciousness.

Notes

1   Wilhelm Busch's 1865 strip *Max and Moritz* is generally credited as the direct basis for Rudolph Dirks's 1897 *Katzenjammer Kids*, which widely popularized a number of visual devices that became standard to comics. Uniquely spanning a period from the nineteenth century to the twenty-first, *Katzenjammer Kids* is the longest-running syndicated strip.

2   A main, distinct comics genre not based on joke forms is the serial fiction strip, including *Dick Tracy*, *Mary Worth*, *Rex Morgan* and a host of superhero strips, such as *Superman* and *Batman*, which share with the others fictionality through some combination of text and depiction in mass medium form.

3   Kant (2007: section 44). Obviously, jokes are not always light, and their points not always agreeable. Any so-called "agreeable art" can be turned to not so agreeable purposes. There is a history of serious comics, including *Maus* and *Doonsbury*, for notable examples, that use the lighter genre's means as a mode of access to deeply troubling matters, dealt with seriously.

4   But, as Aristotle remarked, people "who carry humor to excess are considered buffoons, striving after humor at all costs, aiming more at getting laughs than at saying what is appropriate . . . while those who can neither make a joke nor put up with those who do are considered boorish" (2009: Book IV, Chapter 8).

5   On "sustaining recognition," see Podro (1998).

6   Also for mediocrity. On the drop-off in comics artistry, see Spiegelman (2000).

7   Notably, Carrier (2001). Scott McCloud (1993: Chapter 6) offers general hypotheses about early links between words and images, historically broken.

8   The example and its interpretation are owing to Lisa Bessette, "Corbie Psalter," in Holcomb *et al.* (2009: 36–38). Further comments on medieval drawing touch on themes developed by Melanie Holcomb in "Strokes of Genius: The Draftsman's Art in the Middle Ages", in Holcomb (2009: 3–34).

9   Thus, the sculptor Antony Gormley describes a John Constable: "a small sketch in oil and pigment on board captures that most fleeting of things – the effect of sunlight on water vapour in our atmosphere. Here are ever-changing forms that evoke time, space and the act of being itself, but they are also an invitation to empathise with the exchange systems in our atmosphere. Single dry brushstrokes capture high cirrus against the thin, cold, high air, while rotating brushstrokes evoke the lower nimbus clouds that form hovering masses of white just above our heads. This sketch is another object that locates us within the scheme of things, showing our ability to engage in elemental exchanges" (2010: 15).

10   See Baxandall (1988).

11   This is not the more common question of how depictions can represent things and situations and how we know which ones they do (iconography), although it bears on that.

12   The idea is first stated by Alberti in his *Della Pittura*, and has been refined in a number of places, notably, in the eighteenth century by Brook Taylor, who invented terms such as "vanishing point."

13   These two quotations are from Podro ms (2006) and (2008: 346ff), with insertions from Podro ms (2010: 457), a later draft of (2006). The text also has unnoted elisions for smoothness.

14   Pinker (1997: 215ff). A more careful expression of the influential projective account is psychologist James J. Gibson's (later repudiated by him): "A faithful picture is a delimited physical surface processed in such a way that it reflects (or transmits) a sheaf of light-rays to a given point which is the same as would be the sheaf of rays from the original to that point" (1954: 14). Linear perspective and other projection systems themselves are usually exposited in terms of hypothetical projection from real or notional spatial layouts to surfaces.

15   Gombrich (1960). Gombrich's main insights still go widely unrecognized. Thus neuroscientist V. S. Ramachrandran states that "artists through trial and error, ... genius have discovered the figural primitives of our perceptual grammar. They are tapping into these and creating for your brain the equivalent" of natural stimuli, paraphrasing Gombrich's words nearly fifty years earlier. See Ramachandran (2003).

16   Ramachrandran (2008); also Ramachrandran (Ramachandran, 2003).

17   Tinbergen (1953), using the term "supernormal stimuli." For a short, more recent study of peak shift, see Ryan (1998). Ramachandran's "neuro-aesthetics" features principles of visual response carried over to image-making from environmental perception, including peak shift, grouping, contrast, isolation, perception problem solving, symmetry, closure, balance, metaphor and others. This carries his account well beyond simple "bird brain" neural-structure responses.

18   Ramachandran suggests a method of generating caricatures (possibly funny ones) through peak shift. Some sort of average face image is produced, which is "subtracted" from the same sort of portrayal of the target, the differences showing what is particular to the individual – thus, likely, a striking likeness. These differences are then increased to the extent of caricature required, notably a funny one. While norms may sometimes figure in the process, questionable are his terms "change the image," "hyperbole," "distortion," which appear to have reference to the visual image, which Ramachandran rightly puts aside by the standard homunculus regress argument. Gulls presumably do not compare "supernormal stimuli" to normal ones. Likewise, there is often gratuitous comparison made between comic depiction devices and naturalistic ones, without evidence offered of the former working off the latter – as they do in some cases. Mayan depiction, for example, has instances of what might be comic expression (usually ghastly), absent contact with any naturalistic traditions.

19   Better, for example, than McCloud's diagram (1993: 52 ff.), which arranges comics styles within a triangle, with a "realistic" or "resemblance" corner, allegedly based on "retinal images," besides "meaning" and "abstraction" corners.

20 Thus, advertising designer George Lois, in the film documentary "Art & Copy" (Doug Pray, dir., 2009), asserts that good ads are "poison gas" – see them and tears start (limbic system effect) – capable of "manufacturing any feeling you want."

21 Human Origins Hall, American Museum of Natural History, New York. On this evidence is often inferred probable possession of language.

22 On the basic duality of visual neural streams, see Milner and Goodale (1995).

23 "Odysseus & Boreas", Ashmolean Museum, Oxford, painted skyphos http://www.theoi.com/Gallery/T28.5.html

24 One philosophical visual approach that might appear to address depictive mental content postulates a peculiar kind of visual experience, called "seeing-in," an experience which is said to feature "permeability to thought" (see Wollheim 1998: 224). However Wollheim appears chiefly to mean the possible range of depictive subject-matter, whereas our topic is how subject-matter is presented: as funny, for example.

25 See Tomasello (1999: 84, 91). For earlier and more recent related accounts, see Tomasello and Call (1997) and Tomasello *et al.* (2009).

26 Kant (2007: section 20 ff.) postulates the expectation of a universal commonness of responses ("sensus communis") of delight, in judgments of beauty.

27 Tomasello has revised earlier views about perceiving others' goals as unique to humans, but not his distinct thesis that only humans perceive things in terms of artifacts, in terms of "shared intentionality." A more extended version of the present argument appears in Patrick Maynard, "What Drawing Draws On: The Relevance of Current Vision Research", in *"Disegno,"* ed. R. Casati, *Rivista di Estetica* n.s. 47, 2011: 9–29.

28 Pictorial depictions are carbon-dated to between thirty and forty thousand years ago, carved horn figures to about the same, and claims have been made for much earlier pieces by hominids. The most modern version of our species is dated from around fifty thousand years ago, partly on evidence of these very depictions.

29 Visual design – notably architectural, landscape, city – provides interesting exceptions to this, deserving detailed study as such. That an aspect of design is to make certain features of things more salient to view opens topics of ornament, bodily attire, and so forth. Finally, much of the ambivalence about photography being an art rests precisely on unclarity about what is on purpose, for reasons.

30 Corresponding tools in different cultures often differ for cultural reasons. But learning, for example, to use Asian push or European pull saws, thereby working abductor or adductor muscles, is not well described as acquiring different sawing conventions.

References

Aristotle. *Nicomachean Ethics*, trans. W.D. Ross. Oxford, Clarendon Press, 1908.

Baxandall, M. *Painting and Experience in Fifteenth Century Italy: A Primer in the Social History of Pictorial Style*, 2nd ed., Oxford: Oxford University Press, 1988.

Carrier, D. *The Aesthetics of Comics*, University Park, PA.: Pennsylvania State University Press, 2001.

Gibson, J.J. "A Theory of Pictorial Perception," *Audio-Visual Communication Review* 1, 1954.

Gombrich, E.H. *Art and Illusion: A Study in the Psychology of Pictorial Representation*, London: Phaidon, 1960.

Gormley, A. "Art's Lost Subject," *Saturday Guardian*, 13 February 2010, "Review": 15.

Holcomb, M. *Pen and Parchment: Drawing in the Middle Ages*, New York: Metropolitan Museum of Art, 2009.

Kant, I. *Critique of Judgment*, trans J.C. Meredith, Oxford: Oxford University Press, 2007.

McCloud, S. *Understanding Comics: The Invisible Art*, New York: HarperCollins, 1993.

Milner, D. and M. Goodale, *The Visual Brain in Action*, Oxford: Oxford University Press, 1995.

Pinker, S. *How the Mind Works*, New York: Norton, 1997.

Podro, M. *Depiction*, London: Yale University Press, 1998.

Podro, M. "Truth," Association of Art Historians, "Exchanges at the Interface between Art History and Philosophy" conference, Leeds University, 12 March 2006.

Podro, M. Review of Patrick Maynard, *Drawing Distinctions: The Varieties of Graphic Expression*, *British Journal of Aesthetics* 8 (3), 2008.

Podro, M. "Literalism and Truthfulness in Painting," *British Journal of Aesthetics* 50, October 2010.

Ramachandran, V.S. "The Artful Brain," *3 of The Emerging Mind, BBC Reith Lectures*, 2003.

Ramachrandran, V.S. "Aesthetic Universals and the Neurology of Hindu Art," CISAS lecture, 12 November 2008, available on YouTube.

Ryan, M.J. "Sexual Selection, Receiver Biases, and the Evolution of Sex Differences," *Science* 281, 25 September 1998: 1999–2003.

Spiegelman, A. "Abstract Thought Is a Warm Puppy," *The New Yorker*, February 14, 2000: 61–63.

Tinbergen, N. *The Herring Gull's World*, London: Collins, 1953.

Tomasello, M. *The Cultural Origins of Human Cognition*, Cambridge, MA: Harvard University Press, 1999.

Tomasello, M. and J. Call, *Primate Cognition*, Oxford: Oxford University Press, 1997.

Tomasello, M. et al., *Why We Cooperate*, Cambridge, MA: MIT Press, 2009.

Wollheim, R. "On Pictorial Representation," *Journal of Aesthetics and Art Criticism* 56 (3), 1998: 217–226.

The Language of Comics[1]

Darren Hudson Hick

Introduction

A comic, I take it, consists in a deliberate series of images ("panels"), usually incorporating textual elements, and typically employed for narrative purposes. This is, I admit, a fairly bare description, and, for our purposes here, of limited use. I do not intend it as an essentialist definition of comics. Indeed, I suspect such a definition may not be possible. Rather, the overarching question I seek to answer here is whether it is at all accurate, illuminating, or meaningful to speak of comics as constituting a *language*.

The notion that comics might constitute a language has some history, particularly as offspring to the project of the "language of film," largely sparked by Christian Metz, and the more general project of semiotics – the study of signs and sign systems. Following decades of work on the semiotic project of cinema ("cinesemiotics"), semioticians have more recently turned their collective eye on comics, with particularly focused work undertaken by Ulrich Krafft (1978), Benoît Peeters (1998), and, most notably, Thierry Groensteen (1999/2007). (English-language studies, meanwhile, have largely been the product of practicing comics artists, including Will Eisner (1985) and Scott McCloud (1993)). In the field of analytic philosophy, the general semiotic project is questioned – not because it is necessarily uninteresting, but because it is purportedly based on a misleading, ambiguous, or altogether false conception of language. To the semiotician, a language is simply a culturally-embedded system of signs. On this understanding, there is a language of architecture, a language of music, and even a language of

The Art of Comics: A Philosophical Approach, First Edition.
Edited by Aaron Meskin and Roy T. Cook.
© 2012 Blackwell Publishing Ltd. Published 2012 by Blackwell Publishing Ltd.

fashion. To the semiotician, each of these is a language in very much the same way as English, Welsh, or German is a language. The analytic philosopher of language, conversely, is centrally concerned with *natural* languages (and to a lesser extent constructed and formal languages), to be distinguished from sign systems generally. In this domain, to speak of film – or, in our case, comics – as a language is an anathema.

Much of this article will be framed around an argument by Gregory Currie, in which he works to undermine the semiotic notion of a language of film. Given that not once in Currie's article on the subject does he mention comics, this may seem a strange strategy on my part. However, while Currie's central target is cinesemiotics, his broader target is the seemingly all-encompassing semiotic use of the term "language," and so it is not hard to imagine that if his attack on cinesemiotics is successful, any suggestion of comics as a language will fall under the same barrage (or else, without much difficulty, shortly there-after). I will suggest that although there are difficulties to treating comics as a language comparable to natural languages, it is not unreasonable to discuss the form as being in many ways language-*like*, or as constituting a *pseudo*-language.

A Pre-Emptive Strike

In "The Long Goodbye: The Imaginary Language of Film," Currie argues that while films can indeed be meaningful, this sort of meaning is not *semantic* meaning – the meaning of languages – and so does not imply a language of film. Here, I suspect, Currie would say much the same of comics. Natural languages, Currie centrally contends, are *productive* and *conventional* – productive in that they allow for an indefinite number of expressions within that language, and conventional in that the meaning units of natural languages (typically, words) are determined not because of any natural affinity between them and what they signify (or any natural human disposition to so connect them), but simply because they are used in practice for communication. Put another way, words are entirely arbitrary signifiers of meaning, and come to mean what they mean solely through regularity of use in a speech community. Rules of composition allow us to combine these base meaning units into more complex meaningful sentences. Currie states:

> Since the atoms – words in English – are assigned meanings individually, and since the composition rules make the meaning of the whole a function of the meanings of the parts, we can say that meaning in our language is *acontextual*. The meaning of a given word is determined by its meaning-convention, not by the meanings of other words, and not by anything else; the meanings of sentences depend only on the meanings of the words in them. (Currie 1993/2006: 93)

In other words, on Currie's view, linguistic (semantic) meaning is determined solely by the wholly conventional meanings of the individual words, and the compositional rules of that language.

Conversely, the meaning in film, Currie argues, is *story meaning*, and not semantic meaning *per se*. Story meaning, Currie suggests, is a variety of *utterance meaning*, something that goes beyond mere semantic meaning. Where semantic meaning is acontextual, utterance meaning is heavily contextualized – it is what one would reasonably suppose that an utterer meant in making some given utterance in some given context. A gesture can be meaningful in a given context – that is, it can serve to express an utterance – but it will not thus constitute an element of a language. We understand a gesture because we are rational beings, not because there are *rules* to gestures. Words, too, can express an utterance meaning, but this will be above and beyond the semantic meaning of the sentence spoken. For instance, when asked where my book is, you might respond, "Your book is on your desk." Here, we have a simple case of assertion – a statement of fact. However, if I am proctoring an exam, and it is about to begin, and I say "Your book is on your desk," I am clearly issuing a command – I am telling you to remove it. The semantic meaning in each case might be said to be identical, but the *utterance* meaning differs substantially. Currie thus allows the argument from George Wilson that a given shot in a film (suggested as the basic meaning unit in cinema) will be meaningful because of how it coherently fits into the rest of the film, but he notes this is not unlike the use of language in literature. As we do not want to say that, for example, English literature employs a different *language* than other English writing, Curries argues, we similarly cannot thus use the notion of story meaning as a basis to a language of film.

Currie considers another possible strategy for establishing the existence of such a language: that films employ *appearance meaning*, and that story meaning is equivalent to (or arises from) this. Appearance meaning is, roughly, what event a cinematic image (frame, shot, scene) *seems* to record, and this constructively contributes to the meaning of the film as a whole. However, Currie argues, while appearance meaning may be story meaning, it is non-conventional in nature: "it is not possible to identify any set of conventions that function to confer appearance meaning on cinematic images in anything like the way in which conventions confer (semantic) meaning on language" (Currie 1993/2006: 96). While *productive* (allowing for an indefinite number of expressions), appearance meaning is *non-conventional* in nature. Rather, following Flint Schier, Currie argues that appearance meaning is "naturally generative" – it is because photographic images bear a reliable likeness to their subjects that we can understand them, and not because of any conventionality. Appearance meaning, in other words, cannot ground a language model of film because appearance meaning is non-conventional.

Now, Currie's target is the notion of film-as-a-language, but it seems evident that if his argument is damning for film, it may prove damning for the notion of comics-as-a-language as well. First, as Francis Lacassin points out, many of the elements of film "language" are lifted from, or else mirror those, of comics,[2] and other terms of cinematic vocabulary – *frame, shot, scene* – have become standard comics vocabulary (Lacassin 1972). Second, because of this interrelation, many of the strategies employed by semioticians in arguing for a language of comics are founded upon those used to argue for a language of film. Where falls one, it would seem, there falls the other.

Let us consider first Currie's contention that languages as we normally understand them are composed of wholly conventional meaning-units. On Currie's view, the terms we use in language – *run, of, pickle* – are used arbitrarily, and any other sound/letter combination would work as well. Accordingly, words mean what they mean simply because we use them the way that we do. In his influential essay, "On a New List of Categories," C.S. Peirce outlines a taxonomy of signs, such that a sign (one thing which refers to another) is either an *icon*,[3] an *index*,[4] or a *symbol*. An icon is a sign which refers to an object in virtue of its own character. We might think, for example, of the images used on bathroom doors to indicate men and women – these act as signs and mean what they mean because they resemble the objects they refer to. An index is a sign which refers to an object by virtue of being affected by that object. Smoke, for instance, is taken as a sign of fire: smoke *means* fire.[5] Finally, a symbol, in Peirce's system, is a sign which refers to an object by the fact that it is used and understood as such. As William Alston puts the matter, "[W]hat really demarcates symbols is the fact that they have what meaning they have by virtue of the fact that for each there are rules in force, in some community, that govern their use" (Alston 1964: 57–58). Words in language, Currie contends, are symbols of this kind. Conversely, if appearance meaning *is* meaning (which Currie grants for the sake of argument), it would seem to be so in virtue of being iconic.

However, it is not at all clear that this division is so neat and clean as Peirce – or, for our purposes, Currie – contends. On the one hand, it isn't clear that the meaning units of language (standardly, words) are straightforwardly conventional in the sense of being arbitrary, and on the other, it seems just as unclear that something like appearance meaning is entirely unconventional in how it means. First, there are a number of ways that words may derive their meaning at least in large part from their resemblance to things in the world. We might first look to onomatopoeic words ("phonomimes") – a larger class than one might expect: *bang, boom, chug, click, clump, drip, fizzle, flap, flip, moan, murmur, pop, scratch, sizzle* … It seems fairly clear that such words gain their meaning in virtue of sounding like those things to which they refer. Other words, like the Japanese "*shiin*" (the sound of silence), the English "twinkle" (the blinking of light), and the more specific "bling" (the glinting of light off of precious metals and stones, and the objects themselves), while not sounding *like* anything – because what they "sound" like do not make sounds – nevertheless operate like standard onomatopoeia.[6] Perhaps surprisingly, such mimetic words may not be entirely isolated in kind. Following an experiment by psychologist Wolfgang Köhler (1947), neurologists Vilayanur S. Ramachandran and Edward Hubbard presented English-speaking American and Tamil-speaking Indian college students with two abstract drawings, one jagged in shape, and the other curvy. Participants were asked which was named "kiki" and which "bouba." In each case, 95% to 98% of respondents named the spiky shape "kiki" and the rounded one "bouba." (Ramachandran and Hubbard 2001) Ramachandran and Hubbard suggest that this "kiki/bouba effect" points at a more general non-arbitrariness in the naming of objects, and to a neurological basis for the naming of things.[7] The arbitrariness of language meaning-units may be further eroded by looking to such linguistic systems as American Sign Language and Egyptian hieroglyphs, where meaning-units seem almost entirely selected on mimetic bases. My point is not that language is *non*-conventional – for instance, it seems a matter of convention that water *drips* from a faucet, and does not *plip* – but rather to show that words are not *entirely* arbitrary in their conventionality, and that the line between icons and symbols is not so easily drawn.[8]

Currie's second contention is that the cinematic image is entirely non-conventional. Rather, he argues, it is naturally generative, with the meaning of its appearance depending solely upon a likeness to its subject. This, too, is a contentious matter. E.H. Gombrich, for one, famously questions the "myth of the innocent eye" in his *Art and Illusion*: "Whenever we receive a visual impression, we react by docketing it, filing it, grouping it in one way or another." (Gombrich 1969: 297) Gombrich, along with R.L. Gregory, has shown that even such seemingly non-conventional pictorial cues as depth perception in two-dimensional images are culturally informed. (Gregory and Gombrich 1973; see also Hudson 1960) Nelson Goodman suggests that realism lies:

> not in the quantity of information but in how easily it issues. And this depends on how stereotyped the mode of information is, upon how commonplace the labels and their uses have become. Realism is relative, determined by the system of representative standards given for a given culture or person at a given time. (Goodman 1976: 36–37)

On Goodman's view, an image does not look like its subject in virtue of natural generativity. Rather, "[t]hat a picture looks like nature often means only that it looks the way nature is usually painted" (Goodman 1976: 39).

Realism, Goodman contends, "is a matter of habit." (Goodman 1992: 97). Just how relative representations are to cultural conventions or individual perspectives is a matter of some debate. However, again, my point is not to show that images are *entirely* conventional – that their meaning is not *at all* dependent upon likeness – but to suggest that how we derive meaning from images is not entirely *without* convention. And again, it seems that the line between icons and symbols is a vague one. Rather than a strict distinction between conventional and non-conventional symbols, it would seem more reasonable to suggest that there exists a continuum from entirely conventional signs to entirely non-conventional ones, and that no divisive line can be drawn along this continuum so as to separate languages from non-languages.

Unlike film, comics normally consist of drawings rather than photographs.[9] And as a medium of storytelling, comics have developed a rather complex symbol system. As a sampling, with Western comics, if an artist puts an X in place of each eye in a cartooned character, we know that the character is dead. Spirals in place of the eyes indicate the character is hallucinating, or is under the influence of some other sort of dementia. Stars and/or jagged lines appearing around a part of a character's body tend to mean that that particular body part is in some sort of pain. The Xs on the face should not of course be presumed to actually be *on the face*. Stars and jagged lines do not start shooting out of an injured ankle in the world of the comics, for all the characters to see. These are visual metaphors. Iconography in Japanese comics (*manga*) is only more complex. While incorporating many of the symbols from Western comics,[10] *manga* includes visual metaphors of its own. A single prominent bead of sweat superimposed over the brow-line of a character typically indicates embarrassment or exasperation (while actual sweating is ordinarily depicted more realistically). A floating balloon emanating from a character's nose indicates the character is asleep, while blood dripping from the nose shows sexual or romantic infatuation. A stylized throbbing outline of a cruciform on a character's forehead shows anger or irritation, and heavy shading around a character's eyes typically indicates a vengeful attitude.

To these conventional indicators of internal states, we can add conventional indicators of external states. In particular, despite being composed of static images, comics have developed several conventions for showing motion. In Western comics, the most prominent conventions are speed-lines – lines tracing the movement of characters or things in the image, looking not entirely unlike airplane contrails.[11] In *manga*, quick movement is normally indicated rather by blurring the background around the moving object into a series of parallel lines. However much speed-lines and other visual metaphors might seem obvious, even non-conventional, studies have shown that comprehension of such iconography develops with continued reading, and is not immediately understandable to new readers. (Byram and Garforth 1980; Gross *et al.* 1991; Nakazawa 2005).

Finally, we can add what is probably the most dominant and discussed convention of comics: the speech balloon. Reminiscent of condensed breath in the winter air, speech balloons typically appear as elliptical enclosures of text shown to emanate from speakers in the comics panel according to a "tail" on the balloon pointing at the respective speaker.[12] The shape of the balloon may be modified in particular cases to indicate exclamation (with jagged edges), coldness (with "icicles" dripping from the bottom of the balloon), or mechanical speech (where a given speaker's balloons are squared-off and others' are not). A voice emanating from a truly mechanical source, like a radio, is typically shown with jagged edges and a lightning-bolt shaped tail to the balloon. Any number of variations have been toyed with by artists – some catching on and becoming standard conventions, and others not. Certainly the most revolutionary variant of the speech balloon is the thought bubble, a stylized cloud-shaped space enclosing text indicating a character's thoughts and connecting to the thinker by a chain of smaller ellipses.[13] On occasion, thought bubbles (and even rare speech bubbles) contain not text, but images, greatly expanding the potential of the convention. Despite David Carrier's claim that "almost everyone understands a commonplace comic strip without any need for explanation" (Carrier 2000: 85). whether a variant becomes standardly conventional or not seems to depend upon how easily it is incorporated by artists and grasped by readers.[14]

All this being said, such conventions, while systematic and predictable in effect, are certainly not the primary bearers of meaning in comics, none being essential to the comics form. (Indeed, strictly speaking, none of these conventions are even *peculiar* to comics.[15]) So how *do* comics centrally mean? What does it *mean* for them to mean? Do comics mean in a systematic or predictable manner? And, if so, is their meaning like or unlike the meaning of natural languages?

How Comics Mean

Throughout his essay, Currie holds to the view that words in a language carry individual semantic meaning, and that sentence meaning is merely a function of these and the rules of the language. As such, Currie contends, meaning in language is entirely acontextual.[16] This is a highly debatable view, and not a standard one in philosophy of language. The validity of this position would first seem to depend upon how we count words. Take a simple sentence: "The man went to the bank." On its face, the meaning of this sentence is ambiguous. "Bank," as a noun, can refer to a financial institution, to the edge of a river, or to a number of other things. Whether the sentence is true would seem to depend upon what is being expressed, and second on whether what is being expressed aligns with the world. Strictly speaking, however, sentences per se don't mean *anything* – they cannot be true or false. Rather, sentences typically express *propositions*, which do and can. We might think of a proposition as being the *content* of a sentence. Sentences considered apart from propositions are purely formal – they are just strings of symbols, and different strings of symbols can express the same proposition (for instance, in different languages), and the same string of symbols can express different propositions (as in our bank case).[17] In the best of cases, a sentence will provide accurate access to what is being expressed. But getting a handle on what is being expressed *may* require context. That is, the role of context in *fixing* meaning may be limited,[18] but it will certainly help one to *understand* meaning.

Where the basic units of natural languages are words, the basic units of comics would seem to be panels – discrete images in sequence. It might be said that, like sentences, pictures per se don't *mean* anything either. However, just as sentences can be bearers of meaning by expressing propositions, so too can pictures.

In his oft-referenced essay, "Meaning," Paul Grice outlines a case in which I show to Mr X a photograph of Mr Y "displaying undue familiarity" to Mrs X. Grice contends that this photograph does not *mean* anything (or at least anything non-naturalistic). However, should I *draw* a picture of Mr Y and Mrs X *in flagrante delicto* to show to Mr X, the picture *does* mean something, because the object operates as an utterance (where the photograph is merely a photograph) (Grice 1957/1989: 218–219). Although I question Grice's distinction between the photograph and the drawing, it seems reasonable, first, to think that a picture can express a proposition. However, at least in most cases, a picture will express many – perhaps innumerable – propositions. For example, if drawn from life, my picture of Mr Y and Mrs X will express not only the proposition that they were engaged in an extramarital affair, but that, for example, they were performing such-and-such an act, that he was wearing cowboy boots of such and such a sort, that they were seen from such-and-such an angle, that the lighting was just so, and so on.[19] A picture, as the story goes, is worth a thousand words.

There is a reason, however, that Grice picks just one proposition – it is the *central* or *salient* proposition being expressed in the drawing, with others serving at best in supporting roles. With stand-alone pictures (say, paintings), we have ways of focusing the viewer's attention on some one or more central propositions – by titling the picture, by focusing on particular elements, or by literally foregrounding a subject. Being composed of images, comics have these tricks at their disposal, and others besides, such as giving a central element a special lighting or coloring, bolding that element's outline, and so on.

But comics also provide a further option for focusing our attention on a given panel's salient propositions. Just as the context in which a sentence is uttered can help us to disambiguate its meaning, so too can reading the comics panel in sequence help us to determine the salient propositions expressed. When reading a comic strip or comics page, one understands that a given panel is one in a sequence, such that each panel "anticipates" the next, and refers to the one that came before it. In viewing one panel, we hypothesize a number of salient propositions from that panel, and these hypotheses are confirmed or disconfirmed by the following panels.[20] Of course, this is a simplistic case. A panel may refer back to another panel much earlier in the sequence, such that what seemed hypothetically salient when first reading Panel A, may seem disconfirmed by Panel B, but later reconfirmed by Panel Z. What seems unimportant early in a story may turn out to be critical later on. And it is for this same reason that we might *repeat* some panel again later in the strip, such that in its new sequential setting, different propositions are foregrounded – although it may be that, strictly speaking, all of the same propositions are expressed in the two pictorially identical panels.[21] This motif is used to particular effect, for instance, throughout Alan Moore and Dave Gibbons' *Watchmen*, with identical (or near-identical) panels repeated on the same page, pages later, or even chapters apart. On the third page of the first chapter, for example, we are shown a stocky man in a bathrobe being thrown through a plate-glass window, a smiley-face button, smudged with blood, flying from his chest. At this point in the story, we know only that he is a murder victim, the assailant unknown, with only his deeply-shadowed hands visible. When the same panel appears on the next-to-last page of the second chapter, however, we now know that the victim is Edward Blake, the Comedian, a retired superhero. The button is his only daily reminder of his former life. And when the panel appears this time, it is in the context of a story of *I Pagliacci*, the tragic clowns. It isn't until much later in the story that the identity of the murderer is revealed, and when the panel reappears a third time in the penultimate chapter of the book, it is as the murderer is recounting his actions, surrounding panels showing him committing the act.[22]

Subsequent panels may also intentionally serve only to muddy the issue of determining proposition salience – as in a great deal of poetry, what proposition is expressed or salient at a given point in a given work may be deliberately ambiguous. In this way, the meaning in comics does not seem simply additive, as would be the case with three images randomly placed next to each other, for instance with snapshots randomly arranged on a photo album page. The meaning of comics is not derived simply by summing all of the propositions in Panel A with those of Panel B, and so on. Rather, propositions are foregrounded or backgrounded (or made ambiguous) according to the panel's role(s) in the sequence. It should be noted that I am not centrally claiming that what propositions are *expressed* is context-sensitive (and so too the meaning of the picture), but that which of the propositions is *foregrounded* or made *salient* is contextual within limits. Granted that this is not a fully determinate system, while any one panel may express innumerable propositions, and likewise for each successive panel in the sequence, we might nevertheless reasonably say that we can *understand* that comic as a whole work by focusing on what has been foregrounded as salient in the work.[23]

We are, of course, drifting into what Currie refers to as utterance meaning – what a sentence would reasonably be *taken* to mean in a given context, and what Currie equates with the story meaning of a film. However, as I have shown, the line between semantic meaning and utterance meaning, too, is difficult to draw. A sentence *may* express any number of propositions, and context may help us to discover just which proposition that sentence actually expresses. An image, meanwhile, *does* express any number of propositions – it *means* a lot of things – and context helps us to determine which of these are salient to understanding a comic's narrative.

Part of the problem of discussing the semantics of comics is that the meaning of a comic seems not reducible by paraphrasing. Above, I made the distinction between a sentence and the proposition that it expresses, such that we might understand the sentence as the form and the proposition as its expressed content. On such a view, a given sentence is conversationally replaceable with another sentence that expresses the same proposition. However, as is often argued with regard to literature in general and poetry in particular, the poem's form is just as much a determinant of meaning as are the propositions expressed by its sentences. Dorothy Walsh puts the point nicely: "Poetry, when successful, is […] a fixed precise, unalterable whole in which what is expressed is completely expressed. For this reason, no separation can be made between what is said and how it is said. No re-expression is possible and no translation is possible" (Walsh 1938: 80). Any given word in a poem is not simply replaceable with a synonym. The issue in comics is similar.

Goodman contends that, like literature, pictures consist of a set of signs, and so for this reason can be meaning-bearing. However, he argues, pictorial systems are irreducibly *dense*, both syntactically and semantically (Goodman 1976: 226–227). Any two marks, no matter how small the difference between them, could instantiate different symbols – could point to different referents. That is, he suggests, *every* line, *every* contour, *every* color contributes inexorably to the meaning of a picture. For this reason, Goodman maintains, while literature admits of a notational system (a system of rules for discrete symbol use), pictures do not. Rather, removing or changing any one element changes the meaning of the picture. The meaning of a picture is determined not only by *what* propositions are being expressed by that picture, but also by *how* they are expressed – how they are drawn. We might as such make a comparison here with the semantic distinction between *sense* and *reference*. At least on a rough understanding, Gottlob Frege distinguishes between a given word's referent (that which it picks out in the world) and its sense (the mode of presentation for the referent – *how* it refers to that thing).[24] While both "Mark Twain" and "Samuel Clemens" refer to the same individual, the sentence "Mark Twain *is* Samuel Clemens" is not a vacuously true one. That is, it isn't the same as saying "Mark Twain *is* Mark Twain." Although both names have the same referent, each seems to carry some meaning over and above that of the reference, and this reflects the proposition behind the sentence. Similarly, two drawings may refer to the same scene,[25] but as drawn by two artists (or by the same artist in two styles), will almost certainly *do* so differently. A highly iconographic, stylized, or "cartoony" image may represent the same referent as well as a highly realistic rendering – but, so far as meaning is concerned, the one is not simply equivalent to (exchangeable with) the other. Consider, for example, the origin story of Batman. The story has been told and retold, with details added and removed, but the basic story remains the same: young Bruce Wayne along with his parents, Thomas and Martha, is accosted by a hoodlum, who, in a botched robbery attempt, kills both parents, leaving young Bruce alive. Let us take that single moment when Thomas Wayne is shot. First shown in 1939 (*Batman* #33), Batman's creator Bob Kane depicts the moment from a middle distance, the reader's eye at a position to Thomas Wayne's back-right. Wayne and the killer are the only two shown, bathed in a yellow light, Wayne's hat flying forward as he is shot. In 1948 (*Batman* #47), Kane depicts the same moment, from roughly the same angle, but this time backed up so that Martha and young Bruce are visible, as is the surrounding scenery. In 1976 (*Detective Comics* #457), artist Dick Giordano did not show any of the Waynes at all, instead depicting only the gunman firing his weapon. In 1986 (*Batman: The Dark Knight Returns* #1), meanwhile, Frank Miller shows only the bullet cartridge being expelled from the mugger's pistol. Precisely the same scene at precisely the same moment is depicted, but each artist draws it not only from a different angle and at a different depth of vision, but each also in his own distinctive style. One could not simply be replaced with another without some effect on meaning. Among other things, given their respective styles of drawing, dropping Kane's panel into the middle of Miller's sequence would add an inappropriate humor to the moment, while inserting Giordano's panel into Kane's sequence would make the scene far more gruesome than in the original. Although each panel depicts precisely the same moment in Batman's origin story, to say that one panel *means* the same thing as another is like saying that "Mark Twain" means the same thing as "Samuel Clemens."

The Unified Comic

An apparent difficulty for a language of comics, on this analysis, is that only rarely do comics consist solely in pictorial elements, and to eliminate the written word from an analysis of the language of comics would be as egregious an error as that of including text in an essentialist definition of the form.[26] Words appear in word balloons, thought bubbles, narrative blocks, and free-floating in comics as "sound effects." The difficulty, then, as many attest, is that reading words and reading pictures are essentially different kinds of reading. On Goodman's view, words and pictures involve wildly different symbol systems, and so distinct modes of reading. Carrier contends, "If verbal and visual arts differ in kind, then they demand different, essentially opposed forms of attention" (Carrier 2000: 72).[27] And, as Benedetto Croce maintains, "division destroys the work, just as dividing a living organism into heart, brain, nerves and muscles and so on changes a living thing into a corpse" (Croce 1992: 21–22). The irony, of course, is that the inclusion of textual elements appears to make it more *difficult* to argue that comics constitute a language. If comics involve essentially disparate forms of reading, how – if at all – can comics present a unified reading experience or a unified language? The matter is only further complicated by evidence that different parts of the brain are responsible for conceptualizing language and visuo-spatial input respectively.[28]

At the very least, one cannot seemingly read text at the same time one looks at an accompanying picture. One might think of the experience of watching a subtitled film: at any given time, one must attend either to the image or to the text, but one cannot do both at one and the same time. In comics, this problem is perhaps most evident in such cases as Hal Foster's *Prince Valiant*, consisting of large blocks of narrative and accompanying images, absent speech, or thought balloons. However, the same problem applies to standard cases in which text invades the panel in word balloons, thought bubbles, and sound effects.[29] Viewing pictures and reading words seem like entirely distinct sorts of activities. Dadaist art has often sought to undermine the word/image dichotomy, particularly in collage and photo-montage, by asking us to read pictures, and to view words – to treat each according to the semiotic model for the other, and ultimately to undermine our disparate experiences of visual and literary art forms by intermingling them. Dadaist techniques have been appropriated in comics by such diverse artists as Bill Sienkiewicz (*Stray Toasters*) and Bill Griffiths (*Zippy the Pinhead*), but what is curious about such works is that they largely have *not* been transgressive in their effects, and have not played the same undermining role as in other media – instead, they point at a curious feature about the comics form: here, there is no clear divide between the visual and the verbal.

We *treat* the text in comics as an image, and not merely as a discrete textual element. This is clearest in the use of in-panel sound effects, where text is highly stylized to reflect the sound being represented: loud sounds are represented with large text, quiet sounds with small text, eerie sounds with wiggly text, and so on. Such visual sound effects operate as design elements within the panel, drawing and manipulating the eye of the reader, and telling us something *about* the sound. Titles within the comic may operate similarly. However, sound effects and titles are not the only textual elements we treat as images in comics – they are simply the most obvious. Consider again the subtitled film. In standard cases, within a threshold of legibility, it does not matter what font is used for the subtitles. In this, the text operates much like that in standard cases of literature: a serif font is exchangeable with a sans-serif font with neither gain nor loss in meaning. This is not, however, the case with comics.

In the vast majority of comics, text is hand-rendered or else designed to imitate hand-lettering. Joseph Witek notes, "[F]reehand lettering, no matter how precisely done, always betrays the calligrapher's hand, and thus more closely approximates the nuances of the human voice than does mechanically produced type."[30] In his masterful strip, *Pogo*, Walt Kelly went a step further, lettering particular characters' speech in ornate script, in Gothic lettering, or in the style of circus posters, in each case to add tone or style to the voice. The hand-lettered text in a word-balloon or narrative block cannot simply be replaced with mechanical type without some predictable effect. Hal Foster, for one, used Leroy lettering, a form of clean, sans-serif mechanical type. On occasion, artists will use a Roman typeface. In each case, however, the style of presentation for the text contributes to the work's meaning in much the same manner as an artist's way of drawing a scene contributes inexorably to its meaning. In comics, all text is, in principle, an image, and operates at such. All this is not to say that text ceases to *be* text in comics, but that *as* text, it is not ontologically isolated from the comics' pictorial elements, as it is in illustrated books (including illustrated children's books), newspapers, and even captioned single-panel cartoons. Where the typeface or lettering style in such forms does not standardly contribute to the work's meaning (it is exchangeable with another style), in comics the text's style is never a meaning-neutral element. When text makes up part of the comic, it becomes a part of the irreducibly dense picture-field, in which no visual element is superfluous to meaning, including textual presentation. In other words, when one is reading the text in a comic, one *is* looking at a picture.[31]

So far, we have been speaking of comics as being composed of panels, and these as the basic structural and meaning units of comics. Each panel, I have suggested, expresses innumerable propositions, and the panel's place in the narrative sequence serves to make salient certain of these. However, if Goodman is correct in thinking that pictures are irreducibly dense as conveyors of meaning, to speak of comics panels as discrete meaning-units is itself a misleading abstraction – for each panel is not truly experienced discretely, but as a part of a larger visual matrix: the comics page.[32] Put another way, strictly speaking, a comics page is not composed of several drawings, but of one.[33] In relatively simple cases, panels are arranged on the comics page as a grid, maintaining the conception of panels as simply discrete sequenced pictures read in tiers, left to right, top to bottom.[34] However, as some artists have shown, the matter is not so simple as this.

Figure 7.1 *Xenozoic Tales*, Issue 13, Page 18, by Mark Schultz.
© 1994 Mark Schultz, used with permission of the author.

Consider Figure 7.1, a full page from Mark Schultz's *Xenozoic Tales*. On this page, our hero Tenrec is being hunted by the villain Balclutha. As with a work of prose, the eye habitually gravitates toward the top left corner of the page. Schultz takes advantage of this convention and begins his manipulation of the reader's eye here. The eye will focus first on the most visually prominent element of the top left, the dinosaur. The reader's eye follows the curvature of the dinosaur's body to the beginning of the speed line bisecting the panel. The eye follows the straight speed line, past Tenrec, and to the arrow, which points into panel two. Following the same path, the eye moves past the image of Balclutha, up the twisted vine, and to the foot of the now-fleeing Tenrec. The eye again follows the vine and Tenrec's fleeing foot into panel three. Following the same line across the bottom of this first tier of panels, the eye sees Balclutha climbing the same vine, and follows this vine down to the second tier, where it points almost directly at the image of Balclutha, now running across a tree-bridge. The eye follows the prominent curved tree limb away from Balclutha, down to the swinging Tenrec, and from here down to the third tier, directly into Balclutha's word balloons. The eye moves from the third of the word balloons, down the shaft of the bow, and across the arrow which points into the final panel. The line of the eye moves from the tip of the arrow, to the poised body of Tenrec, along the bent tree limb, through Tenrec's word balloon, and ends at the image of Balclutha, hunched unawares.

To look at this page as being composed simply of six discrete panels is a myopic view. Certainly, Schultz works more than most with the page as a single visual field – as a single drawing – but as Harvey notes, "Only in the comics can the field of vision be so manipulated: the size and arrangement of images control our perception to the events depicted, contributing dramatically to the narrative effects produced" (Harvey 1996: 162). Comics are not merely a narrative medium; each comics page is at one and the same time also a static picture. And just as composition operates within each comics panel, so too does it operate within the comics page as a whole. And so, while the narrative positioning of a panel serves to make salient certain propositions expressed in that panel, the panel as a whole also operates as an aspect of the larger visual field, one deliberately designed. Just as the panel, as a unit, is irreducible in meaning, so too, as a unit, is the comics page – a visual field much greater in meaning than the sum of its discrete parts. Although not all comics artists will treat it as such, each comics page is in essence a single, stand-alone image, distinct from, but at the same overlapping, the narrative aspect of the comic.

Conclusion

We have, throughout the foregoing, investigated some of the many and unique ways in which comics serve as a partly-conventional, meaning-bearing, and (to at least some degree) predictably operant form of proposition communication. Comics express propositions through sequential images which serve to make salient certain of these propositions by virtue of each panel's role in the sequence. The inclusion of linguistic text in the comics form serves to complicate this system, but still operates in part as a meaning-bearing image. The comics sequence itself is typically broken down and organized on discrete pages, or else in strips, each of these serving as a visual unit, itself an irreducibly dense vehicle of meaning. Is all this enough to constitute a *language* of comics? One of the problems with comics is that rarely if ever do we encounter them in a non-narrative form – even the in-flight instruction pamphlets on airplanes use comics in a narrative manner.[35] This being the case, it is difficult to speak of a "language of comics" in any truly abstracted way. Indeed, treating comics as analogous to natural languages presents an array of perhaps intractable difficulties not discussed by Currie. While this chapter has focused largely on semantic issues, the notion of a *syntax* of comics is a difficult concept to even wrap one's head around.[36] Although we have been treating comics panels (and perhaps pages) as basic syntactic units, given their irreducible denseness, it is not at all clear how (if at all) systematized concatenation rules might even be described – and if there *are* such formalizable rules, we certainly don't know them. Moreover, while the comics form seems especially well suited to storytelling, how the form might be used to, say, pose a question, feels strange to even ask.[37] However, as I believe I have shown, the line that Currie seeks to draw between languages and non-languages is substantially blurrier than he presents it. And although discussing comics *as* a natural language is perhaps a stretch, it seems not unreasonable to talk of them as being language-*like* – as constituting a *pseudo*-language – operating in *many* ways like a natural language. As such, while perhaps not *entirely* accurate, the notion of a "language of comics" seems nevertheless both illuminating and meaningful, and not merely metaphorical.

Notes

1   My thanks to Christopher Hom, Heidi Tiedke, and David Miguel Gray for their input in my development of this essay, as well as to the editors, Aaron Meskin and Roy T. Cook, for their helpful comments. A substantial portion of this chapter is based on research undertaken for my M.Phil in 1998 at the University of Wales, Lampeter, under the late R.A. Sharpe.

2   Lacassin gives examples of aerial views, medium close-ups, extreme close-ups, and silhouetted figures.

3   Alternatively, a likeness or semblance.

4 Sometimes referred to as an indication, and sometimes simply as a sign.

5 On this view, smoke *means* fire "naturally."

6 Such words are sometimes called non-auditory onomatopoeia or phenomimes.

7 Ramachandran and Hubbard (2001).

8 Scott McCloud explores in detail and charts the gradiated "picture plane" of comics in Chapter 2 of *Understanding Comics* (see especially McCloud 1993: 52–53).

9 Currie puts aside discussion of animated film, and I will put aside comics composed of sequential photographs (as in the Italian tradition) – but not because I believe they will complicate my view.

10 Osama Tezuka, revered as the "father of manga," borrowed much of his character design and iconography from classic American animation, which employ many of the same symbol systems as comics.

11 Quick movement is also occasionally indicated by a series of strobe-like after-images of the moving object, or by a blurring of the lines of the moving object itself.

12 Variations on this formula are many, and the shapes of balloons may vary widely. On occasion, balloons may be done away with entirely with text simply floating in a neutral space over characters with a mere line pointing at the speaker (as in Garry Trudeau's *Doonesbury*). In Richard Outcault's *The Yellow Kid*, the title character "speaks" by having words appear on his long tunic. As well, comics may represent nonspecific speech by replacing text with illegible squiggles, nonspecific exclamation by using only question marks or exclamation marks in word balloons, or speechlessness by using entirely empty balloons. The Italian word for comics, *fumetti*, translated literally, means "little puffs of smoke," referring to speech balloons.

13 In *manga*, thought is normally depicted not in a thought bubble, but in a halo of exploding lines situated near the thinker. The distinction between speech balloons and thought bubbles is eroded in such comic strips as *Peanuts* and *Garfield*, in which animals "speak" in thought bubbles typically only understandable by other animals in the strips.

14 Wellman *et al.* note that while few three- and four-year-olds grasped the function of a thought bubble without instruction, if simply told that they show what characters are thinking, the vast majority of children easily understood the convention. See Wellman, Hollander, and Schult.

15 The iconography representing internal states of comics characters is used widely in animation. Even the speech balloon traces its origin back to Gothic painting (in which characters' speech is depicted on a scrolls emanating from the speakers' mouths), and perhaps to Pre-Colombian Mesoamerica, and is now used widely outside comics, particularly in advertising.

16 Presumably, Currie will have to allow for *some* contextuality in meaning, for such cases as indexicals (e.g., "here," "there," "I," "you").

17 It is worth noting that, while widespread, this propositional account of language is not without its detractors. That being said, I believe my argument could easily account for other competing accounts of meaning.

18   Here, for the sake of argument, I put aside such seemingly context-dependence semantic elements as indexicals (*I, you, here, there*).

19   It might be said that the picture expresses a single, complex proposition, itself composed of many "simple" propositions.

20   Much of literature in general, and poetry in particular, works along similar lines.

21   Groensteen walks through a related exercise. See Groensteen (1999/2007: 134–141).

22   Other good examples of this technique can be found in the work of Frank Miller (especially *Sin City*) and Daniel Clowes (e.g., *David Boring*).

23   Nakazawa treats an ability of readers to do just this as the test for comics "literacy." See Nakazawa (2005: 33–35).

24   See Frege (1984). I put aside, for the sake of simplicity, the fact that what is referred to in most – though by no means all – comics is fictional. While this causes problems for semantic theories generally, for the sake of argument, I hold to a view like Amie Thomasson's, that fictional objects are real things brought into existence in the act of artistic creation (involving referring to non-existent things), and are thereafter referred to in a relatively ordinary way. See Thomasson (1998).

25   Goodman contends, "A picture that represents – like a passage that describes – an object refers to and, more particularly, *denotes* it" (Goodman 1976: 5).

26   Despite the weight of counterexamples, some have continued to insist that the word-image relationship is essential to comics. See Carrier (2000: 4), Harvey (1996: 3), Harvey (2001: 75), Witek (1989: 6) for example.

27   Scott McCloud calls the word/image relationship in comics "more alchemy than science" (McCloud 1993: 161); R.C. Harvey calls it "an uneasy marriage" (Harvey 1996: 263).

28   To begin, see Sperry (1968).

29   This problem is not *peculiar* to comics in that all manner of media employ both word and image – newspapers, catalogues, illustrated texts, advertisements. The difference is that rarely does one encounter claims regarding the *language* of newspapers, catalogues, or illustrated texts (although advertisements are a semiotician's playground).

30   Witek (1989: 23). Today, many comics publishers use specially-designed fonts, although these still mimic hand-lettering.

31   See also Meskin (2009: 231).

32   I speak here of the print comics page, but we might also speak of the comic strip, or the double-page spread in comic books. Online comics offer an array of other possibilities.

33   Groensteen talks of the comics page as a "multiframe" (Groensteen 1999/2007: 24); Eisner calls it a "meta-panel" (Eisner 1985: 63).

34   In *manga*, following the reading convention in Japanese, panels are read right to left, top to bottom.

35   We might, however, look for examples of non-narrative comics in, for instance, Andrei Molotiu's edited comics anthology, *Abstract Comics* (Fantagraphics Books: 2009).

36   This is not to say that some have not tried. See Groensteen (1999/2007) and Saraceni (2003), for example. Following Metz (and before him Ferdinand de

Saussure), some have argued that film constitutes a *language*, but not a *langue* – that is, it is a meaning-bearing system, but lacking the strict grammar and syntax of a natural language.

37 Of course, this much seems equally true of a number of non-natural languages.

References

Alston, W.P. *Philosophy of Language*, Englewood Cliffs, NJ: Prentice Hall, 1964.

Byram, M. and C. Garforth. "Research and Testing Nonformal Education Materials: A Multi-media Extension Project in Botswana." *Educational Broadcasting International*, 13, 1980: 190–194.

Carrier, D. *The Aesthetics of Comics*, University Park, PA: Pennsylvania State University Press, 2000.

Croce, B. *The Aesthetic as the Science of Expression and of the Linguistic in General*, trans. C. Lyas, Cambridge: Cambridge University Press, 1992.

Currie, G. "The Long Goodbye: The Imaginary Language of Film," in N. Carroll and J. Choi (eds), *Philosophy of Film and Motion Pictures: An Anthology*, Oxford: Blackwell, 2006: 91–99 (originally published in *British Journal of Aesthetics*, 33(3), 1993: 207–219).

Eisner, W. *Comics and Sequential Art, Extended Edition*, Tamarac, FL: Poorhouse Press, 1985/1991.

Frege, G. "On *Sinn* and *Bedeutung*." in B. McGuinness (ed.), *Collected Papers on Mathematics, Logic, and Philosophy*, trans M. Black, Oxford: Blackwell, 1984: 56–78.

Gombrich, E.H. *Art and Illusion: A Study in the Psychology of Pictorial Representation*, 2nd ed., Princeton, NJ: Princeton University Press, 1969.

Gombrich, E.H. *The Essential Gombrich, ed.* R. Woodfield. London: Phaidon Press Limited, 1996.

Goodman, N. *Languages of Art: An Approach to a Theory of Symbols*, 2nd ed., Indianapolis, IN: Hackett Publishing Company, 1976.

Goodman, N. "Reality Remade: A Denotation Theory of Representation." in P. Alperson (ed.), *The Philosophy of the Visual Arts*. Oxford: Oxford University Press, 1992: 88–102.

Gregory, R.L. and E.H. Gombrich. *Illusion in Art and Nature*, London: Duckworth, 1973.

Grice, H.P. "Meaning," in *Studies in the Way of Words*. Cambridge: Harvard University Press, 1989: 213–223 (originally published in *Philosophical Review* 66, 1957: 377–388).

Groensteen, T. *The System of Comics*, trans. B. Beaty and N. Nguyen, Jackson, MS: University Press of Mississippi, 2007 (originally published as *Système de la bande dessinée*, Paris: Presses Universitaires de France, 1999).

Gross, D., N. Soken, K.S. Rosengren, A.D. Pick, B.H. Pillow, and P. Melendez "Children's Understanding of Action Lines and the Static Representation of Speed of Locomotion." *Child Development* 62(5), 1991: 1124–1141.

Harvey, R.C. *The Art of the Comic Book: An Aesthetic History*, Jackson, MS: University Press of Mississippi, 1996.

Harvey, R.C. "Comedy at the Juncture of Word and Image," in R. Varnum and C.T. Gibbons (eds), *The Language of Comics: Word and Image*, Jackson, MS: University Press of Mississippi, 2001: 75–96.

Hudson, W. "Pictorial Depth Perception in Sub-Cultural Groups in Africa." *Journal of Social Psychology*, 52, 1960: 183–208.

Köhler, W. *Gestalt Psychology*, 2nd ed., New York: Liveright, 1947.

Krafft, U. *Comics Lesen: Untersuchungen zur Textualität von Comics*, Stuttgart: Klett-Cotta, 1978.

Lacassin, F. "The Comic Strip and Film Language," *Film Quarterly* 26(1), 1972: 11–23.

McCloud, S. *Understanding Comics: The Invisible Art*, Northampton, MA: Kitchen Sink Press, 1993.

Meskin, A. "Comics as Literature?" *British Journal of Aesthetics* 49(3), 2009: 219–239.

Nakazawa, J. "Development of Manga (Comic Book) Literacy in Children," in D. Shwalb, J. Nakazawa, and B. Shwalb (eds), *Applied Developmental Psychology: Theory, Practice, and Research from Japan*, Greenwich, CT: Information Age Publishing, 2005: 23–42.

Peirce, C.S. "On a New List of Categories." *Proceedings of the American Academy of Arts and Sciences*, 7, 1868: 287–298.

Peeters, B. *Case, planche, récit. comment lire une bande dessinée.* Tournai: Casterman, 1998.

Ramachandran, V.S. and E.M. Hubbard. "Synaesthesia: A Window into Perception, Thought, and Language." *Journal of Conscious Studies* 8(12), 2001: 3–34.

Saraceni, M. *The Language of Comics*. New York: Routledge, 2003.

Sperry, R.W. "Hemisphere Deconnection and Unity in Conscious Experience." *American Psychologist* 23, 1968: 723–733.

Thomasson, A. *Fiction and Metaphysics*, Cambridge: Cambridge University Press, 1998.

Walsh, D. "The Poetic Use of Language," *Journal of Philosophy* 35(3), 1938: 73–81.

Wellman, H.M., M. Hollander, and C.A. Schult, C.A. "Young Children's Understanding of Thought Bubbles and of Thoughts." *Child Development* 67, 1996: 768–788.

Witek, J. *Comic Books as History: The Narrative Art of Jack Jackson, Art Spiegelman, and Harvey Pekar*, Jackson, MS: University Press of Mississippi, 1989.

Part Three

Comics and the Other Arts

Making Comics into Film

Henry John Pratt

Film has always been an art form that depends heavily on adaptation from other media, including literature, theater, folk tales, video games, and even amusement park rides. The oldest surviving American feature film is an adaptation of Shakespeare's *Richard III*, and in fact, the American film industry originally settled in Hollywood partly in an effort to escape paying for the rights to literature published in New York.

Recently, films adapted from or based on comics have become commonplace. By my count, including only those in English that have received cinematic release, at least 125 films have been adapted from comic books; similar numbers have been adapted from newspaper strips. Over half of these films were made in the last decade alone, and many more are in development. Comics have also provided the basis for some of the highest grossing films of all time (as of this writing, *The Dark Knight* (2008) stands at number six).

What explains the recent popularity of comic-to-film adaptations? At one level, this question is not difficult, and perhaps not even philosophically interesting; indeed, I begin with a few quick answers to it based on a moderate amount of socio-cultural speculation. But at a deeper level, the philosophical problems grow more complex. I shall be arguing that comics and film are intimately connected by certain specific traits of the media that comprise them. The trend of adapting comics into film is a sign of this connection – and leads to the more radical thesis, which I defend in the first portion of this article, that comics is more suited than any other medium for adaptation into film. This is a view that needs to be spelled out with some nuance, however. For, as I argue in the second portion of this article, even

The Art of Comics: A Philosophical Approach, First Edition.
Edited by Aaron Meskin and Roy T. Cook.
© 2012 Blackwell Publishing Ltd. Published 2012 by Blackwell Publishing Ltd.

though nothing adapts into film better than comics, such film adaptations can never achieve the ideal of perfect fidelity. That is, because of medium-specific constraints, there are features of comics that cannot be fully captured in a film.

Some of the factors that explain the explosion of interest in comics as sources for film are straightforward and largely socio-cultural. I conjecture that these include the following:

1   The medium of comics is a mature one, that presents a rich trove of resources for an industry – film – that is starved for original ideas (as evidenced by upcoming film adaptations of board games). Plots, characters, and the fictional worlds in which they are embedded are highly developed in comics and present boundless, untapped opportunities for adaptation.

2   Certain comics, particularly those of the superhero ilk, feature well-known characters such as Batman, Superman, and Spiderman. These characters are highly iconic and highly marketable in films and related licensing opportunities including action figures and video games – as the current business models of large comics publishers like Marvel and DC attest.

3   Films featuring (formerly) obscure comics characters such as Blade and Hellboy retain their marketability, simply because audiences like to see superheroes in epic battles between the forces of good and evil.

4   The advent of more sophisticated computer-generated imagery (CGI) has made plausible-looking exercise of super powers increasingly possible. The web-slinging and swinging from buildings in *Spiderman* (2002) and its sequels could not have been depicted so well even twenty years ago. CGI is allowing films to show viewers practically anything that can be imagined on the comics page, at a relatively low cost.

5   The art form of comics is increasingly esteemed, and is beginning to be considered on a par with forms of literature such as the novel. College courses are taught on comics; entire aesthetics anthologies are now devoted to them. Accordingly, basing a film on a comic does not carry the social stigma that it once did. Adapting a renowned alternative comic such as *Ghost World* or *Black Hole* is an act that brings critical praise rather than mockery.

These are my explanations for why comics *are* currently important sources for film adaptations. What remains to be shown is that comics are the *best* sources for film adaptations (except for film-to-film adaptations, of course). Arguing as much requires a short discussion of the position known as *medium specificity*.

Medium specificity traces back at least as far as Gotthold Lessing's *Laocoön*. Lessing argues that painting and poetry, in virtue of the media from which they are composed, have very different capacities for representation: the former is best suited for representing how things appear in a single moment of time, while the latter is best suited for representing events unfolding through time. Extending this idea beyond painting and poetry, the generalized version of medium specificity would be that the media (material components and the processes by which those components are manipulated) associated with a given art form entail specific possibilities for and constraints on representation and expression. Simply put, due to their media, some art forms are (*ceteris paribus*) better at certain tasks than others.

Medium specificity has attracted controversy and criticism, chiefly when it comes to whether its postulates can or ought to be employed by artists in the effort to produce valuable works. That is, one might think that the medium-specific characteristics of an art form provide a normative framework for what artists working in it ought to attempt. Noël Carroll, for one, rejects this view, on the grounds that successfully replicating the qualities that are alleged to be specific to an art form – making a film that employs to the fullest particularly cinematic techniques, for example – is insufficient for producing a good work (2008: 45–51).

The proponent of medium specificity, however, need not adopt the aspects of the position that Carroll finds to be so objectionable. One may endorse the view that different media carry with them different capacities, and hence that each art form is naturally better at doing some things than at doing others, without at the same time holding that the success criteria for each art form are fixed by all and only those capacities specific to it. Carroll rejects the latter, and rightly so, but his worries do not extend to the former. And it is the former that is at once the indispensable element of medium specificity and the key to understanding the particular suitability of comics for adaptation into film.

Comics and film have parallel histories. They became popular at about the same time; both have faced censorship pressures (leading, respectively, to the Comics Code Authority and the Hays Code) as well as a lowbrow reputation and a prevailing sentiment that they are not art. Both are considered mass media, technologically reproducible at a great scale and designed for popular audiences. But while these connections are intriguing, they pale in significance compared to the narrative aspects specific to comics and film.

Film and comics alike admit of an avant-garde. There are non-narrative films, like Peter Kubelka's *Arnuf Rainer* (1960) and Godfrey Reggio's *Koyaanisqatsi* (1983). The existence of non-narrative comics is more controversial.[1] I tend to think that works like Ibn Al Rabin's *Cidre et Schnaps* and Andrei Molotiu's "blotcomics" are not comics at all. However, even if I am mistaken, the fact is that the art form of comics, like film, is *predominantly* narrative. That is, the vast majority of comics and films that are produced tell stories; non-narrative works are unusual exceptions.

The reasons why comics and film alike tend strongly to be narrative are medium-specific. Films are (partially) constituted by images that succeed each other in actual time but appear to the viewer in the same actual space. Comics are (partially) constituted by images that succeed each other in actual space but appear to the reader at the same actual time. While this means that the processes of reading comics and viewing films involve different skills, it is also notable that each medium requires us to make sense of a sequence of images. And the simplest way to do this – to come to terms with a sequence as a unified whole – is through narrative, understanding the sequence as the telling of two or more events in a causal relation.

Here we have our first reason why the medium of comics is the best for adaptation into film: for both comics and film, medium-specific qualities exert a strong pressure toward narrativity. As such, comics are better sources for film adaptation than media that carry with them strong biases *against* narrativity, such as paintings, photographs, and sculpture.

Of course, there are plenty of other media (literature and theater, for instance) that tend to be narrative. Comics had better be more closely related to film than these if my thesis is to be defensible. And, indeed, the relation is close. Consider first the *type* of narration that is typically employed in comics and film. Narratologists since Aristotle have been aware of a distinction between *mimetic* and *diegetic* narration. Mimetic narration occurs when the storytelling act is one of showing, with no direct narrator (as in *Hamlet*). Diegetic narration occurs when the storytelling act is one of telling, directly by a narrator (as in *Moby Dick*).

Many narratives blend together both types of narration, though some are purely one way or the other. A particular comic or film can employ both mimetic and diegetic narration. In comics, diegetic narration typically takes the form of boxed words that express the thoughts of the narrator (who may or may not be personified). In film, diegetic narration usually arrives in the form of voiceovers and intertitles. Diegetic narration in comics and film, however, is purely optional. Not all works in those media, and not all narrative components of individual works – panels, pages, shots, and so on – rely on direct acts of narration, as any survey of either will demonstrate. In contrast, comics and film alike overwhelmingly employ mimetic narration: in most (if not all) panels and shots, the reader or viewer is directly shown narrative events. Why are comics and film this way?

Again, the reasons are medium-specific. The media that comprise each are essentially (if not exclusively) visual, rather than tactile, auditory, olfactory, and so on. That is, to be experienced properly, they must be perceived through sight. One *watches* a film. And though one *reads* a comic, this is a special kind of reading that requires attention not merely to the words of the comic (which may not always be present, given the possibility of wordless comics), but also to the pictorial images that comprise it.[2]

Comics are highly adaptable into film, then, because the media of both are visual, and it is advantageous to adapt from one visual art form into another. This stands in contrast to typical literature, in which visual appearances do not have any effect on the narrative – for most literary works, note, the story remains the same no matter the typeface. Literary forms like novels and epic poetry are more awkward than comics to adapt into film because the media that they employ force them to rely predominantly on diegetic narration. To capture the details of a novel coherently in a film, diegetic narration in the form of a voiceover is often shoehorned in, sometimes to disastrous results (as in *Dune* (1984) or the original cut of *Blade Runner* (1982)). When adapting into a mimetic medium, better to keep everything mimetic, including, if possible, the source narrative.

So far, I have argued that comics are better suited to adaptation into film than works in media that are non-narrative or non-visual. Think, however, of theater: a mimetic art form, an act of showing, where visual appearances are crucial. Arguably, the media of theater relate it much more closely than comics to film. Theatrically performed narratives show us actual motion; as Carroll argues, the possibility of motion is a crucial characteristic of film (2008: 58–63). Theater has the capacity to engage senses other than sight, since we can hear what the actors have to say. Since the 1920s, synchronized dialogue and other recorded sounds have given film the same capacity – even if sound is not essential to film, it is, at present, expected. Theatrical works take actual time to perform, and the time it takes to perform a scene generally corresponds directly to the *diegetic time* of that scene (the time that elapses during that scene in the world of the narrative). Just so for film: movies have an actual screening time, and the scenes depicted therein may (and often do) elapse in "real time." Finally, theater provides us with direct perceptual access to real human beings. If photography is transparent, as Kendall Walton famously claims ("Transparent Pictures"), cinema provides us with the same access.

Comics have none of these features; they are engaged exclusively through the process of visually reading still, silent pictures. Actual motion and sound are impossibilities in a print medium. While these features may be added in electronic media, the category of comics would be stretched to the breaking point by including works that move and make noise. Furthermore, the time frame in which a comic is read is largely severed entirely from the diegetic time that elapses within its narrative. This is not to say that comics cannot be read in "real time": Jeff Smith's *Bone*, for example, contains a sequence ("Eyes of the Storm") in which reading time and diegetic time are supposed to be identical. But rarely do narrative elements like dialogue and movement play out in comics at anything like the rate at which we would experience them in real life, to say nothing of on stage or in film. The medium of comics is also prototypically non-transparent. Though there are photo comics (which are more common in Europe than in America), the dominant form of comics is drawn by hand or on a computer. Such comics, unlike theater and film, do not provide us with perceptual access to any real people.

Theater and film appear to be closely related, and adaptations from the former to the latter are not unusual. However, adapting theater to film can be awkward and difficult. To do so requires more than merely placing a camera in front of a theatrical performance. In some ways there is a disconnect between the media, a source of difference that presents challenges to the task of adaptation. Understanding how this could be so provides further support for the claim that comics are the best sources for adaptation into film.

Let us think about the ways in which theatrical works are organized. Typically, each work consists of one or more scenes, each of which, as previously noted, takes place in real time. That is, within each scene, diegetic time is largely identical to performance time. Temporal gaps – jumps in diegetic time – conventionally occur only between scenes.

The spatial organization of theatrical works is managed in much the same way. The viewer's relationships to the diegetic space represented in each scene are stable, in virtue of relatively stationary positioning vis-à-vis the actors and set. The spatial relations between viewer and diegetic space generally change only when there are scene changes, which may toggle the viewer between, for instance, a blasted heath and a Scottish castle.

Film and comics, by way of contrast, are organized in very different fashion. While these art forms also tend to be divided into scenes, each scene contains (necessarily, for comics, and typically, for films) a number of discrete units that may be discontinuous both in diegetic time and diegetic space. Consider film first. Scenes may be composed of only one shot; ordinarily, they are composed of more. With a few exceptions, successive shots are taken from different angles, but the viewer understands that he or she is seeing the same scene – just from a different perspective, at a later time. Accordingly, it is appropriate to say that films are prototypically "gappy": the relationship between the viewer and the diegetic time and space is constantly shifting. In fact, classical film theorists such as Rudolph Arnheim and V.I. Pudovkin went so far as to locate the essence and the particular value of the film medium in its ability reconstitute reality through the intentional production of gaps, achieved through editing techniques such as montage.[3]

The comics medium works in similar fashion. One of the fundamental units of comics is the panel (the page is another – more on this later). The particular visual devices used to define a panel vary from comic to comic, but each serves the purpose of bracketing off images from each other. Spaces between panels – gutters – require the reader to fill in aspects of the narrative through a process that, following Scott McCloud, has come to be called *closure* (1993: 63). The panels of a comic can show the reader the same scene from the same perspective, requiring minimal closure on the part of the reader. More common, however, are transitions whereby the perspective from which the scene is depicted, like a camera angle, varies in the interests of graphic liveliness and to focus the reader's attention. Except for cases in which successive panels show us the same moment from a different perspective (one of the least common transitions in American and European comics, according to McCloud (1993: 75–76)), diegetic time elapses in between panels. Readers must reconstruct the events that occur in these temporal and spatial gaps in order to make sense of a comic's narrative.[4]

Panels and the transitions between them are to comics what shots and the transitions between them are to film. The art form of comics, like film, is prototypically gappy; just as classical film theorists were drawn to the idea that the capacity for gaps is essential to film, theorists attempting to come to terms with comics – McCloud included – have been drawn to the idea that gaps and the process of closure are definitive features of comics. While essentialist characterizations that rely on such features are controversial and have attracted a great deal of criticism, it is clear that filmmakers are drawn to the use of editing techniques that exploit gappiness; in comics, manipulating the gutter and the closure process is the gateway to managing reader perceptions of diegetic time and space.[5]

The media of the theater, by way of contrast, admit of no readily identifiable organizing device comparable to the shot or the panel. Not even the scene: while scenes *could* theoretically be arranged to track exactly the diegetic content of each panel of a comic or shot of a film, this would be an avant-garde strategy of performance at best (and a technical and narrative disaster at worst). The fact is that theater is not well-suited to the same types of narrative breakdowns that are so naturally present in comics and film.

Theater, then, *lacks* a vital affinity to film that comics share. And here we find further support for my overall thesis: adapting from one gappy art form into another is much more natural and straightforward than adapting from a non-gappy art form into a gappy art form. So comics are better sources for film adaptation than theatrical works are.

One more affinity between comics and film will serve to drive the point home. Theater, film, and comics each employ a range of visual techniques to direct the attention of the percipient to (or, in some cases, away from) narratively salient elements. In theater, these techniques include *blocking* – the ways actors are to move about onstage – and lighting (the spotlight, for example). In film, they include (as Carroll describes them in "The Power of Movies") *indexing*, guiding the viewer's attention via camera movement like pans, zooms, and tracking shots; *bracketing*, framing each shot so as to include or exclude certain features of the diegetic world; and *scaling*, positioning the camera in such a way as to foreground prominent and (often) narratively significant objects and events while minimizing others. In comics, indexing is achieved through a succession of panels that alter the reader's viewpoint with respect to the distance or orientation of an object, or by showing us where a character is looking (called a "point-glance" shot in film). Bracketing is done in comics of necessity: since panels cannot be infinitely wide or tall – even those that bleed to the edge of the printed page – they must exclude some of the diegetic space. Scaling is a similarly straightforward effect, accomplished by drawing represented objects as if seen from various distances.

Comics and film are more closely related to each other than to theater in terms of the attention-directing techniques that they employ. True, the effects achieved by these techniques are similar in all three media: if the narrative is presented adequately, the audience will know where to look. But the degree of control allowed by comics and film far surpasses that allowed by conventional theater. For instance, in theater, it is extremely difficult and awkward to alter significantly and quickly the audience's perspective of the characters and the props – consider the challenges of transitioning from a panoramic view to a tight view of an actor's face, or of foregrounding a small object such as a telephone or knife. In comics and film, manipulating such spatial relations is easy and natural. Creators of comics and film can control fluidly the percipient's access to any object, from any perspective.

Because the degree to which they admit of visual control over presentation of the narrative is roughly equivalent to that found in film, comics can serve as a basis for film adaptation to an extent unknown to other media. A comic, in ways a theatrical performance (to say nothing of a theatrical script) does not, has already broken down the visual presentation into the equivalent of shot transitions. And comics offer ideas about how to use the camera within a shot. It is no accident that storyboards for films look almost exactly like comics. Even when a filmmaker is not adapting a comic, the filmmaking process is strengthened by acting – through the creation of the storyboard – *as if* the film was based on a comic all along. (The point I make here is very general and – as we will see shortly – should not be taken to imply that every comic can be straightforwardly adapted for film.)

Some examples in which directors of comic-to-film adaptations used the comics as storyboards may prove helpful at this point. The famous opening page of Alan Moore and Dave Gibbons's *Watchmen* is imitated directly in Zach Snyder's film adaptation (2009) in the shot immediately following the opening credits (from 11:12 to 11:39). Both comic and film begin the sequence with a tight close-up depicting the bloody happy face button and then transition through a succession of images that bring us up from the street level to the skyscraper window from which the Comedian was pushed (this zoom in the film even includes Rorschach, who we see quickly in panel three of the comic).

For *Sin City* (2005), the use of Frank Miller's comics as a storyboard is evident from beginning to end (Miller even gets credit as a co-director). There is no point (or space here) in describing all of the ways in which the shots of the film are synchronized with the panels of the comic. To get a taste of the correspondence, watch the film from 13:02 to 16:21 and follow along in *Frank Miller's Sin City Volume 1: The Hard Goodbye* from pages 10 to 28. Save for a few extraneous images and a few snippets of narration in the comic that do not appear in the voiceover, the film uses the framing, focus, and narrative of the comic as much as can possibly be achieved in a cross-media context.

My argument so far, then, is that close attention to the media of comics and film reveals a number of striking commonalities. Both tend strongly toward the narrative; both employ largely mimetic, visual narration; both are prototypically gappy; and both control the percipient's attention to a similar degree and with similar techniques. No other medium – neither literature, nor theater – shares these affinities with film to the same degree that comics does. Accordingly, comics provide the best possible source for adaptation into film.

Nonetheless, we should recognize that there is a certain risk associated with talking about comics in the same way that one talks about film. As Douglas Wolk puts it in *Reading Comics*,

> The most thoroughly ingrained error in the language used to discuss comics is treating them as if they were particularly weird, or failed examples of an entirely different medium altogether. Good comics are sometimes described as being "cinematic"... It's almost an insult, though, to treat [such claims] as compliments. Using them as praise implies that comics *as a form* aspire (more or less unsuccessfully) to being movies. (2007: 13)[6]

Wolk's point is well taken. The danger in the claim that comics provide the best bases for film adaptation is that we may begin to think of comics as merely inert, static, technologically unsophisticated precursors of films that can be made from them. This is bad for the status of the medium of comics – demoting them to very low level on the totem pole of artistic potential – but may also have troubling effects on the creativity of comics creators. For if *they* begin to share Wolk's worry that comics are poor imitations of other media, they will either give up on comics or do whatever they can to make comics most like the medium they are trying to emulate. And it may well be detrimental to comics as a whole if creators and readers alike equate success with the cinematic, since a comic can never fully achieve that which a film can achieve quite easily (movement and sound, for instance).

I do not think that these worries are decisive against my argument in the foregoing. For it is entirely possible both that comics are best suited, among media, for film adaptation, and that such adaptations can never fully capture the comics on which they are based. The latter would be the case if there is something distinctive that the medium of comics has to offer, something that means comics cannot be adapted with perfect fidelity, something that they can do that film cannot.

Perhaps the best place to begin looking for these distinctive features of comics is at various assertions that certain adaptations are "impossible." I will turn to some of these shortly. First, though, we need to consider briefly what it is for an adaptation to be impossible. Whatever sense of possibility is deployed here must be very weak, for anything, one might think, can be adapted into anything else – just not very well. Those who claim that an adaptation is impossible, then, are most plausibly understood to mean that there is something about the original that cannot be fully captured in any adaptation of it: perfect fidelity cannot be achieved.

What would perfect fidelity involve? Transposition of the story across media, certainly, causally prompted by the original. Strict story identity seems to be required as well: a perfect adaptation would maintain, in Seymour Chatman's words, "the continuum of events [of the original,] presupposing the total set of all conceivable details, that is, those that can be projected by the normal laws of the physical universe" (1978: 28). These points are commonplace, but I want to add something else to them. A perfect adaptation would preserve the style of the original. As Ernst Gombrich argues forcefully in *Art and Illusion*, each artist (or, we might add, collective of artists) has a distinctive temperament or mental set that explains why his or her works turn out differently than the works made by others (even in the circumstances where all the artists are using the same technology and attempting to represent the same things). If all of the characters and events of a story are captured perfectly by an adaptation but the style is different, the adaptation has less than perfect fidelity.

Perfect fidelity in this sense is too strong a requirement when we are trying merely to determine what counts as an adaptation in the first place. The claim that an adaptation is possible is not equivalent to the claim that perfect fidelity can be achieved. Correspondingly, the claim that an adaptation is impossible is not the claim that perfect fidelity in a particular case cannot be achieved. Perfect fidelity, in short, comes apart from typical claims about the impossibility of adaptation, since there may be good reason to think that at least some adaptations are possible even though perfect fidelity cannot be achieved under any circumstances.[7] Better, then, to retreat to a weaker position: when it is asserted that a certain work is impossible to adapt, the idea is that no reasonable degree of fidelity can be achieved. Generally, as we shall see, such claims are not only ontological but also evaluative. When adaptations are said to be impossible, there is something about the value of the original that is thought to be lost, necessarily, in the adaptation.

Time to turn to specific examples. Consider, first, Jorge Gracia's rather general statements about film and literature:

> A film cannot do the same things that a written work can do. For example, films need to be relatively short, whereas a written work can have thousands of pages.... Moreover, in films, visual images are directly presented to the audience and take precedence over words, whereas in a written work, images are always mediated through words, the primary medium of meaning. (Gracia 2007: 200–201)

Gracia is not writing directly about adaptations of comics, but his ideas are relevant because comics generally feature printed words (in word balloons, narrative boxes, and so on). Are comics impossible to adapt because, like literature, they are (at least partially) written?

No – at least, not on Gracia's grounds. While it is true that films usually have a relatively short viewing time, this presents no difficulty if the comic to be adapted is also short (as is the case with *Ghost World* and *Sin City*). Longer comics can, in theory, be adapted into longer films that would preserve all of the comics' dialogue and narration. Sheer amount of text is not a problem for adaptation *per se*. And while the non-pictorial nature of most literature does provide a challenge for adaptation into film – making such literature difficult to adapt, as I argued in the foregoing – it is a challenge that comics do not present, since they are pictorial.

So let us move on to an argument more specific to comics. Wolk, discussing David B's *Epileptic*, writes:

> The book is also a very clear demonstration of what comics can do, as drawn narratives that require the reader's imagination to play along, that nothing else can. And it's impossible to imagine it being adapted into any other medium: to lose the specific work of B.'s drawing hand would be to lose *Epileptic* itself. (2007: 141)

Wolk is making two assertions. First, no other medium can deploy the reader's imagination (by which Wolk is presumably referring to the exercise of closure) in the same way as the drawn narrative that constitutes a comic. At the least, it is unclear that this is correct. Film, we have seen, uses closure in much the same way as comics, and it is entirely possible that the imaginative faculties are engaged in the same way by each medium.

Second, Wolk focuses on style. Adaptation of *Epileptic* is impossible, he holds, because David B's drawings are so distinctive and personal. Note that this does seem to be at once an ontological and an evaluative point; any attempted adaptation of *Epileptic* would result in the *loss* of the work, which, since it is a good work, would not maintain value.

Epileptic may, in fact, be impossible to adapt to film, but it is not evident that this is due to barriers having to do with the comic's visual style. The look of B's drawings could at least be captured with an *animated* film. Marjane Satrapi's *Persepolis*, heavily influenced by *Epileptic*, was animated in a way that preserved its style. Wolk even compares the style of *Persepolis* directly to that of *Epileptic*: if the *style* of the former was successfully preserved in adaptation, then it ought to be possible to do so for the latter as well (regardless of whether all the *content* of *Epileptic* can be preserved).

Perhaps it will be responded that we have been thinking about photographically based film adaptations all along, and that bringing animation in at this stage is changing the subject. Very well. Photographs can be made that correspond identifiably with an artist's drawing style. As Guillermo Del Toro acknowledges in his director's commentary on the DVD release, the film *Hellboy* (2004) was designed (successfully, I would argue) to preserve closely the visual sensibility of the comic's artist, Mike Mignola. So too for *Ghost World*: the events constitutive of the narrative of Dan Clowes's comic are largely vestigial in the film, but Clowes's artistic sensibility is evident throughout. The fact that a comic is drawn, I conclude, does not provide an insurmountable barrier to adaptation into film, even film that is photographically based.

The final examples of "it cannot be adapted" claims I shall consider all center around *Watchmen*. Wolk says, "*Watchmen* [the comic], bless its twisted heart, is totally unfilmable – not that people haven't been trying to figure out how to turn it into a movie for twenty years, but it's so heavily invested in *being a comic book* that to take it away from its native medium would be to rip all its bones out" (2007: 241). Alan Moore, who wrote it, claims:

> There are things that we did with *Watchmen* that could only work in a comic, and were indeed designed to show off things that other media can't.... I increasingly fear that nothing good can come of almost any adaptation, and obviously that's sweeping. There are a couple of adaptations that are perhaps as good or better than the original work. But the vast majority of them are pointless. (2008: 1)

The views of Wolk and Moore, formulated separately, share several salient features. For one, each is ultimately making an evaluative point; an adaptation of *Watchmen* would "rip all its bones out," or be "pointless." And it is fortunate for them that their assertions are about value, since the film adaptation of *Watchmen* has been made, released after the statements quoted above. Adapting *Watchmen*, we have now learned, is not ontologically impossible. Even so, Wolk and Moore seem to be grounding their evaluative stances in an ontological base. There is something specific to the medium of comics that *Watchmen* (the comic) exploited to the fullest but which, when adapted for film, is lost. And *that*, whatever it is, is why adapting *Watchmen* while preserving its value is impossible.

So what is lost? Perhaps it has something to do with the sophistication of the content of the *Watchmen* comic, combined with the provocative worldview that it expresses. The comic has a complex narrative structure rife with allusion, and presents a great deal of intellectual challenge. In addition, it calls into question the nature of right and wrong and the ultimate significance of humanity in the universe. Heady stuff.

Much of this content is, in fact, lost in the film. Part of the problem has to do with the fact that *Watchmen* is about superheroes. In mainstream Hollywood-style cinema, superhero movies involve beautiful men and women with extravagant superpowers who are engaged in energetic battles with supervillains or other forces of evil. Plenty of action and excitement is required, but not a lot of thought. The overriding mentality is one that prioritizes spectacle and profits.

Watchmen does not fit comfortably into this framework. In many ways, its theme is the antithesis of traditional superhero comics. The "costumed heroes" depicted in the comic, save Dr. Manhattan, have no actual superpowers. But the film succumbs to the temptation to show otherwise, as we see right from the initial fight sequence, in which an ostensibly normal human being punches through a cement wall. (This is why seeing Ozymandias catch a bullet with his hand is remarkable in the comic but not in the movie: in the latter but not the former, the audience expects it.)

One "impossibility" in adapting *Watchmen*, then, is that it is extremely unlikely that a mainstream anti-superhero superhero movie can be made.[8] The problem is reminiscent of François Truffaut's famous statement that no war movie can be made without portraying war as fun. No mainstream superhero movie can be made without portraying superheroes in action as *awesome*, but that is exactly what an adaptation of *Watchmen* requires. (Even *The Dark Knight* succumbed to this temptation. As one of my friends put it, "Batman is the world's greatest detective, not the world's greatest head-puncher.") Of course, what this really means is that given the realities of the movie business, a faithful adaptation of *Watchmen* is highly unlikely. It does not mean that because of *medium-specific* features, a faithful adaptation of *Watchmen* is impossible, and that, in part, seems to be what Wolk and Moore are asserting.

Despite the many similarities raised earlier between the media of film and comics, there is one glaring dissimilarity that has the potential to interfere with adaptation – and which explains why *Watchmen* might be thought to be beyond adaptation. The images that comprise a comic are juxtaposed in space but are simultaneously present in time. In this way, comics are like the random access memory characteristic of a computer hard drive: any panel, regardless of its location in the book and its relations to previous panels, can be called up for attention at any given moment. The images that comprise a film, in contrast, are juxtaposed in time but are perceived in a single space. Film, then, is more like a tape drive, where memory is stored sequentially: frames are only seen in relation to those previous to them. (DVD's and similar technologies allow for random access to frames, but typically, films are watched in sequence.)

Because of these medium-specific features, comics allow for types of control that cannot be achieved in film, in the processes of both reading and creation. First, reading: film manages "watching time" *for* the viewer. One has no choice but to experience the narrative at the rate of the mechanical succession of the frames. The pace of reading comics, in contrast, is like that of reading literature. Readers of comics are largely responsible for their own rate of processing the narrative, and can freely direct attention back and forth among its images and events.[9]

A comic like *Watchmen* exploits this to the fullest. Consider the sequences of a comic (*The Black Freighter*) within a comic. Here we have two simultaneous narratives running in parallel, each of which continually comments on and enriches the other. It is possible and relatively easy for readers to process this kind of embedding. It is *not* easy to do so in film, and maybe not even possible. While a film can toggle back and forth between different narratives, it cannot present them simultaneously (as in a split screen) with any expectation of a reasonable degree of comprehension.

Inclusion of the *Black Freighter* parts in the *Watchmen* film, shown on the screen concurrently with the main narrative, would have made both narratives largely incomprehensible (in notable contrast to the comic). On the other hand, interposing the *Black Freighter* portions consecutively with the main narrative (as happens in the "ultimate cut" of the DVD release) disjoints the film and eliminates the subtlety with which the narratives in the comic are intertwined and mutually reinforcing. The only other alternative is to separate the two narratives entirely – *Tales of the Black Freighter* (2009) was originally released as a self-contained, animated feature – but, of course, this brings the adaptation of *Watchmen* farther and farther away from the comic itself.

Moore bears out and expands on this point in an interview at blather.net:

> With *Watchmen*, what we tried to do was give it a truly kind of crystalline structure, where it's like this kind of jewel with hundreds and hundreds of facets and almost each of the facets is commenting on all of the other facets and you can kind of look at the jewel through any of the facets and still get a coherent reading. Yeah, basically, there are single panels there, single images, that somehow kind of tie up the whole book. (2010: 3)

Because the medium of comics juxtaposes panels in space, readers have the luxury of being able to process and understand such complex narrative structures. Because the medium of film juxtaposes frames in time, viewers do not have that luxury.

I claimed earlier that the medium-specific features of comics allow for a type of creative activity that cannot be achieved in film. Let me explain. As a number of comics theorists have noticed, comics creators have two types of panel organization to consider.[10] One is sequential: how are the panels going to follow one after the other on the page? The other is tabular: how is each page in its entirety going to be arranged graphically? Tabular organization is of crucial importance. Most comics artists will tell you that the fundamental unit of comics is not the panel but the page. Yet those who create films cannot concern themselves with tabular organization. Since film images are not spatially juxtaposed, the viewer can only be aware of one image at a given time. (Split-screen, again, is an exception, but one that only awkwardly attempts to simulate the experience of comics, as in Ang Lee's disastrous *Hulk* (2003).)

The pages of *Watchmen* are arranged largely on a three-by-three panel grid. Even within this framework, graphic choices are made that have vital effects on the reader's experience. We notice how colors, symbols, characters, and motifs recur across the page. Moreover, the grid is occasionally broken up by larger panels. Through this technique – in essence, a version of scaling available uniquely to comics – the artists not only add depth and variety to the comic, but also draw attention to salient aspects of the narrative in ways unavailable in film, which is constrained by a stable frame dimension.

There are many points at which tabular organization is used to maximum effect in *Watchmen*, but perhaps two examples will suffice. First, the entirety of Chapter V, "Fearful Symmetry," consists of pages that are mirror images of each other in layout, color, overall design, and even narrative event: the last page mirrors the first, the second-to-last mirrors the second, and so on, until they meet in the middle. Without the possibilities afforded by tabular construction, this effect cannot be achieved. Second, *Watchmen* contains no splash pages whatsoever until Chapter XII, "A Stronger Loving World," which begins with six of them consecutively. The scenes depicted, not accidentally, are the horrifying climax of a plot that the reader has been gradually becoming aware of throughout the comic. By choosing to withhold the tabular arrangement of the splash page until this part of the story, Moore and Gibbons greatly enhance its impact.

Perhaps these are the medium-specific features of comics behind the claims that *Watchmen* is impossible to adapt into film. So long as the sense of "impossible" here is a weak one, such claims are more than plausible. Significant aspects of the comic cannot be preserved in film. This does not entail, however, that the medium of comics is superior; one could, no doubt, produce a parallel argument having to do with ways in which certain films cannot be adapted into comics. Nor does it entail that comics are poor choices for adaptation into film. Comics are still the best sources for film adaptation, but "best" does not mean "perfect."[11]

Notes

1   For a defence of non-narrative comics, see Meskin (2007); for a response, see Pratt (2011).
2   I have argued in the past that comics are essentially pictorial: see Hayman and Pratt (2005). Scott McCloud's influential definition of comics, as "juxtaposed pictorial and other images in deliberate sequence" carries the same implication (1993: 9). Note that if comics are essentially pictorial, then each comic shows the reader at least something, implying that comics is an essentially mimetic medium.
3   For Arnheim's view and his summary of Pudovkin's treatment of montage, see *Film as Art* (87–102).
4   For a detailed treatment of the ways in which comics manage time and space, see Pratt (2009).
5   The reliance of classical film theorists on gappiness has been criticized a number of times by Noël Carroll (2008: Chapter 2); Meskin (2007) has cast doubt on the possibility of any essentialist definition of comics.
6   Frank Miller makes a similar claim: "The whole reference to comics being movies on paper is a corrupt one, because it makes us sound so inferior" (Eisner and Miller 2005: 87).
7   See Smuts (2009).
8   An interesting related issue is whether readers can recognize the existence of a mainstream anti-superhero superhero *comic*: perhaps even *Watchmen* fails in this!
9   These are points I have made in greater length and detail in Pratt (2009).
10   See Hatfield (2009: 139–144), Witek (2009: 153–155), and Pratt (2009: 114–115).
11   I would like to acknowledge the aid of the editors of this volume in the preparation of this article, as well as Andrei Buckareff, John Holbo, Ian Hummel,

Christy Mag Uidhir, and Cathleen Muller. Earlier versions were presented at the American Society for Aesthetics Annual Meeting in November of 2008 – where Roy T. Cook's comments were particularly helpful – and at Marist College in February of 2009.

References

Arnheim, R. *Film as Art*. Berkeley, CA: University of California Press, 1956.

Carroll, N. "The Power of Movies," *Daedalus* 114, 1985: 79–103.

Carroll, N. *The Philosophy of Motion Pictures*. Oxford: Wiley-Blackwell, 2008.

Caswell, L.S. and D. Filipi. *Jeff Smith: Bone and Beyond*, Columbus, OH: Wexner Center for the Arts, 2008.

Chatman, S. *Story and Discourse*. Ithaca, NY: Cornell University Press, 1978.

Eisner, W. and F. Miller. *Eisner/Miller*. Milwaukie, OR: Dark Horse, 2005.

Gombrich, E. *Art and Illusion*. London: Phaidon, 1959.

Gracia, J.E. "From Horror to Hero: Film Interpretations of Stoker's Dracula," in W. Irwin and J.E. Gracia (eds), *Philosophy and the Interpretation of Pop Culture*, Lanham, MD: Rowman and Littlefield Publishers, 2007: 187–214.

Hatfield, C. "An Art of Tensions," in J. Heer and K. Worcester (eds), *A Comics Studies Reader*, Jackson, MS: University Press of Mississippi, 2009: 132–148.

Hayman, G. and H.J. Pratt. "What Are Comics?" in D. Goldblatt and L.B. Brown (eds), *Aesthetics: A Reader in Philosophy of the Art*, 2nd ed., Upper Saddle River, NJ: Pearson Prentice Hall, 2005: 419–424.

Lessing, G. *Laocoön: An Essay Upon the Limits of Painting and Poetry*, trans. Ellen Frothingham, Boston: Little, Brown, and Company, 1910 (original work published 1766).

Meskin, A. "Defining Comics?" *Journal of Aesthetics and Art Criticism* 65, 2007: 369–379.

Miller, F. *Frank Miller's Sin City Volume 1: The Hard Goodbye*, Milwaukie, OR: Dark Horse Books, 2005.

McCloud, S. *Understanding Comics*, Northhampton, MA: Kitchen Sink Press, 1993.

McCloud, S. *Making Comics*, New York: HarperCollins Publishers, 2006.

Moore, A. and D. Gibbons. *Watchmen*, New York: DC Comics, 1987.

Moore A. and D. Gibbons. Interview by B. Kavanagh. "The Alan Moore Interview: *Watchmen*, Microcosms and Details." Oct. 17, 2000. Blather.net. Mar. 14, 2010. Available online at http://blather.net/articles/amoore/watchmen3.html (accessed August 6, 2011).

Moore A. and D. Gibbons. Interview by N. Gopalan. "Alan Moore Still Knows the Score." Jul. 18, 2008. *EW.com*. Jul. 22, 2008. Available online at http://www.ew.com/ew/article/0,20213004,00.html (accessed August 6, 2011).

Pudovkin, V.I. *Film Acting and Film Technique*, London: Vision Press, 1958.

Pratt, H.J. "Narrative in Comics," *Journal of Aesthetics and Art Criticism* 67, 2009: 107–117.

Pratt, H.J. "Relating Comics, Cartoons, and Animation," in D. Goldblatt and L.B. Brown (eds), *Aesthetics: A Reader in Philosophy of the Arts*, 3rd ed., Upper Saddle River, NJ: Pearson-Prentice Hall, 2011: 369–373.

Smuts, A. "Story Identity and Story Type," *Journal of Aesthetics and Art Criticism* 67, 2009: 5–13.

Walton, K. "Transparent Pictures: On the Nature of Photographic Realism," *Critical Inquiry* 11, 1984: 246–277.

Witek, J. "The Arrow and the Grid," in J. Heer, and K. Worcester (eds), *A Comics Studies Reader*, Jackson, MS: University Press of Mississippi, 2009: 149–156.

Wolk, D. *Reading Comics*. Cambridge, MA: Da Capo Press, 2007.

Why Comics Are Not Films: Metacomics and Medium-Specific Conventions[1]

Roy T. Cook

The Problem

This chapter begins with a question that was put to me by a prominent philosopher of film.[2] After sitting in the audience during a recent panel on the aesthetics of comics at a meeting of the *American Society for Aesthetics*, the philosopher in question asked whether we truly needed a (separate) philosophical account of the nature and structure of comics. After all, he noted, we have a rich literature already extant on the philosophy of film. Since comics appear to be, in most relevant respects, little more than static films on paper, won't we find all the critical and evaluative tools we need for our examination of comics already developed and ready for use in the literature on film? In other words, the suggestion was that a separate philosophical account of comics threatens to be a case of reinventing the wheel.

We can put the worry a bit more carefully: given any particular comic, we can imagine the sequence of images (and text, etc.) contained in the comic projected on a screen – either projecting each image in sequence, or projecting each page entire in sequence. The result, clearly, will be a film – not a particularly thrilling film, perhaps, but a film nonetheless. Thus, so the worry goes, comics, properly understood, are (or are equivalent to) a subspecies of film, and as a result all of the tools and techniques we need to evaluate and understand them can be found within film theory and the philosophy of film. I shall call this argument (which we shall fine tune a bit below) the *Filmstrip Argument*.

The Art of Comics: A Philosophical Approach, First Edition.
Edited by Aaron Meskin and Roy T. Cook.
© 2012 Blackwell Publishing Ltd. Published 2012 by Blackwell Publishing Ltd.

It is this view of comics, and the aesthetics of comics, that I will argue against here. The argument will proceed in three stages. First, I shall formulate (what I take to be) the strongest version of the *Filmstrip Argument*. I shall then examine two particular comics in some detail, and argue that these comics (and, of course, many others like them in relevant respects) provide counterexamples to the *Filmstrip Argument*.

Of course, the *Filmstrip Argument* is a particular instance of a more general thought. Given the obvious (and in some cases not-so-obvious) structural similarities and historical connections between comics and film, one might think that comics do not raise any distinctive, substantial philosophical questions that are not already raised by films. As a result, one might be tempted to think that, even if the particular pattern of reasoning found in the *Filmstrip Argument* is shown to fail, that the more general point might stand. Fortunately, the counterexamples discussed below do not merely demonstrate that the *Filmstrip Argument* itself is flawed. In addition, they provide valuable guidance towards seeing the flaws in this more general line of thought.

If the point of this chapter were merely to demonstrate the rather commonsensical view that comics are not (equivalent to) a species of film, however, then it would be of very meager interest. More important than defending this thesis, however, are the lessons to be learned along the way regarding the nature of comics and the subtler relationships between comics and cinema. The idea that (some) comics work very differently from film is, of course, not new. Comics critic Douglas Wolk, for example, (echoing writer Alan Moore's own comments) describes *Watchmen* as:

> ... totally unfilmable ... it's so heavily invested in *being a comic book* that to take it away from its native medium would be to rip all its bones out. (2007: 241)

The real purpose of this chapter is to flesh out one understanding of Wolk's idea that a comic can be "heavily invested in being a comic book" – an understanding that can underwrite substantial differences between the nature and structure of (some) comics and the nature and structure of films, and which can block the *Filmstrip Argument* and arguments like it. With this in mind, the chapter concludes with a discussion of what the failure of the *Filmstrip Argument* teaches us more generally about the nature and structure of comics.

Before embarking on our examination of the *Filmstrip Argument*, however, it is worth getting a few preliminary issues out of the way. First, we should note that the *Filmstrip Argument* does not require the assumption that we have a *complete* account of the nature of film already to hand, which we of course do not yet have, and likely will not have for some time (if ever). The point of the argument is that, if comics are identical or equivalent to a subspecies of film in some relevant sense, then our efforts should be aimed at further developing our account of the nature of film (whatever that account ultimately looks like), and not on developing a completely new (and unnecessary) sub-discipline aimed at comics.

Second, the tools we have developed for interpretation, evaluation, and so on, of film are spread amongst a number of somewhat disparate academic disciplines, including philosophy, film theory, communications, critical theory, and many more. As a result, in order to simplify the discussion I shall use the catch-all term *film-theoretic tools* to refer to whatever tools and techniques have been (or will be) developed specifically for the study of film within any and all of these disciplines.

Third, we should recognize at the outset that there are philosophically substantial reasons to take the *Filmstrip Argument* seriously – or, at the very least, to take the intuitions that motivate the argument seriously. First, and foremost, there is the fact that film-theoretic tools have been extremely useful for the philosopher of comics. Hans-Christian Christiansen emphasizes both the similarities between comics and film and the fact that comics scholarship has, in virtue of such similarity, borrowed heavily from film-theoretic work in the first paragraphs of his "Comics and Film: A Narrative Approach":

> Aesthetic and narrative analysis of comics has been dominated, within criticism and theoretical debate, by a paradigm which relates comic art to other media, particularly film.
> There is also, of course, evidence of general conceptual continuity from medium to medium. (2000: 107)

This is no doubt that these formal similarities[3] between comics and film – the same similarities that motivate the *Filmstrip Argument* – are what bring about this overlap of resources, and it would be foolish to deny these resources to the blossoming field of philosophy of comics. It would be equally foolish, however, to immediately conclude that these similarities in method and approach entail that these two fields are, in fact, one and the same, and that the only theoretical resources that the study of comics requires are film-theoretic tools.

Another connection between comics and films that could be used to motivate the *Filmstrip Argument* are the deep historical connections between the development of film and the development of comics and the effect which these connections have had on the way that creators think about, and how they create, comics. For example, in *Eisner/Miller*, the extended conversation between Will Eisner and Frank Miller, Eisner states that:

> When people talk about the cinematic quality of *The Spirit*, that is because I realized when I was doing *The Spirit* that movies were creating a visual language and I had to use the same language, because when you are writing to an audience that is speaking Swahili, you'd better write in Swahili. (2005: 88)

Along similar lines, Jim Steranko comments that:

> I learned to draw from the comics, but all my storytelling techniques and processes are derivative of cinematic aesthetics. (Dooley and Heller 2005: 6)

(Note the rather disturbing implication that one can learn to draw from comics, but one only learns how to tell stories from film.) These connections are so evident that Scott McCloud, in *Understanding Comics*, claims that a film (celluloid, not digital), laid out and perceived frame by frame, *is* a comic – in other words, he accepts a converse version of the *Filmstrip Argument*! (1993: 8).

Thus, comics creators have relied on the techniques developed in the (younger, but arguably more mature) field of cinema in order to create great (or at least, quite good) comics. The patterns of mutual influence do not end here, however: films are often planned out in the form of storyboards – sequences of images mapping out the shots that will constitute the film, roughly delineating what shall be shown in each shot and from what perspective. Even if there are principled philosophical reasons for denying the status of comics to storyboards (as is suggested in Meskin 2007), there is no denying their close structural relationship to comics. (This observation regarding storyboards being, or at least being similar to, comics also suggests that theorists interested in the nature of film should also be interested in the nature of comics).

Thus, there are intimate connections between cinema and comics, and these connections come in two varieties. The first type consists of the formal similarities – pictorial, narrative, sequential, and so on, – inherent in and constitutive of the art forms themselves. The second type consists of more historically contingent factors – for example, the influence that filmmaking techniques have had on the methods and approaches of comic book creators, and the fact that comic creators often evaluate their own works in terms of criteria lifted straight from cinema.[4] Although such connections fall far short of a fully developed defense of anything like the *Filmstrip Argument* – after all, similarity is not identity – they do suggest that we should take arguments along these lines seriously. Thus, our next task is to formulate, and then to evaluate, the *Filmstrip Argument* a bit more carefully.

The Filmstrip Argument

In the previous section we sketched the *Filmstrip Argument* roughly as follows. Given any comic, we can project that comic filmstrip-style onto a screen. The result is a film, but also retains all of the relevant aesthetic properties of the original comic. Thus, we don't need a separate account of the aesthetics of comics, since we can study, evaluate, critique, and so on, the projected filmstrip version just as effectively using film-theoretic tools.

This simple description above hides, as is the norm in simple summaries of complex philosophical issues, a number of separate steps in the argument that need to be isolated and examined individually. First, given any comic Σ, we shall refer to the filmstrip projection of the comic as FS(Σ). Second, we offer the following definition:

Df: Given a comic Σ, a filmstrip projection FS(Σ) is *faithful* if and only if it preserves all of the intrinsic aesthetic properties of Σ.

Of course, this definition is incomplete until we specify what is meant by intrinsic aesthetic properties of Σ. Loosely speaking, what is meant here is that FS(Σ) preserves the aesthetically relevant physical properties of Σ – for example, the images, their relative size, their ordering and/or relative position, and so on. In particular, a faithful filmstrip projection of Σ should preserve any properties that are necessary conditions for being a comic in the first place, but faithfulness involves far more than this – it also requires preservation of at least many of those properties of the comic that make it the comic that it is, such as its pictorial content and the structural arrangement of that content (the reader should note that "faithful" is used here as a technical term, unconnected to any other uses the word might have in the philosophical and critical literature).

While this still leaves the definition of faithfulness a bit loose, it is sufficient for our purposes, since the main objection to the *Filmstrip Argument* developed below is independent of how, exactly, we define faithfulness. The *Filmstrip Argument* can now be fleshed out as follows:

Given any comic Σ:
(1) There could exist a faithful filmstrip projection FS(Σ) of Σ.
(2) FS(Σ) is a film.
(3) All of the aesthetically, critically, and evaluatively relevant features of Σ are preserved in FS(Σ).
(4) The analysis, evaluation, critique, and so on, of FS(Σ) can be carried out using film-theoretic tools (this follows from (2) and the fact that the

analysis, evaluation, and critique of a film requires only film-theoretic tools).

(5) The analysis, evaluation, critique, and so on, of Σ can be carried out using film-theoretic tools (since, by (4), FS(Σ) can be analyzed, evaluated, and critiqued using only film-theoretic tools, and, by (2), all of the aesthetically relevant features of Σ are also present in FS(Σ)).

(6) We do not need a separate theoretical account of comics (since (1) – (5) shows this for any arbitrary comic Σ).

The first thing to notice about this argument is that it is valid. In other words, if we grant premises (1) – (3), then claims (4) and (5), and thus the conclusion (6), follow. Thus, if the *Filmstrip Argument* is to be blocked, and the need for a purpose-built philosophical account of comics is to be defended, then it had better be the case that one of our three premises is false.

It turns out that premise (3) *is* false, and that for many comics Σ, any filmstrip projection FS(Σ) of Σ, whether faithful or not, will fail to preserve some *extrinsic* but aesthetically relevant properties of Σ. In other words, even if the filmstrip projection FS(Σ) preserves all aesthetically relevant *intrinsic* properties of the original comic Σ (i.e., loosely put, it "looks the same") it will fail to preserve more complex characteristics of Σ that depend on the relationship between Σ itself and the particular history and context within which Σ was produced. Since these properties are lacking in FS(Σ), one cannot do full justice to the aesthetic qualities of a comic Σ by relying solely on the application of film-theoretic tools to FS(Σ). I shall examine two such comics in some detail in the next section. Before doing so, however, it is worth taking a bit of a closer look at the other two premises.

There might be reasons to doubt premise (2) – the claim that a filmstrip projection of a comic is, in fact, a film. In "Defining the Moving Image" Noël Carroll argues that something is a film only if it "belongs to the class of things from which the impression of movement is technically possible" (1996: 130). Intuitively, this definition might entail that filmstrips are not films, since they do not (and could not?) provide the requisite impression of motion. Nevertheless, Carroll's account of the nature of film and accounts like it, while widely influential, are not uncontroversial. In addition, the claim that filmstrips do not provide an impression of movement – even possibly – is contestable. (After all, how are we to draw sharp dividing lines between pre-digital, traditionally projected films and sped-up filmstrips?)

The situation is further complicated by so-called "motion comics," such as the recent *Watchmen* motion comic. Motion comics seem, at first glance, to be comics (or, at least, something very much like comics) and at the same time filmstrip projections (and thus films). In other words, if a motion comic

Σ is in fact a comic, then it provides a case where $FS(\Sigma) = \Sigma$. As a result, the *Filmstrip Argument* is particularly plausible when applied to motion comics. Nevertheless, although the truth of premise (2) clearly has ramifications regarding the nature of both comics and film, since we have bigger (comic-theoretic) fish to fry elsewhere, we shall for the sake of argument grant the truth of premise (2).

Premise (1) is another story, however. It turns out that there are (at least) two distinct reasons one might doubt (1), although, as we shall see, only one of these stands up to close scrutiny.

First, if one thinks that being printed (as opposed to projected) is a necessary condition for being comic, as Anne Elizabeth Moore suggests (see the preface to Pekar 2006: x), then the *Filmstrip Argument* – in the form sketched here, at least – is a non-starter: Filmstrip projections of a comic would not preserve this intrinsic formal property of the comic being projected. Since there are independent reasons for thinking that comics need not be printed – for example, this conception of the art form rules out web-comics – we shall set this worry aside, however, and move on to the second worry regarding premise (1).

The second objection to premise (1) relies on the idea that there are comics where the ordering between the panels is of a more complex type than can be faithfully represented on a screen, no matter what editorial trickery is employed. Intuitions to the contrary can be traced to a simplification that seems to have been uncritically adopted in most discussions of the structure of both comics and of cinema: that both comics and films consist of sequences (read: linear ordering) of "units" (in the case of comics, the units are individual panels, tiers, or pages; in the case of films the units are shots or scenes). While this simplification is no doubt useful in many cases, and perhaps harmless in most, the possibility of more complex orderings amongst such "units" turns out to be critical in our evaluation of premise (1). The reason is simple: it is likely that comics allow for more complex structural relationships between "units" than can be reproduced in film.

Although using techniques such as split-screen and the like allow for the simultaneous projection of multiple units on the screen (and further, there seems to be no in-principle upper bound on the number of distinct such "units" that can be simultaneously displayed, assuming arbitrarily high resolution and arbitrarily large screens), the fact that such images must be projected onto a flat screen in real time entails that the relationships holding between these "units" must be, at the very least, a *strict weak ordering*. An ordering $<$ on a collection of objects is a strict weak ordering if and only if $<$ is a *strict partial ordering*:

< is irreflexive:
   For any x, it is not the case that x < x.
< is transitive:
   For any x, y, and x, if x < y and y < z, then x < z.

and, in addition, the incomparability relation:

x and y are *incomparable* $=_{df}$ it is not the case that either x < y or y < x.

is also transitive:

For any x, y, and z, if x and y are incomparable, and y and z are incomparable, then x and z are incomparable.

Comics, however, are less limited, and panels can be arranged in any ordering that corresponds to a *planar directed graph*. A *directed graph* (or digraph) is an ordered pair < N, E > where N is any collection of objects (the nodes of the digraph) and E is any relation on N × N (the edges of the digraph). Intuitively, a digraph is just a collection of points with arrows connecting some of the points to others (and where, for any two points, there is no more than one arrow going in each direction). A directed graph is *planar* if and only if it can be embedded into the Euclidean plane – loosely put, if it can be drawn on a piece of paper in such a way that none of the arrows intersect.

Further, the use of thought and speech balloon tails, and of trails (or directional arrows), once reserved for clarifying the panel progressions in early comics, and now used by, for example, Chris Ware in his structurally complex comics (e.g., *Quimby the Mouse*), arguably allows for the arrangement of "units" within comics corresponding to any directed graph whatsoever, planar or not.

We need not get bogged down in the technical characteristics of these mathematical notions here. The crucial mathematical point is that every strict weak ordering corresponds to a directed graph, but not vice versa, demonstrating that the order-theoretic possibilities within comics are more complex than the corresponding set of possible orderings of units in film. This can be demonstrated with a simple example. The four panels in Figure 9.1 are ordered (via balloon tails) in a circular pattern. Such patterns of panel dependence are easy to achieve within comics (i.e., they correspond to planar directed graphs), but it is impossible to project four distinct scenes within a film so that the ordering between them is circular in this way (i.e., the panels in this particular example are not arranged in a strict weak ordering).

Figure 9.1 'Circular Panel Comic' from "Comic Theory 101: Loopy Framing". Used with permission of Tymothi Godek and Neil Cohn.

Of course, it can be objected that this claim about the impossibility of reproducing, in a filmstrip projection, the structural relationships between panels only applies if we imagine the panels being projected one-by-one (or perhaps in slightly more complex split-screen arrangements). If we project each entire page on to the screen, one at a time, then, at least at first glance, it seems that we can reproduce any panel arrangement from a comic in a filmstrip projection – after all we can just reproduce the page exactly, trails and all.

Even projecting entire pages (or even pairs of pages, to preserve multi-page splash panels and the like), it is not clear that *all* structural features will be retained, however. The fact that scenes in a film are projected – that is, their order and duration are controlled solely by the filmmakers (and perhaps the projectionist) – while panels in a comic can be perused in whatever order we decide – paging back and forth, comparing earlier and later images – suggests that it is not just the order of the relevant units, but the nature of this ordering, that is different. For example, it is hard to see how one could faithfully reproduce the celebrated symmetric structure of issue #5 of Alan Moore and Dave Gibbon's *Watchmen*, since an appreciation of the formal structure of the comic requires comparing panels on the first page to panels on the last, panels on the second page to panels on the second-to-last page, and so on. A similar direct comparison between non-adjacent scenes in a film is impossible (at least, impossible within the intended context – viewing the film publicly in a theater). Of course, it is possible that in our DVD saturated, post-TIVO world some films are designed with the intention of such non-linear comparisons between "units" – that is, a cinematic analogue of such "flipping back through the pages." Even so, a crucial difference remains: the intended manner of experiencing comics encourages such "back-and-forth" comparison, while similar phenomena in films requires that one not be in the primary intended context for viewing films.

At any rate, even if our brief discussion of these thorny issues is far from complete or conclusive, we have at the very least shown that the truth of premise (1) of the *Filmstrip Argument* is neither obvious nor trivial. Now that we have noted this, however, we shall set worries about (1) aside, and concentrate on premise (3).

Metacomics

In order to show that premise (3) is false, and thus that the *Filmstrip Argument* fails, it is enough to provide a single counterexample – that is, a comic whose aesthetic properties cannot be reproduced within any filmstrip projection. In fact, we shall look at two similar counterexamples. Both are instances of a sub-category of comics known as metacomics, which is itself a species of the more general category of metafiction. Although her target is metafictional novels, Patricia Waugh provides the following working definition of metafiction:

> Metafiction is a term given to fictional writing which self-consciously and systematically draws attention to its status as an artefact in order to pose questions about the relationship between fiction and reality. In providing a critique of their own methods of construction, such writings ... examine the fundamental structures of narrative fiction ... (1984: 2)

Put simply, according to Waugh metafiction is fiction that, in addition to presenting a narrative, purposely highlights the fact that the narrative is, in fact, a narrative – a fiction. In doing so, metafiction typically involves an implicit manipulation and/or critique of the conventions of the storytelling tradition within which it is produced (novels in Waugh's study, comics here). Waugh fleshes this idea out a bit further:

> Metafictional novels tend to be constructed on the principle of a fundamental and sustained opposition: the construction of a fictional illusion, and the laying bare of that illusion. In other words, the lowest common denominator of metafiction is simultaneously to create a fiction and to make a statement about the creation of that fiction. (1984: 6)

Along similar lines, a metacomic is a comic that is "about" comics in one sense or another, where this "meta" aspect of the narrative is intended not only to further the narrative, but also to comment on the nature of narrative itself. Thus, in fashionable jargon, metacomics are "reflexive" or "self-referential" of "self-conscious" comics.

It is worth noting that in this context I find both "reflexive" and "self-referential" misleading, however, since both terms suggest that the comic in question is somehow "about" itself, when a metafictional comic might be about the comics world in one of a number of broader senses. This also highlights a point at which we are diverging from Waugh's treatment of the matter: Waugh claims that a work metafiction must "make a statement about the creation of that fiction." Here, we are understanding the terms "metafiction" and "metacomic" more broadly, to encompass any work that makes a statement about either the fiction itself or about the creation and reception of that *type* of fiction.

Metacomics come in a number of varieties, depending on how, and to what purpose, the metafictional content is constructed. The following rough taxonomy is sufficient for our purposes here:

- A *narrative metacomic* is a comic whose plot involves the production, consumption, or collection of comics (or any other aspect of the comics subculture and its trappings).
- A *cameo metacomic* is a comic whose plot involves interaction with characters, locales, or other elements that are not in the same continuity, or whose plot involves parodying or spoofing other comics.
- A *self-aware metacomic* is a comic whose protagonist (or perhaps some other character) is aware that he or she is a character in a comic.
- An *intertextual comic* is a comic whose content interacts, in some manner, with the content of some other text or artwork.[5]
- An *authorial metacomic* is a comic whose plot involves the appearance of the writer, artist, or other creator as a character in the comic.
- A *formal metacomic* is a comic whose plot involves formal manipulation of the conventions of the comic medium.

A few examples: Mort Walker and Jerry Dumas' *Sam's Strip*, which revolves around Sam's attempts to run his newspaper strip as a business, is a narrative metacomic.[6] Any of the number of "cross-over" comics involving characters from two or more different continuities (such as those collected in Conway *et al.* 1997) are cameo metacomics.[7] John Byrne's celebrated 1980s run on the *Sensational She Hulk* (and, to a lesser extent, continued in Dan Slott's run on the more recent *She-Hulk*), where She-Hulk is aware that she inhabits a comic book and continuously breaks the fourth wall to interact with readers, the writer, and the editor, is a well-known example of a self-aware metacomic. The conclusion of Grant Morrison *et al.*'s *Animal Man*, where Animal Man meets Morrison – his "creator" – during an existential breakdown, is perhaps the paradigm instance of an authorial metacomic. Finally, we shall look at two striking instances of formal metacomics below.

These categories are not, of course, exclusive: many comics can be instances of more than one type of metacomic (for example, issue #50 of Byrne's *She-Hulk* arguably fits into all six categories!). In addition, I make no claims for this list being exhaustive: This list is meant merely to be a taxonomy that I have found useful when thinking about metacomics, and which has managed to fruitfully categorize all examples that I have come across so far. Finally, it should be noted that, although this taxonomy is distinct from the taxonomy of metacomics developed by others (e.g., Jones 2005; Inge 1995), it has benefited greatly from insights found this prior work.

The category of metacomics that shall be of interest to us here are formal metacomics. The reason this category is of interest in the present context is not hard to identify: formal metacomics rely on conventions regarding how narratives are constructed within comics – conventions that might have no analogues in the contingent norms governing narrative construction in other media (such as films!). As a result, even if all of the intrinsic formal elements of a comic are reproduced within a filmstrip projection of that comic, the absence of the relevant conventions within the cinematic context will prevent the filmstrip projection from achieving the same metafictional ends as are achieved in the original. As a result, any analysis of the comic that proceeds by analyzing the filmstrip projection using merely film-theoretic tools will fail to do justice to certain aesthetically relevant aspects of the original comic. In short – regardless of the obvious similarities between the two media – the tools and techniques developed for the study of film will be insufficient for the study of comics.

Thus, the general shape of the argument is clear. Of course, the argument only works if, first, there are conventions governing the construction of comics that have no analogue within film and, second, if there are (or could be) formal metacomics that involve the manipulation of these conventions. Fortunately, there are such conventions, and there are such comics. The examples we shall look at are Jimmie Robinson's *Bomb Queen* and Grant Morrison's *The Filth*. After examining these comics in some detail in the next two sections, we shall then examine the particular metafictional effects achieved by these comics and argue that at least some of these effects involve conventions that are particular to comics and thus can neither be replicated within films nor understood using only film-theoretic tools.

Before doing any of this, however, a warning is in order: Both of these comics are intended for adults (as attested to by warnings on their covers), and both involve explicit and sometimes very extreme sexual content (although not in the sections I shall discuss). In the case of Robinson's *Bomb Queen*, the adult content is in service to the parody of the so-called "Bad Girl" trend which dominated the mainstream comics industry during the 1990s (another metafictional aspect of the comic), and in Morrison's *The Filth*, it serves similar narrative and aesthetic goals. Thus, although in both cases the adult content is justified in terms of substantial and (in my opinion) successfully achieved aesthetic ends, the reader should not expect the traditional, clean-cut, "good guys win and all is right with the world" content familiar from more mainstream fare.

Bomb Queen's Editor Girl

Editor Girl is a supporting character in Jimmie Robinson's *Bomb Queen*, a comic starring the eponymous supervillain dictator who rules New Port City, an independent urban center where evil is encouraged, superheroes are outlawed, and criminality is the norm. Although the federal government tolerates Bomb Queen's rule, due mainly to the decreased crime rates throughout the rest of the nation, the plot of the comic typically revolves around various superheroic attempts to clean up New Port City and bring Bomb Queen to justice.

Editor Girl (based on Kris Simon, editor of Jim Valentino's *Shadowline* imprint at *Image Comics*) is one such superheroine. Editor Girl first appears in issue #2 of *Bomb Queen* Volume 4, teamed up with Nyx (also known as She-Spawn) in an attempt to free Bomb Queen and her city from the influence of the demon Desarak (formerly Bomb Queen's cat, Ashe).

The subtleties of the plot (although interesting) are not our main concern here, however. The most interesting aspect of this comic, for our purposes, is Editor Girl and, in particular, her superpowers. Like many of her colleagues, Editor Girl can fly, but much more interesting is her magic red Sharpie pen. Editor Girl can use this pen to edit the contents of speech balloons – the resulting, post-edit text then comes true (interestingly, Editor Girl's powers do not seem to extend into the psychic, since there is no evidence either that she can see thought balloons or that she can modify their contents in the same manner as she does with speech balloons). For example, in her first appearance Editor Girl is set upon by a pair of hoods. When one of them shouts "I'll drop you with this gun, bitch!," Editor Girl, in the subsequent panel, crosses out three words so that the word balloon says "I'll drop ~~you with~~ this gun, ~~bitch~~!," which he promptly does (see Figure 9.2). Similarly, on the next page, the same thug shouts "But it didn't make you bulletproof!," which she alters to say "But It didn~~'t~~ make you bulletproof!?" rendering his subsequent gunplay ineffective.

Figure 9.2   Bomb Queen Vol IV, Issue 2, page 13.
Bomb Queen TM and © Jimmie Robinson. Editor Girl TM and © Kristen K.
Simon. Used with permission of Image Comics.

One particularly interesting aspect of the depiction of Editor Girl's powers is that in depicting them, Robinson must violate one of the generally agreed-upon rules governing the depiction of balloons in comics – that there be no *objectified* thought or speech balloons.[8] A balloon is objectified when it is placed in such a way as to force the reader to interpret the balloon as part of the physical universe inhabited by the characters and objects depicted in a particular panel – for example, if part of a balloon is "under" a character's foot, or if it is depicted as behind objects which are located far from the speaker or thinker to whom the balloon is attached. Editor Girl's powers, on the other hand, *require* that balloons be objectified – she would not be able to interact with them otherwise, and her act of writing on them forces the reader to interpret the balloons as parts of the physical world she inhabits. Disturbingly, the more one reads the comic, the more confused one becomes regarding the metaphysical nature of the universe Editor Girl inhabits and how that universe must appear to Editor Girl herself.

The fact that Editor Girl's pen-wielding superpowers involve not just a convention specific to comics – the use of speech balloons – but also involve violating subtler conventions and norms governing how such balloons are depicted in more straightforward, non-metafictional comics, emphasizes how the resulting metafictional effect is deeply dependent on these conventions. As a result, the aesthetic effects achieved in the panels depicting Editor Girl are impossible to replicate in a filmstrip projection – at least, such replication is impossible if the filmstrip projection is interpreted using merely film-theoretic tools. Before examining this failure in detail, however, it is worth looking at another example in order to ensure that the phenomenon in question, while uncommon, is not singular.

The Filth's Max Thunderstone

Max Thunderstone is a supporting character in Grant Morrison's *The Filth*, a thirteen-issue miniseries detailing Ned Slade/Greg Freely's re-induction into a shadowy government organization called The Hand, whose mission is to insure that society continues to enjoy "Status Q." With the help of a Communist chimpanzee assassin and a beautiful agent named Miami, Slade attempts to, uh, um, … #$%&!, as they say in the comics! A short synopsis of this comic will be about as coherent as any short synopsis of any of Morrison's non-mainstream work (e.g., *The Invisibles, Doom Patrol*). Thus, instead of attempting the impossible, I shall concentrate on that portion of the comic directly relevant to our purposes.

The Filth, like *Bomb Queen* (and like the majority of Morrison's non-mainstream work), is a metacomic, and one of the metafictional aspects of the comic – the one we shall focus on here – involves Morrison's non-standard manipulation of the conventions governing balloons – in this case, thought balloons. During issue #10, The Hand is called in to deal with self-made superhero Max Thunderstone. After winning the lottery, Thunderstone devoted his newfound resources to becoming a superhero and saving mankind (with a particularly warped idea of what constitutes both "superhero" and "saving"). While torturing a Hand agent, Thunderstone relates his history and motivation in what appears to be a standard internal monologue depicted in thought balloons. Halfway through the fifth page of Thunderstone's narration, however, these 'thought balloons' reveal a surprise – "I even have my own **superpowers**, see?... A consciousness so focused and so disciplined, it can actually manifest words in a **cloud** above my head ... That's right, visible thought" (see Figure 9.3). In other words, the thought balloons above Thunderstone's head are no such thing – at least, they are not the thought balloons we are used to, visible to the reader but not the characters. Instead, Thunderstone's thought "clouds" (similarly to speech balloons in Editor Girl's world) are real, physical constituents of his world.

Perhaps the most interesting aspect of Thunderstone's thought clouds is the difficulty readers have in sustaining their correct interpretation – a difficulty that Morrison is clearly aware of, and takes advantage of. Thunderstone continues to provide narrative on the action within these clouds above his head for another dozen pages or so. Inevitably – at least, inevitably amongst the two-dozen or so readers with whom I have discussed this comic – the reader reverts to interpreting the thought clouds manifested above Thunderstone's head as traditional thought balloons. As a result, when towards the end of this sequence, a reporter asks a police officer "Who's the guy with the batwings, and what's all the smoke coming off his brains?," the reader is thrown for a loop, so to speak – realizing that she had been misinterpreting the preceding pages, since Thunderstone's thoughts are not private, as is indicated by traditional thought balloons, but are instead on public display for the other characters to see and understand.

Like Editor Girl's modification of the content of speech balloons, Morrison's non-standard use of thought balloons in *The Filth* requires that the balloons be objectified. The difficulty of correctly interpreting the portions of this comic involving Thunderstone, however, demonstrate that the conventions governing speech and thought balloons are not *merely* conventions – that is, specific contingent rules that we have adopted when creating and interpreting comics. In addition, experienced comics readers have completely internalized these conventions to the extent that they are extremely hard to "turn off" when this is required by the narrative. As a result, violations of these conventions such as those explored by Robinson in *Bomb Queen* and Morrison in *The Filth* are more than merely technical

Figure 9.3 The Filth, Issue 10, page 6.
© Grant Morrision and Chris Weston. Used with permission of DC Comics.

tricks – instead, they force us to reevaluate the conventional aspects of comics and how those conventions shape our ideas of what comics are and what they can do.

Conventions and Aesthetic Analysis

Now that we have our two data points, we can return to the *Filmstrip Argument*. Recall that, in order for the *Filmstrip Argument* to succeed, it needs to be the case that, for any comic Σ, there is a filmstrip projection FS(Σ) of Σ such that FS(Σ), viewed as a film (and evaluated solely in terms of film-theoretic tools), preserves all of the aesthetically relevant features of Σ. The problem, of course, is that, no matter how we manufacture the filmstrip projections of either *Bomb Queen* or of *The Filth*, we will lose some aesthetically relevant properties present in the original comics. The reason is that, even if we perfectly reproduce the non-standard manipulations of thought or speech balloons in the filmstrip projections, these manipulations will lose much of their aesthetic force (or, at best, they will have a very different aesthetic effect) since speech and thought balloons are not standard conventional ingredients of films.

It is worth emphasizing a point already implicit in the last statement of the previous paragraph. It is not that we cannot have speech or word balloons as ingredients of films – quite the contrary, speech or thought balloons can be used just as easily within film as they are within comics. The point is that, as used within film, they are already a non-standard feature, typically functioning as an explicit reference to comics (as is done quite effectively in the film adaptation of Harvey Pekar's *American Splendor* – thus, films utilizing speech or thought balloons might be classified as *intertextual metafilms*, in parallel with our taxonomy for metacomics given above).

To formulate the point more carefully in terms of our two counterexamples: the metafictional effect of Editor Girl's superpowers depends upon Robinson's subverting our expectations regarding the role that speech balloons play, replacing the commonplace and conventional with something much weirder. Since speech balloons are, within film, already non-standard and unconventional, there are no expectations to subvert – the presence of balloons would already be weird. Likewise, the bizarre effect that Max Thunderstone's visible thought clouds have on the reader (and on other characters) cannot be reproduced within film, since it depends on their being well-entrenched conventions regarding how to interpret thought balloons. In film there are no such conventions, so we are less likely to find ourselves involuntarily reverting back to the standard (but incorrect) interpretation of his thought clouds as conventional thought balloons.

Thus, the filmstrip argument fails, and there is a genuine need for a separate aesthetic account of comics. Before moving on to conclusions and extensions, however, a few points regarding what this argument does not show are in order.

First, the fact that some formal trick involving the manipulation of conventional aspects of comics (such as the ones discussed above) cannot be reproduced within film does not imply that clever filmmakers cannot discover other formal tricks – tricks involving the formal manipulation of conventional aspects of film itself – that achieve a parallel effect. One good example of this is "Tales of the Black Freighter," the comic-within-a-comic in Alan Moore and Dave Gibbon's *Watchmen*. "Tales of the Black Freighter" is a pirate comic that is read, in installments, by one of the supporting characters in *Watchmen*, and the structure and narrative of this comic closely parallels the main superhero narrative. Of course, much of the point would be lost if the filmmakers adapting *Watchmen* to the screen had merely had the same character reading a comic. Instead, they filmed an animated version of "Tales of the Black Freighter" which would serve a similar role, replacing the comic-within-a-comic with a film-within-a-film. Of course, the aesthetic effect of the comic-within-a-comic and the film-within-a-film are distinct, but they are structurally parallel in important ways. There seems to be no reason why someone could not adapt Editor Girl or Max Thunderstone to film using similarly parallel devices (for example, Editor Girl might have a magic tape recorder that could rewind and edit first-person narration, or Thunderstone might recite a film-noir style voice-over narration that the other characters can somehow hear).

Second, the fact that for some comics there is no filmstrip projection that, when evaluated using film-theoretic tools, preserves all of the aesthetically relevant features of the original comic does not mean that we cannot properly interpret and evaluate comics when looking at filmstrip projections of them, any more than an argument showing that the conventions of photography and painting differ shows that we cannot properly interpret and evaluate paintings by looking at photographs of them. The point is not that filmstrip projections cannot play the same, or a similar, role to direct interaction with the comics themselves (after all, as anyone who has taught courses on comics knows, such filmstrip projections, typically achieved via Powerpoint, are unavoidable if one wants to expose students to a great variety of comics). The point is that, when viewing a filmstrip projection of a comic, one needs to use tools specifically developed for the evaluation and interpretation of comics in order to properly analyze the comic being projected. Application of the theoretical tools developed for evaluating and interpreting films merely because the projection is, strictly speaking, a film and not a comic, would result in an analysis of the filmstrip projection, but not of the comic itself.[9]

Conclusions

If the argument above is correct, then there is a genuine need for a separate account of the structure and aesthetics of comics. Applying the tools of film theory and the philosophy of film to comics (or to filmstrip projections of comics), while often immensely fruitful, will not tell us the whole story, since such an approach will fail to do justice to the conventional aspects of comics in general, and will fail to provide us with the tools required to analyze and interpret metacomics in particular. In the technical jargon introduced above, the filmstrip projection of a comic might preserve the intrinsic aesthetic features of that comic (such as the pictures, their arrangement, etc.), but for at least some comics these are not the only aesthetically relevant properties. In addition, some comics – some metacomics in particular – have additional, extrinsic features involving the relationship of the comic to the larger context within which they occur. These features depend on the work in question being a work of a particular kind – a comic – and as a result might not be retained by the filmstrip projection. Thus, film-theoretic tools are not sufficient for the evaluation and philosophical analysis of film. The points made here have a somewhat wider scope than merely defending this (some might say rather obvious) thesis, however.

In particular, the argument given above highlights the fact that the uniqueness of each art form depends not only on the formal characteristics of that art form, but also on the conventions adopted with respect to how that art form functions and how we should interpret and evaluate instances of it. As a result, we might find (as is at least plausible in the case at hand – comics and film) that there are art forms that are structurally quite similar, but which nevertheless function very differently due to dramatic differences in the conventions we have adopted with respect to each. Of particular interest is the following theoretical possibility: there could be two art forms A and B such that the formal methods utilized in A and B are *identical,* and it is only the conventions adopted with respect to the two art forms that differentiate them. In fact, one could understand the striking differences between Western comics and Manga in exactly these terms: these are two distinct (albeit importantly interrelated and, in the relevant sense, structurally isomorphic) art forms in virtue of the very different conventions governing how narratives and visual effects are constructed within them and how these narratives and effects are interpreted (I do not mean to suggest that this is the *correct* way of viewing the situation, but merely to point out that such a position seems to be a viable one on the theoretical map).

In addition, the argument above also emphasizes the importance of the study of metacomics (or metafiction, or "meta-art" more generally) as a tool for examining and understanding the conventions adopted and utilized by comics creators and readers (or writers more generally, or artists and their audience). After all, one of the most promising methods for understanding the conventions inherent in a particular art form, and for distinguishing the conventional aspects of that art form from its less contingent structural characteristics, is to examine artworks that consciously subvert or manipulate those conventions. *Bomb Queen* and *The Filth* are useful examples in the arguments above for exactly this reason – they provide us with a useful way to interrogate our assumptions and conventional wisdom regarding the ways that thought balloons and speech balloons are used, and should be used, within comics.

Of course, meta-level manipulations of conventional elements are not restricted to comics, or even to narrative art forms – one need merely glance at the history of twentieth- and twenty-first-century painting to be convinced that meta-level considerations and manipulations have become one of the primary foci. It is worth noting, however, that comics seem particularly saturated with conventional elements – for example, thought and speech balloons, panel borders, motion lines, emanata, and so on – when compared to other art forms, and thus seem a particularly fruitful medium for metafictional manipulation. For some art forms, such as narrative fiction, "meta" considerations have generated a great deal of attention (for example, in the case of literature, Waugh (1984) and the literature springing from it). Comics scholarship, however, has barely scratched the surface in its examination of this very important sub-category (with the exception of Jones (2005), who restricts his attention to erotic comics, and Inge (1995), who restricts his attention to newspaper comic strips). There thus remains a great deal to be done.

Notes

1 Thanks are due to John Holbo, Aaron Meskin, Henry Pratt, Marcus Rossberg, Christy Mag Uidhir, and the students in my yearly Comics as Art Freshman Seminar for fruitful and collegial conversations on this and related topics and for suggestions that improved this chapter.

2 I will not name the philosopher of film here. It is worth noting that subsequent discussion made it clear that the question was intended to foster discussion, and that he was not, in fact, seriously suggesting that we abandon the enterprise taken up in this volume and elsewhere.

3 See Christiansen (2000) and Henry Pratt's contribution to this volume for more sustained examinations of the formal similarities (and dissimilarities) between comics and film.

4   The extent to which comic evaluation is tied to cinematic criteria is evidenced in the following observation by Will Eisner:

> Comics artists feel that their success in this field is when they take a strip and make a movie of it – then they've "arrived." (Eisner and Miller: 319)

5   In order to distinguish intertextual metacomics from cameo metacomics, we assume that the artwork to which reference is made in an intertextual metacomic is not a comic. Thus, typically the metafictional content of an intertextual metacomic involves drawing contrasts or connections between it and other art forms.

6   Note that this definition implies that any autobiographical comic is, in some minimal sense, a narrative metacomic, since any such comic will be about the creator of that comic.

7   Also worth mentioning here is the tradition of newspaper cartoonists honoring other creators who are retiring or have passed away by including the departing creator's characters in their strips (e.g. the spate of newspaper cartoons which featured *Peanuts* characters (or characters depicted in the *Peanuts* style) when Charles Schulz retired).

8   For detailed analyses of the evolution of speech and thought balloons, and the conventions governing them, the reader is encouraged to consult Lefèvre (2006) and Smolderen (2006).

9   This is not to say that an analysis of the filmstrip using solely film-theoretic tools will not be interesting or worthwhile – after all, the filmstrip projection of a comic might turn out to be a particularly interesting film in and of itself.

References

Byrne, J. *Sensational She-Hulk*, New York: Marvel Comics, 1992.

Carroll, N. "Defining the Moving Image" (1996), in N. Carroll and J. Choi (eds), *Philosophy of Film and Motion Picture: An Anthology*, Oxford: Blackwell, 2006: 113–134.

Christiansen, H. "Comics and Film: A Narrative Perspective," in A. Magnussen and H. Christiansen (eds), *Comics and Culture: Analytical and Theoretical Approaches to Comics*, Copenhagen: University of Copenhagen Press, 2000, 107–122.

Conway, G. *et al.*, *The Marvel/DC Collection: Crossover Classics Vol. 1*, New York: Marvel Comics, 1997.

Dooley, M. and S. Heller (eds.) *The Education of a Comics Artist*, New York: Allworth Press, 2005.

Eisner, W. and F. Miller. *Eisner/Miller*, Milwaukee, WI: Dark Horse Books, 2005.

Inge, M. *Anything Can Happen in a Comic Strip: Centennial Reflections on an American Art Form*, Columbus, OH: Ohio State University Libraries, 1995.

Jones, M. "Running Head: Reflexive Comics," *The International Journal of Comic Art 7*, 2005: 270–286.

Lefèvre, P. "The Battle over The Balloon: The Conflictual Institutionalization of the Speech Balloon in Various European Cultures," *Image & Narrative* 14, 2006. Available online at: http://www.imageandnarrative.be/painting/pascal_lefevre. htm, Retrieved February 25, 2010.

McCloud, S. *Understanding Comics: The Invisible Art*, New York: Harper Collins, 1993.

Meskin, A. "Defining Comics?," *Journal of Aesthetics and Art Criticism* 65, 2007: 369–379.

Moore, A. and D. Gibbons. *Watchmen: Absolute Edition*, New York: DC Comics, 2005.

Morrison, G. *et al. Animal Man*, Vols. 1–3, New York: DC Comics, 2001–2003.

Morrison, G. *et al. The Invisibles*, Vols. 1–7, New York: DC Comics, 1996–2002.

Morrison, G. *et al. Doom Patrol*, Vols. 1–6, New York, DC Comics, 2000–2008.

Morrison, G. *et al. The Filth*, New York, DC Comics, 2004.

Pekar, H. (ed.) *The Best American Comics 2006*, New York, Houghton Mifflin, 2006.

Robinson, J. *Bomb Queen*, Vols. 1–5, Chicago: Image Comics, 2006–2009.

Slott, D. *et al. She-Hulk* Vols. 1–5, New York: Marvel Comics, 2005–2007.

Smolderen, T. "Of labels, loops, and bubbles," *Comic Art* 8, 2006: 90–112.

Walker, M. and J. Dumas. *Sam's Strip: The Comic about Comics*, Seattle, WA: Fantagraphics Books, 2009.

Ware, C. *Quimby the Mouse*, New York: Random House, 2003.

Waugh, P. *Metafiction: The Theory and Practice of Self-Conscious Fiction*, London: Routledge, 1984.

Wolk, D. *Reading Comics: How Graphic Novels Work and What They Mean*, Cambridge, MA: Da Capo Press, 2007.

Proust's *In Search of Lost Time*: The Comics Version

David Carrier

Like motion pictures, comic strips are a novel art form, the creation of modernist culture. Traditional arts like old master painting were primarily for the elites. But in a democratic society, there is a demand for mass art. Some decades after the birth of photography, film was invented and it was discovered how to project sequences of mechanically produced images. Soon enough, then, came the addition of sound and the invention of color filming. The birth of comics, by contrast, did not depend upon new inventions. Shortly after the invention of printing, books combining images and words were published.[1] They constructed narratives using written words and hand made pictures. But comics did not become important until the early twentieth century. At that point American newspapers needed to be accessible to immigrants, who often had limited English. Comics were ideal, for they supplement written materials with images.

These circumstances surrounding the origin of comics do not in themselves identify their aesthetic value, or tell us how to interpret them. Early on there was a great deal of discussion about whether cinema was an art. Nowadays, however, film has its canons and numerous highly sophisticated academic interpretations. Comics, by contrast, although widely read, are as yet of marginal academic interest. Identified in America, at least, as an art meant for teenage-boys, they are often sold in specialized bookstores. Recently there has been a great deal of discussion about the ways in which art historians should study visual artifacts found outside the museum. And of course much contemporary art, which does attract the attention of art historians, employs novel media. But when researching my *The Aesthetics of*

The Art of Comics: A Philosophical Approach, First Edition.
Edited by Aaron Meskin and Roy T. Cook.
© 2012 Blackwell Publishing Ltd. Published 2012 by Blackwell Publishing Ltd.

Comics, I was surprised to discover how little interest art historians took in comics. (There is discussion by cultural historians, focused on the content of comics.) That is very disappointing, for comics are amazingly visually inventive. Some old master painters created extended visual narratives, but none of them employed systematically the devices, the closely spaced narrative sequences of images and the word balloon, that the great comics artists use.

Here, building upon the account in that earlier published book, I focus on a single case study, the recent presentation of Marcel Proust by the comics artist Stéphane Heuet. This example is richly suggestive. Adaptations of classic novels made these books accessible to readers with weak language skills, for the comic book versions are shorter and the pictures make the narrative easier to follow. Because *In Search of Lost Time* is such a long novel, with an intricate literary style, adapting it as a comic is very challenging. Recently my *Proust/Warhol: Analytical Philosophy of Art* examined Proust's aesthetic theory. This essay extends that discussion. What, I ask, is the relationship between the novel *In Search of Lost Time* and Heuet's comics version?

I speak of Proust's novel and call its hero Marcel. As *In Search of Lost Time* explains, although much of it is written from the first-person point of view of a narrator named Marcel, Marcel is not identical with Marcel Proust. Marcel is straight and seems to be a gentile; he is an only child, while Proust was gay and had a Jewish mother and a brother. At the end of Proust's novel, Marcel is ready to write his book which is described in the novel we have just finished reading. That book cannot be the novel *In Search of Lost Time*. There are many significant differences between Marcel and Proust.

We can read *Swann's Way*, the first volume of *In Search of Lost Time* in English thanks to the fluent translation by Lydia Davis. And we can see Proust translated into comics thanks to Heuet. I thus speak of translation to refer to both the translation of the French original into English, and the translation of that text into Heuet's images and words. Proust scholars are expected to study him in French, for in English-language translation, something of the original is lost. Usually the translation is a lesser work of art than the original, but in principle, a gifted translator might create something greater. French commentators offer very high praise for Charles Baudelaire's translations of Edgar Allen Poe, which is surprising to Americans who know only the English-language originals. Heuet published his original comic with the words in French and now that adaptation has been published with the words in English. The words require translation, though of course the images do not. But since what concerns me here is the relationship between the novel and its translation into a comic, I will discuss only the English-language version of Heuet.

Just as a literary work can be translated from one language to another, so also a novel can be translated from its original medium to another, to become a film, an opera, or a comic book. In a translation, then, *the same story* is told in another medium, in another language or in a different art form. Like Proust's novel, Heuet's comic tells Marcel's story. But where Proust uses just words, Heuet uses words and also images. Many of Proust's words are left out of the comic, but images are added. To speak, then, of Heuet's comic as telling *the same story* as Proust's *In Search of Lost Time* raises complex questions. How can a picture substitute for words in the storytelling? When a very long novel is translated into the relatively short sequences of images and words of a comic book, what is preserved? What, we are asking, is the distinction between Proust's original story as such and Heuet's version? Making this distinction leads to another obvious question. How does translating Proust's novel into a comic change our aesthetic experience of his story?

We have in English four volumes of Heuet's translation of Proust into comics: *Combray, Part Two: Within a Budding Grove*, volumes 1 and 2; and *Part Three: Swann in Love*. Heuet presents the story in the same order as Proust, his four comics books taking us not quite all the way through volume one, *Swann's Way* of the seven-volume novel. The Combray episode, which occupies 188 pages in the new English translation of Proust, is presented by Heuet in just sixty-nine pages, with fewer words but many images on every page.

When Proust's novel *À la recherche du temps perdu* was translated into English, first as *Remembrance of Things Past* and, more recently, as *In Search of Lost Time*, the translators face the much-discussed problems of finding English-language equivalents for his French prose. The older poetic title, alluding to Shakespeare, has been replaced by a more literal translation of the French original. And Proust's famous opening sentence:

Longtemps, je me suis couché de bonne heure. (Proust 1987: 3)

became in the first English version:

For a long time I used to go to bed early. (Proust 1982: 3)

or, in the newer translation:

For a long time, I went to bed early. (Proust 2003: 3)

Translating Proust into comics requires a much more radical transformation of the original. In Heuet's comic, the words:

For a long time, I would go to bed early. (Heuet 2001: 3)

are set above an image showing a window with closed shutters, a detail not in the novel.

Combray begins with Marcel's first-person narrative. We have an extended reverie; four pages about his difficulty at getting asleep; his recollections of sleepless nights in hotels; his childhood fear of having his curls pulled by his great-uncle; his erotic fantasies of being in bed with a woman; his experiences of dozing off in an armchair after dinner; and, finally, his recollections at some point in later life of Combray. He could spend the better part of the night, Marcel explains, remembering such experiences. This description of these fleeting memory images leads him then into one particular recollection of childhood, important for my present purposes, the magic lantern.

The comic narrative begins quite differently. We start by looking from outside towards the room in which Marcel the insomniac reflects. And where in the novel, in French or English the next sentence, which describes how Marcel would awaken unaware of his location, follows immediately, Heuet gives us a second image, showing Marcel in bed. He then supplements Proust's account of Marcel's reverie with a collage of images from later scenes, showing a Zeppelin over the Eiffel tower, from World War II; the Grand Hotel at Balbec where later Marcel visits; Venice; and an automobile. At the start of his book Proust doesn't describe all of these details, some of which are presented only in later parts of the novel, which were not yet written when *Combray* was published.

Proust never saw a movie, even though by the time of his death film theaters were commonplace Parisian attractions. But the magic lantern, which projects a sequence of images in a darkened room, was an optical device which anticipated films. Just as a modern day parent might calm a restless child at bedtime with television, so Marcel's mother soothes him with this device. The story it presents, however, is oddly unsettling, for as Marcel explains, this narrative in which a faithful wife, Genevieve de Brabant, is falsely accused of adultery frightens him. And then when soon he meets the Duchess de Guermantes, a descendent of that woman, his view of the nobility is much affected by his experience of this magic lantern show. In the comic, this important narrative connection isn't apparent. Proust's opening scene tells a deal about Marcel's feelings and thoughts, giving much more information than Heuet can present. But the novel does not allow us to see Combray.

Proust created a literary narrative. Heuet's different task is to find a verbal-and-visual equivalent for that written story. But where the novel reports his memories, the comic can show them. Marcel's reverie thus is realized visually. What do Proust's characters and their settings look like? This, I grant, may seem to be an inappropriate, even a silly question, for the characters and settings mostly are just fictional and so have only the identity given by him in the novel. Still, asking how Proust's imaginary people and settings look is a natural question to raise when reading a novel that contains many lovingly detailed descriptions of people and places; appearances do matter for Proust. We know what the novelist looked like, for he was photographed. But Marcel and all of Proust's other fictional figures exist only as he describes them. Some of Proust's settings, like the public spaces in Paris and Venice, are real, but others, Marcel's house in Combray for example, are merely fictional. That town is now called Illiers-Combray, in a gesture alluding to the novel.[2] Tourists come to see Marcel Proust's house. But they cannot view Marcel's home.

You see in Heuet's book young Marcel, Albertine, Swann, Odette, Baron Charlus and the other Proustian figures. And Swann's hair, blond, almost red, is faithfully shown. We have also the pleasure of seeing the settings of Marcel's family home in Combray; the grand hotel at Balbec; and the Paris street scenes. And in *Swann in Love*, we view Swann's enormous two-story library and see an elaborate visual presentation of his reverie during Vinteuil's sonata, with musical notes superimposed upon close up images of Swann set against the house where the performance takes place and a landscape scene. Heuet is very good at presenting visually Swann's confused response to the music. But given what Proust says about the limitations of photographs, which can never explain why someone is loved, what exactly can Heuet's representation of Albertine reveal? She is Marcel's true love, and so looks special to him; but to the reader she's simply another young French girl, dressed like the others we see in Balbec in period costumes. The comic doesn't, and perhaps cannot, explain visually why Marcel loves her.

It's easy to unintentionally impose modern styles of dress on Proust's imaginary figures. When long ago I first read *Within a Budding Grove* I imagined the adolescents, Marcel and Albertine, dressed in modern styles. And so it's a useful shock to be reminded by Heuet that at the beach Marcel wears coat, tie and hat, and carries a walking stick; and that Albertine and her girlfriends dress in skirts, not bikinis. (At one point Marcel is shown in a bathing costume, wearing a shirt.) Just as the train to Balbec and the grand hotel, where Marcel and his grandmother stay, are very different from modern day trains and beach resort hotels, so too the styles of dress have changed. Readers of Proust become sensitized to such changes. At the end of *Swann's Way* we see that Odette de Crécy has become Madame Swann, in a new world filled with automobiles, not the horse driven carriages of Marcel's youth. And at the end of *In Search of Lost Time* when Marcel reenters society, he has difficulty re-identifying the aged friends of his youth. An early twenty-first-century reader of Proust merely experiences these changes in a more dramatic way.

Proust took a serious interest in visual art when he was young, and wrote some marvelous essays about painting. And so it's not surprising that his novel is filled with references to paintings and sculptures. In *Combray* the pregnant kitchen-girl is compared to Giotto's figure of Charity in the Arena Chapel. Proust asks us to envisage this comparison, drawing on the fact that in his era Giotto's painting was familiar to most sophisticated readers. In his more literal pictorial narrative, Heuet shows this maid next to images from Giotto's fresco, making the comparison explicit. Swann compulsively identifies people he knows with figures in paintings. Comparing Odette with a figure by Botticelli in a Sistine Chapel fresco, for example, Swann justifies his admiration for her beauty. In Heuet's *Swann in Love* we see these comparisons illustrated. When the comic directly compares Odette to the Botticelli, we understand the absurdity of this procedure and, also, why Swann still finds it so seductive. Even if Odette looks like Botticelli's figure, why should that give Swann a reason to love her? In the comic, more so than in reading, the visual dimensions of Proust's novel come to life.

Recently a beautifully produced, very literal-minded book sought to elucidate Proust's uses of painting and sculpture by illustrating all of the visual works of art mentioned in the novel (Karpeles 2008). This procedure is a variation of the strategy of the older standard biography of Proust by George Painter, which seeks in Proust's life real sources for every person, place and situation in the book. The problem, as Joshua Landy (2004) has very effectively shown, is that this procedure fails to give proper credit to Proust's literary creativity. In creating literature, the novelist employs and transforms his personal experience. Proust's Marcel is a fictional character who owes much to his creator. But we cannot legitimately treat every detail in the novel as a transposition of its author's life experience. Seeking sources for the art in the writer's art is an issue with many modernist novelists. Virginia Woolf is not her fictional character, Orlando, who does share some of her personality. But it is a special concern with Proust, for Marcel is in very many ways closely identified with the creator of *In Search of Lost Time*. Marcel supposedly writes that novel, and so it is natural to identify him with Proust. But the fictional character is not identical with his creator, for *In Search of Lost Time* is not an autobiography.

What initially attracted my interest as an art writer to Proust's novel was one short scene in volume two, *Within a Budding Grove*, the episode where young Marcel visits the great imaginary painter Elstir.[3] Like most art critics, I do studio visits. An artist invites me to write a catalogue essay, or just to look. And rather quickly I need to size up what he or she is doing. Such studio visits are an important art world institution. Before an artist shows in the public spaces, the galleries, or museum, that person needs to make contact with art writers and curators. In the gallery, you can quickly choose whether to look at the art on display. Being in the studio is a more complex situation, for if you like the artist but don't appreciate his or her art, then it's not easy to graciously extricate yourself.

Proust didn't do studio visits, and so the way in which he anticipates the concerns of art critics is extremely fascinating. Young Marcel, who knows nothing about visual art, impulsively decides that he and his aristocratic friend Robert Saint-Loup would like to do a studio visit. Elstir invites Marcel only, who then postpones the visit until his nana pesters him. He finds Elstir's studio in an unattractive house some distance from the beach. But when Marcel gets there, we have a magic moment, one that is very rich in art historical allusions. At this point a more sophisticated intellectual than the young Marcel takes charge of the narrative. Proust is the source. Or, if you will, this account is the product of Marcel when he becomes a novelist, in that long process described by Proust in his last volume.

In Elstir's studio Marcel is looking at Elstir's masterpiece, *Harbour at Carquethuit*, a painting that is described in close detail. What do you visualize when reading the scene that Proust describes in words? Art historians are much concerned with verbal descriptions of visual works of art. Traditional art history employed word painting, *ekphrasis* to use its technical name, to provide such descriptions.[4] When inexpensive photographic images became available, then the nature of art writing changed. No longer did the interpreter need to describe the picture in words, for it was possible to refer to reproductions, which can show the whole picture and its sources. One difference between Vasari and his present day successors is that nowadays we can set written accounts against good color reproductions of the painting. No longer, then, do art writers need to conjure up in words the pictures they interpret. But inspired in part by Proust's youthful reading of John Ruskin, whose books he translated, his novel adopts a frankly traditional procedure of description of paintings.

Proust's account of *Harbour at Carquethuit* has attracted the attention of art historians and literary scholars.[5] His description of this imaginary seascape draws on his extensive experience of contemporary art. We find here allusions to Degas, Manet, Monet, Gustave Moreau, Renoir and Whistler, and of course to Turner, whose greatest champion was Ruskin. Proust encountered the works of these artists during his youth. He never mentions, either in the novel or in his letters, the two best-known French painters who did seascapes during his lifetime, Seurat and Matisse. By the time he was writing his novel, Proust no longer took an active interest in contemporary visual art. His visual sensibility was formed in the nineteenth century.

Vacations at the beach were a relatively new development when Proust was young. Recent scholarship has had a great deal to say about the relationship of avant-garde French art to this gentrification of the seashore. Monet and other painters worked in Normandy, preparing the way for tourists. Thanks to the new trains, prosperous Parisians like Proust's family took extended summer beach vacations, staying in grand hotels like the one Marcel inhabits. The setting of Elstir's studio and the subjects of his art are fictional constructions based upon this solid reality.

Elstir's imaginary picture challenges Heuet, for illustrating *Harbour at Carquethuit* poses obvious problems. How can a comic book present Proust's concept of visual metamorphosis? Just as verbal metaphors compare one thing to another, so Elstir's paintings recreate what is seen, most frequently by comparing what is on land to what's at sea, blurring this distinction. But how can that idea be shown? When you read the account of *Harbour at Carquethuit* you are given a long sequence of descriptions of picture elements, intermixed with some observations about Elstir's mental processes, in an analysis which takes the better part of four pages. The painting, we are told, shows the inlets of the sea near Balbec. (Here we have visual metamorphosis, objects at sea appearing to be on land, and vice versa.) Then we have the beach, where men push boats and women gather shrimp. More details then follow: we learn of fishermen coming out of the town; tourists setting out to sea; and a recent thunderstorm. There is a church, which appears to rise out of the waters, and ships tossing in the waters. One part is calm, while another is stormy. But it is not easy to see how these scenes fit together.

Just as the fact that *Harbour at Carquethuit* has many art historical sources makes it hard to envisage its style, so that the picture shows all these scenes makes that composition hard to imagine. Try sketching the painting and you will see this problem. How do all of these parts fit together? Proust doesn't specify exactly how large the painting is, but certainly it's an easel picture, not a mural. For a writer, that the painting includes beach and sea, tourists and a fisherman, without working out an account of these spatial relationships, is no problem. Proust only needs an extended description, not a visual plan. But since Heuet seeks to illustrate the story, he needs to come up with an image. And doing that is not easy.

Figure 10.1 Elstir's *Harbour at Carquethuit*.
Heuet, S. Remembrance of Things Past: Combray (J. Johnson Trans.). New York: Nantier-Beall-Minoustchine, 2001. pp. 14–15, in *Remembrance*: Part Two; *Within a Budding Grove*, Vol. 2. Used with permission of Delcourt Publishing.

Figure 10.2   Elstir's *Harbour at Carquethuit*.
Heuet, S. Remembrance of Things Past: Combray (J. Johnson Trans.). New York: Nantier-Beall-Minoustchine, 2001. pp. 14–15, in *Remembrance*: Part Two; *Within a Budding Grove*, Vol. 2. Used with permission of Delcourt Publishing.

On pages 14 and 15 of *Remembrance of Things Past: Part Two: Within a Budding Grove*: Volume 2 Marcel visits Elstir's studio (see Figures 10.1 and 10.2). The bottom of page 15 includes seven scenes copying the novel's account of *Harbour at Carquethuit*. And at the center top of these pictorial fragments is an image of Marcel looking at the back of the painting, in a scene which looks oddly like Velázquez depicting himself before his masterpiece *Las Meninas*. Heuet's version of *Harbour at Carquethuit* is puzzling. How could the three scenes showing calm waters be part of the same painting as the four other fragments showing rough waves? Literary commentators enumerate Proust's visual sources, without asking: what does *Harbour at Carquethuit* look like? Because the comic shows images, it focuses attention on this problem, without resolving it.

In principle, every detail of *In Search of Lost Time* could be translated into a comic. In practice, however, comics usually abbreviate, as does Heuet. But even if a comic included every detail of a novel, still the result would be different. A work of art in one medium can be translated into another. Shakespeare's *Othello* became Rossini's and also Verdi's *Otello*; and several of Jane Austen's novels have become good films. In such translations, something is gained and something lost. In opera we lose Shakespeare's full language, but gain the music; in film, we lose much of Austen's language but gain the visual drama. An artist who translates is not necessarily lesser, for Verdi is as great as Shakespeare, and some film producers are greater artists than the novelists whose books they adopt.

The Aesthetics of Comics argues that the classical comic relies upon two devices: the word balloon, which allows us to see the thoughts of the characters; and the narrative sequence of images. Comics are in-between art works, neither just image nor merely verbal narrative, but both at once. Any story that can be presented in a novel can, I believe, also be told in a comic. But there of course it comes out differently. Comics are a bastard art form, impure because they combine words and images. The pejorative sense of that description identifies problems that many commentators have with such impure arts.

In his discussion of opera, Roger Fry condemns such impure arts (1–57). To view an opera, he argues, is to simultaneously see a play, hear music, and look at sets, which is like viewing paintings. And that means that our attention is diluted, for seeing a play or hearing music or looking each by themselves are fully engaging experiences. The obvious reply is that ideally at the opera the music and sets contribute to our experience of the drama. If they are effective, then the acting and set should contribute to our experience of the music. This, after all, is why all things being equal a fully staged opera is superior to a musical performance in which the singers merely perform their roles, minus costumes and set. Exactly the same argument applies to comics compared to novels. When reading a comic the words and images should work together.

Everything that can be said in words can also be shown in images and words, but that narrative comes out differently. A novel has but one way of conveying information, words, while a comic has two: words and images. This analysis makes the comic sound richer, but of course it must get the words to work alongside the images. Do this as an experiment, turn from Proust's novel to Heuet's comic, comparing back and forth. What is most surprising is the effortless way that when reading Heuet we shift between words and images. There is no felt discontinuity going from Heuet's words to images, nor any sense that there is a difference in kind between experience of his mode of narration and Proust's. Indeed, it seems possible to make seamless transitions between reading the novel and the comic. But perhaps that is easy for me because I bring to that experience considerable familiarity with the novel.

In Search of Lost Time sometimes employs a first-person narrative. In the Combray episode, the narrator is Marcel. But at other places, the narrative is impersonal, as with *Swann in Love*. And in the very last volume of the book, whose title is translated as *Finding Time Again,* Proust reverts to a first-person narrative, since that part of the novel is about Marcel who will write the story that we have just read. In fact, it could be argued, the entire novel is implicitly written in the first-person point of view. It is Marcel's book, the story of his life, the narrative telling how he becomes a writer. Employing the first-person account means that we only know what Marcel knows, though Proust complicates this strategy even early on by sometimes taking us ahead in time. At the very start, for example, the narrator's reflections about insomnia describe the experience of the older Marcel, whose inability to sleep is traced to the young Marcel's life in Combray. Much of the virtuosity of Proust's presentation comes in the way he moves us backwards and forwards in time, which is very appropriate since his long last sentence compares the limited place people occupy in space with their extended presence in time, in which:

> They are in simultaneous contact, like giants immersed in the years, with such distant periods of their lives, between which so many days have taken up their place – in Time. (Proust 2002: 358)

It is very important that "time" is the last word in the book, for the novel is about the changing identity of people and things through time.

Occasionally Heuet uses images using the point of view of a character. At the beginning of *Combray*, as I mentioned, we see Marcel's reverie about events in his adult life. And in *Swann in Love* we have images of Swann's fantasies, as when he imagines Odette seen in the style of Watteau drawings. But almost always the comic adapts the visual equivalent of an impersonal narrative point of view. In *Combray* we begin by seeing Marcel's family dining, episodes from the life of Swann, and then the episode where Marcel is sent to bed alone. Sometimes we look down from high above, often we have close ups, and occasionally we see the scene looking up. This constant motion, which is not dictated by Proust's text, gives energy to Heuet's narrative. The rhythm given by Proust's sentences can hardly be captured by the comic, which frequently quotes only fragments of the novel. The novel tells the story from the viewpoint of Marvel, his knowledge and memories, though frequently shifting to the future; while the comic moves the implicit point of view around, as if creating a movie.

Try this experiment, read a few pages of the novel then turn to the comic. Since Proust offers a slow-motion narration, it will at first seem strange, even cruel to find the story presented so quickly in Heuet's comic. And yet, the comic has its own pleasures. The subtly of Proust's prose disappears in the soundbites of Heuet's comic. But sometimes something interesting is added. Because the bathroom door can be locked, Marcel explains, it's the place where he engages in his four solitary activities: reading, reverie, tears and "sensuous pleasure." Heuet doesn't illustrate that. But he does give us an image of Swann in the bedroom with one of his mistresses, showing both of them getting dressed, showing a scene isn't in the novel. When we are presented with Gilberte's indecent gesture, then Heuet fails us. And we do get the marvelous image of Marcel going up the steep stairs following by Françoise, and then putting on his nightshirt, which isn't in the book. So there are loses *and* gains. Sometimes Heuet uses many words, but occasionally, as when he introduces Baron de Charlus, he offers a long, almost wordless sequence of images. And then when the Baron walks with Marcel's party, we see him eyeing workers and sailors, images that give readers an early hint about the Baron's erotic interests. But when Proust explains that the Combray church has a stained glass window, which looks like the tarot cards used to entertain Charles VI, that detail doesn't come into the comic.

If Heuet loses something because he must cut the original text, he does add a great deal because he can show the scenes which Proust merely describes. I especially admire the large drawing of *Within a Budding Grove: Volume 2* (39). Looking at the beach from high above, the distant girls encircle Marcel who is far below a soaring seagull. Proust merely tells of the transformative effect of the Madeleine scene, where Marcel suddenly discovers the power of involuntary memory. But Heuet devotes two magnificent pages of his *Combray* to showing that metamorphosis, in a remarkable cinematic style, devoting a full-page image, which is unusual in his book, to depicting Combray as envisaged by Marcel.

Philosophers of mind have said much about how, from the fragmentary scattered sense data, we assemble coherent view of the world. Analogously, what is fascinating about film, commentators have noted, is how, from images jumping often from one viewpoint to another, we construct a unified narrative. When, for example, the movie jumps from one scene to the next, we read that as a plausible transition. Our ability to learn the conventions of film is very surprising. Comics, too call for such learning, for they require that we master somewhat different conventions. To follow Heuet's narrative, we need to see the words in his word balloons as spoken by the characters depicted in his drawings, with those words supplemented by the narrative above and below the drawings.

Compared to Proust's novel, Heuet's *Remembrance of Things Past* is only a slight work of art. And yet, I would not scorn the comic, both because Heuet's book does raise extremely interesting philosophical questions about the nature of visual and verbal narratives and, also, because it's fun rereading the novel alongside the comic. When you do that, so I have argued, you will find that Heuet's little books can teach us something about Proust's great novel.[6]

This essay is for Joshua Landy, in thanks for his contributions to our understanding of Proust published in his great *Philosophy as Fiction: Self, Deception, and Knowledge in Proust* and, also, for his generous support of my research. *Art Outside the Art System*, a forthcoming book I co-author with Joachim Pissarro, will discuss art forms which have been marginalized. Comics are one important example.

Notes

1 See Kunzle (1973).
2 See http://www.tourisme28.com/uk-illiers-combray-the-village-that-inspired-marcel-proust/uk-illiers-combray-the-village-that-inspired-marcel-proust.php.
3 See Carrier (2005).
4 See Carrier (1987).
5 See Carrier (2008).
6 Chute (2008) offers a valuable up-to-date survey of the literature.

References

Carrier, D. "Ekphrasis and Interpretation: Two Modes of Art History Writing," *British Journal of Aesthetics* 27(1), 1987: 20–31.
Carrier, D. *The Aesthetics of Comics*, University Park PA: Penn State University Press, 2000.
Carrier, D. "Marcel's studio visit with Elstir," *ArtUS* 9, 2005: 29–39.
Carrier, D. *Proust/Warhol: Analytical Philosophy of Art*, New York: Peter Lang, 2008.
Chute, H. "Comics as Literature? Reading Graphic Narrative," *PMLA* 123(2), 2008: 452–465.
Fry, R. *Transformations: Critical and Speculative Essays on Art*. Garden City, NY: Doubleday and Company, 1956.

Heuet, S. *Remembrance of Things Past: Combray*, trans J. Johnson. New York: Nantier-Beall-Monoustchine, 2001.

Heuet, S. *Remembrance of Things Past:* Part Two: Within a Budding Grove, Vol. I., trans. J. Johnson, New York: Nantier-Beall-Monoustchine, 2002.

Heuet, S. *Remembrance of Things Past:* Part Two: Within a Budding Grove, Vol. II. trans. J. Johnson, New York: Nantier-Beall-Monoustchine, 2003.

Heuet, S. *Remembrance of Things Past:* Part Three: Swann in Love, trans. J. Johnson Trans, New York: Nantier-Beall-Monoustchine, 2008.

Karpeles, E. *Paintings in Proust: A Visual Companion to "In Search of Lost Time."* London: Thames and Hudson 2008.

Kunzle, D. *The Early Comic Strip: Narrative Strips and Picture Stories in the European Broadsheet from c.1450 to 1825 (History of the Comic Strip, Volume 1)* 1st ed., Berkeley, CA: University of California Press, 1973.

Landy, J. *Philosophy as Fiction: Self, Deception, and Knowledge in Proust*, New York: Oxford University Press, 2004.

Painter, M.D. *Marcel Proust: A Biography* New York: Random House, 1989.

Proust, M. *Swann's Way*, trans. C.K. Scott Moncrieff and T. Kilmartin, New York: Random House, 1982.

Proust, M. *A la recherche du temps perdu I.* Paris: Gallimard, 1987.

Proust, M. *Finding Time Again*, trans. I. Patterson, London: Penguin, 2002.

Proust, M. *Swann's* Way, trans. Lydia Davis, New York: Penguin, 2003.

Index

The Art of Comics: A Philosophical Approach, First Edition.
Edited by Aaron Meskin and Roy T. Cook.
© 2012 Blackwell Publishing Ltd. Published 2012 by Blackwell Publishing Ltd.

Printed and bound by CPI Group (UK) Ltd, Croydon, CR0 4YY

13/04/2025

14656562-0003